Doing
Educational
Research

Doing
Educational
Research

A Guide to First-Time Researchers

Clive Opie

with
Pat Sikes, David Hyatt, Jon Scaife,
Ann-Marie Bathmaker, Michael Pomerantz

SAGE Publications
London • Thousand Oaks • New Delhi

SAGE Publications Ltd
1 Oliver's Yard
55 City Road
London EC1Y 1SP

SAGE Publications Inc.
2455 Teller Road
Thousand Oaks, California 91320

SAGE Publications India Pvt Ltd
B-42, Panchsheel Enclave
Post Box 4109
New Delhi 100 017

British Library Cataloguing in Publication data

A catalogue record for this book is available
from the British Library

ISBN 0 7619 7001 0
ISBN 0 7619 7002 9 (pbk)

Library of Congress Control Number 2003109262

Typeset by C&M Digitals (P) Ltd., Chennai, India
Printed in Great Britain by The Cromwell Press Ltd, Trowbridge, Wiltshire

Summary of Contents

Contents

Notes on Contributors

Ann-Marie Bathmaker is a lecturer at the University of Sheffield. She started her career in education as a teacher of English as a Second Language, later becoming a local authority coordinator for the Technical and Vocational Education Initiative. She worked at the University of Wolverhampton for six years, becoming Principal Lecturer with responsibility for teaching and learning. Her areas of research and publication include policy and practice in post-compulsory education and training, teacher and learner identity, young people's transitions and qualifications and training for teaching and learning professionals.

David Hyatt works in the University of Sheffield where he is the Director of the MEd in English Language Teaching Programme and the Singapore Distance Learning Programme. He is also a tutor on the MEd Literacy and Language in Education Programme. David has considerable experience in the supervision of postgraduate students and regularly leads sessions on academic literacy and critical reading for study. David's present research interests centre around political and media discourse, critical literacy and academic literacy, and he is currently researching feedback on postgraduate work.

Clive Opie is a Deputy Director of the Institute of Education at Manchester Metropolitan University. His research interests have centred on the use of ICT to support and enhance teaching and learning with a variety of groups such as teachers and pupils in schools, students on initial teacher education courses and those undertaking higher degree courses. He has had substantial experience of teaching and tutoring students on MEd courses where, amongst other areas, he has taught research procedures and data analysis both of which have included the exploration of using computers to assist in such work. In June 2002 the Open University published a text jointly authored with Judith Bell *Learning from Research: Getting More from your Data*.

Mike Pomerantz is an Associate Tutor to the MSc Course and the EdD Programme both in Educational Psychology at the University of Sheffield where he has been teaching for almost 20 years. His teaching interests focus on assessment and interventions with emotional and behavioural difficulties, group dynamics, professional well-being and information technology. He is a Senior Educational Psychologist and team manager in Derbyshire providing services to a range of primary, secondary and special schools including assessments, interventions, consultation, work with parents, conflict resolution, staff development and Child Protection work. He was the Convener of the Standing Committee on Supervision of DECP (British Psychology Society) during 1984–93. This group produced professional guidelines and organised National Conferences in 1987, 1988 and 1993 at the Tavistock Clinic and the Institute of Education. The work culminated in a series of articles published in I. Lunt and M. Pomerantz (eds) (1993) 'Supervision and Psychologists' Professional Work', *Educational and Child Psychology*, 10:2. His more recent research concerns database development, confidentiality in record keeping, evaluation of Educational Psychology Services and under-achievement especially amongst able pupils. In August 2002 David Fulton and NACE published his latest work (co-authored by Kathryn A. Pomerantz) entitled *Listening to Able Underachievers: Creating Opportunities for Change*.

Jon Scaife is a lecturer at the University of Sheffield. He has a particular interest in learning and in the nature of knowledge and the construction of meanings. These interests underpin his research interests in the relationship between learning and teaching, in Interpersonal Process Recall, and in the construction of rich learning environments. He studied and taught Physics and Mathematics and in the field of Science Education has written on learning, on equity and equality, and on uses of ICT. He directs Educational Studies courses for doctoral students and for PGCE students at Sheffield University.

Pat Sikes is a lecturer at the University of Sheffield. Throughout her academic career, the study of aspects of teachers' lives and careers through qualitative research methodologies in general and life history/narrative approaches in particular, have been the central strand of her research interest and activity. In pursuit of this interest her work has focused on, and developed in, four main interrelated areas. These are: teachers' lives and life cycles; life history methodology; social justice issues, and qualitative research methodology. She has published extensively in all of these fields, and, in addition is Series Editor of an Open University Press series entitled Doing Research in Educational Settings. Her current research project: Strengthening the Research Base in A New University, takes an auto-ethnographic, reflexive, collaborative, action research approach to the task of strengthening and developing the research base of, and research activity within a school in a new university.

Preface

Although this is a book about educational research it differs from the proliferation of texts that already exist in this field in that it is written specifically with the needs in mind of those embarking for the first time into educational research. The undeniable value of many of the existing texts in educational research is not in question. Neither is the fact that they provide comprehensive and informative discussion of areas such as research methodology, research procedures (methods) and the use of technology in supporting qualitative and quantitative data analysis. The point is, though, that the very comprehensiveness of such texts often results in a level of redundancy of information for the beginner researcher. So while no criticism of existing texts is intended there is recognition, from the experience of those contributing here, that for the beginning researcher they often offer far more than is required. The argument made is that those commencing educational research need to be provided with a carefully orchestrated source of information, which while being necessarily correct is reduced to a digestible size and level of comprehensibility so as to provide the supportive framework essential to their stage of development. This book sets out to do just this.

Collectively, the authors have brought together over 60 years of experience in the field of educational research, to provide a text aimed at meeting the particular needs of Masters students new to its intricacies. These needs include simplicity of expression of apparently complex issues such as those associated with methodological and ethical concerns; support strategies for the academic writing required for a dissertation; straightforward presentation of standard aspects of research approaches and procedures (methods); informative, but clear and helpful, frameworks for exploring data analysis; and a comprehensible insight into the world of statistics at a level appropriate to the beginning educational researcher.

Others will undoubtedly argue this book misses out key areas, or is too superficial in places. Such criticism may or may not be legitimate and the educational fraternity will inevitably continue to argue over such points. However, while making no excuse for focusing on a grounding in the basics of educational research, its use of a wide range of references sets out to provide a springboard for further exploration should it be required. The chapters and their contents have arisen from much discussion with colleagues involved in Masters teaching and, importantly, students embarking upon educational research for the first time. It is supported throughout with 'teaching points' and exemplars from actual student material. The intention is then that while meeting the needs of Masters students, equally it will provide a starting point for higher degrees such as PhD.

Each of the chapters can be read independently although they make reference to each other for the purposes of coherence. The first chapter offers a general overview of educational research and sets out to answer the fundamental question asked by all newcomers, 'Can I do Educational Research'? The answer is an unequivocal 'yes' and the reader is led to this result through a process of reflection of a number of 'typical' views held by beginning researchers. Having attempted to allay any fears that educational research is not just the prerogative of a chosen few, the chapters that follow each present a key issue involved in its undertaking.

In Chapter 2 Pat Sikes provides an eloquent insight into methodological issues clarifying the distinction between this and research procedures (methods). It is worth noting at this point that throughout this book the term 'procedures' is used in preference to 'methods' as experience indicates that the latter term throws up unnecessary confusion with the term methodology. The chapter also addresses the central importance of considering the ethical issues, which arise when undertaking educational research.

Many beginners' level of anxiety rises sharply when faced with the actual process of undertaking academic writing. The view often held is that such writing is shrouded in mystique, which only the very gifted writers can handle. Nothing could be further from the truth. Admittedly conventions exist but there is nothing mystical about them that a suitably presented analysis cannot unravel. Such an analysis is provided in the third chapter by David Hyatt who uses his years of experience as an ELT expert to provide a down to earth approach at unravelling the apparent intricacies of academic writing.

Another key issue for those commencing educational research is how to make appropriate claims and construct credible accounts of their research so as to gain and maintain the confidence of their readers, in short to gain the reader's sense of trust in what he or she is reading. This forms the basis of the fourth chapter by Jon Scaife. Although addressing issues such as validity, reliability and causality the focus is not on the technical issues associated with these areas but, and arguably more importantly, on the quality of the communication between the reader and writer.

More often than not students new to educational research show an emphasis for the practice of doing it, that is, the approach to be taken and the procedures used, rather than considering the theoretical issues that should underpin it. This is not surprising as 'doing' the research is seen as synonymous to collection of real data, which in turn provides the material for analysis and presentation of conclusions and after all isn't this what research is all about? The actual approach taken to any research and the procedures used are, though, of no more importance than the contents of the earlier sections, arguably they are less so as without thought being given to methodological issues the whole *raison d'être* for the research approach and procedures cannot exist.

It is for this reason, and like many other texts, that the 'doing' aspects of research are only now raised. Chapter 5 details three main approaches to research – Case Study, Action Research and Experiments – and the decision to focus on these has been guided by the consideration outlined earlier, namely their suitability for the beginning researcher undertaking a Master's degree. Each approach is defined and then explored through student example(s). There is also a consideration of Grounded Theory which although deemed unlikely to find wide use at Master's level is raised as it links to later chapters which consider the use of qualitative data analysis software in the organisation and analysis of the data obtained from using such an approach.

Questionnaires, Interviews and Observational research are considered within the next chapter on research procedures. Each is discussed in terms of its appropriateness to the methodological stance underpinning the educational research being undertaken and in terms of the particular issues raised, such as question types, interview styles and the types of observations, which might be undertaken.

Too often thoughts of data analysis are left until after the data have been collected. This is fatal and any researcher needs to keep in the forefront of their mind that shoddy, ill-conceived or inappropriate data analysis can make an otherwise sound research project worthless. To help understand this, the next chapter begins by looking at the types of quantitative data one could collect and the kind of analysis it lends itself to.

It is also at this point that the introduction of computer data analysis programs such as Microsoft Excel and, the Sage product SphinxSurvey are introduced. These are powerful and useful tools for quantitative data analysis but equally can be the bane of a reader's life as this chapter goes on to consider. Graphs, pie charts, tables in a variety of formats and colours are achievable at the press of a few buttons. Used wisely, they present data in an informative, easy to understand and simple to read format. Used indiscriminately, they do more to confuse and frustrate the reader than help him or her to appreciate the significance of the research findings.

Given the small volume of qualitative data which is likely to arise from Masters research much can be said for simply reading what is collected and extracting various points using the in-built facility of a word-processor to search for keywords. The value however, of looking at the potential of computer data analysis programs to enhance any such analysis should not be underestimated. As such exploration of the Lexica edition of SphinxSurvey as a relatively simple to use, but still powerful, text analysis program is given some prominence in the last section of this chapter.

Had this book done no more it is likely it would have provided sufficient introductory material for the beginning Masters students to help them embark upon their research. The recognition that technology is increasingly advancing the ease at which both quantitative and qualitative data analysis can be undertaken and that statistical analysis used correctly is important prompted the addition of three further chapters.

Chapters 8 and 9 provide a carefully orchestrated venture into two computer assisted qualitative data analysis software (CAQDAS) programs. Both authors reflect on their own research work and ask the important question 'How did it help me'?

Ann-Marie Bathmaker provides an extremely salutary excursion into the potential of using the Sage software NUD·IST (now upgraded and-renamed Nvivo 2.0) for the analysis of the semi-structured interviews she undertook with staff and students in a further education college and which formed the basis for a case study of teaching and learning in further education. Although NUD·IST helped her bring together relevant texts a great deal more easily than if she had attempted to do so by manually cutting and pasting, the interpretation of the data, and telling the story, came from detailed reading of the interviews, talking about them to others as well as reading the excerpts placed under each theme produced by the software. She makes an important point when she advises others to try out such software using tutorials provided and to not be seduced by what it can do, but to ask 'Did I *want* to do that'?

In Chapter 9 Mike Pomerantz, an educational psychologist, also discusses his own research, which was exploring, through interviews, the needs of able, underachieving pupils in one Local Education Authority in the UK and how he used another Sage software product ATLAS.ti. His chapter provides a valuable narrative of his own inroads into the world of qualitative analysis as well as a comprehensive insight into the value of CAQDAS programs to assist in supporting the Grounded Theory approach he used. What is possibly even more interesting and perhaps reflects the symbiotic relationship of manual and computer based analysis is that his partner Kathryn, also an educational psychologist, elected to examine the interview transcripts without the benefit of ATLAS.ti. Although she used notes in margins and coloured highlights, they found congruence. There is though perhaps the additional value of using CAQDAS in that it provides the potential for readily revisiting the data in search of that 'elusive' something else.

The final chapter may seem somewhat out of character in as much as it is written in the format of a glossary of terms associated with quantitative analysis. This was done purposefully. Arguably many of the terms and details could have been included in Chapter 7. However, many need not concern beginners to educational research and so including them just for the sake of completeness seemed inappropriate. As editor, the final decision, rested with me and as such I have argued that while an understanding of many of the terms included here could be of value at Masters level their inclusion in other chapters was not justified. Too often students shy away when confronted with statistical terms – this is not the intention of this book. What is offered then is a glossary of terms associated with quantitative analysis, which should provide the reader with all the necessary information he or she might need but without making their reading conditional.

This is a beginner's text, which although necessarily minimalising the discussion of a range of issues does not marginalise their importance or significance to educational research. The authors hope you enjoy reading and using this text and find its contents useful and stimulating and its references substantially wide to allow further depth of exploration should you require it. The first chapter ends by stating to all those new to educational research and worried about their ability to undertake it – 'You can do it' – and we sincerely hope this book will help you in doing so.

Clive Opie

Acknowledgements

My grateful thanks go to a number of people for their help and support in ensuring this book ever saw final publication. First, to all my colleagues based at the University of Sheffield not only for contributing selflessly to the writing of their chapters but in providing me with the encouragement to ensure my own were completed. Without their various expert contributions the worth of this book would be sorely reduced. To Zoë Elliott from Sage for her patience, guidance, constructive criticism and unwavering support. To all the hundreds of students who I have had the pleasure of working and, more importantly, learning from. Constraints of space permit but a few to be cited but they have all, in their own way, helped me in the development of my thoughts. Finally to my wife and family for their patience and willingness to give up countless weekends in allowing me to complete this book. To you all I owe a great debt of gratitude.

1 What is Educational Research?

Clive Opie

This first chapter seeks answers to the question in its title and a second one, 'Can I do it?'. The answer to the first seems to require an exploration of various terminologies, for example positivism, interpretivist paradigm, ontology, epistemology, symbolic interactionism, action research, ethnography, grounded theory, critical theory and so on. Now, before these terms start to perhaps 'blow your mind' and you think about putting this text down, read on.

These terms, and the many others not mentioned, can, at first sight, seem baffling and complicated and only readily understandable by those who have been working in the area of educational research for many years. The truth of the matter is that to 'do' educational research at the Masters level one need only grasp a subset of such terms – and these are kept to a minimum and form the basis of this and the other chapters in this book.

This latter paragraph will undoubtedly raise eyebrows and criticism from some in the educational fraternity. What terms should be included? What criteria for their selection have been used? Why are those that have been excluded so treated? What is the validity (a term which will be explored more fully later in this book) for making these choices? One could, and rightly so, be criticised for a level of personal subjectivity in selection of the terminology deemed to be 'appropriate' at Masters level. Those chosen though are based on over a decade of experience of working with distance learning students and discussions with the colleagues who have worked with them in completion of their degrees. In this way the terminology presented here takes on a level of objectivity.

I would argue that in reality the majority of Masters students finish their degree blissfully unaware of much of the amassed educational research terminology, which exists. Should the educational research world be worried? Unless their student is undertaking a specific Research Masters designed as a prerequisite for a PhD as, for example, required by the recently introduced Educational and Social Research Council '1 + 3' (ESRC, 2001) guidelines, then surely the answer has to be no. What is more important is that a

Masters student, who, perhaps typically is not seeking to further their studies to a higher level (e.g. PhD), is aware of the main aspects of educational research terminology and crucially how these impinge upon the actual research they are seeking to undertake and the research procedures they need to employ.

To reiterate the context for this book is to provide a text, which meets the needs of beginner researchers. Limiting the terminology to be engaged with is one way of doing this. There are also numerous other eloquently written texts on the market, which more than adequately cover any 'deemed missing' terminology (Cohen et al., 2000; Walliman, 2001) should the reader wish to extend his or her knowledge of educational research terminology.

Having, I hope, indicated how I intend to answer the first of these two questions how about the second? This is much easier – the answer is yes – and hopefully you will come to this conclusion yourself as you work through this and the others chapters in this book.

Many of the chapters require you, the reader, to start from position of personal reflection. What do you think? What do you understand by? What are your views? This format is intentional as it begins to get you to explore various aspects of educational research from your personal perspective, knowledge and present understanding. You may, as some cultures do, feel this is relinquishing responsibility as a not uncommon view from those beginning research is that the MEd tutors are the experts so they should tell those less versed in this field what to do.

What this does though is deny the inherent knowledge and personal educational experiences, which any new researcher brings to the task. Experiences of working with children and colleagues, introducing and co-ordinating teaching schemes, reflecting on teaching problems, managing resources and the myriad of other day-to-day activities all add up to a wealth of knowledge which will almost certainly have some pertinence for any research being proposed. Where the MEd tutor is of value is in refining the research to be done and providing, as we shall see later, a systematic approach to its undertaking.

So, let's start from your perspective of research, as shown in Figure 1.1. We shall not consider any answers to the third sentence(c) in Figure 1.1, although the normal paucity of answers, which usually occurs, is probably indicative of some of the issues we will raise in answering the first two. Hopefully though by the time we have worked our way through these you will have any worries about undertaking educational research dispelled, and realise you can do educational research.

What is educational research?

(a) Research is …

What are your views of Research?

1   Complete the following sentences:

   (a) Research is ...
   (b) Research is something that requires ...
   (c) Research is done by ...

2   List around five or so words you associate with the word Research.
3   Now jot down some research that has either influenced your teaching, or your own learning, or has influenced another aspect of your life perhaps, in a non-academic sense. Note, if you can, who did this research? Why was it influential?

Figure 1.1   Views of educational research

Seeking through methodical processes to add to one's body of knowledge and, hopefully, to that of others, by the discovery of non-trivial facts and insights. (Howard and Sharpe, 1983: 6)

A search or investigation directed to the discovery of some fact by careful consideration or study of a subject; a course of critical or scientific inquiry. (OED, 2001)

You may not have arrived at such specific definitions but hopefully you will have begun to appreciate that research aims to overcome the limitations of 'common-sense knowing' (Cohen et al., 2000: 3–5). You will undoubtedly have jotted down other terms such as 'systematic process' and concepts such as 'control' and we will address these later in this book. For now it is sufficient to keep the principle of the definitions above in mind. A lot of what will be written refers to social science research in its most general sense. But, as the social sciences cover a vast array of subject areas it is also worth providing a definition of educational research and its importance in the context of prac-tising teachers, as it is these points we will be focusing on throughout this book. Educational research can then be viewed as 'the collection and analysis of information on the world of education so as to understand and explain it better', with a significance for practising teachers in that it should be

viewed as a critical, reflexive, and professionally orientated activity ... regarded as a crucial ingredient in the teacher's professional role ... generating self-knowledge and personal development in such a way that practice can be improved. (Hitchcock and Hughes, 1989: 3–4)

(b) Research is something that requires ...

- the collection of quite large amounts of data
- results which can be generalised

- a hypothesis
- the undertaking of experiments
- objectivity rather than subjectivity
- the use of statistics
- that something is proved
- specific expertise, as it is difficult.

Those new to educational research often come up with answers not too dissimilar to those above. This list is not definitive and its order is no more than for convenience of this text, but it gives a fair picture of 'typical' views. None of them is necessarily correct although each will have its own significance depending on the kind of research being undertaken. Let us though look at each of these points in the context of the kind of research likely to be undertaken in the context of an MEd dissertation and the timescale within which to do it, typically six months.

Collection of large amounts of data

Educational research of the type involved at Masters level will be relatively small scale. This is not to say it may not have significant impact upon personal practice or that of others, or add 'new' knowledge to a particular field of enquiry. It will though in most cases *not require the collection of large amounts of data* – although again the definition of large is open to interpretation.

Typically one may be working with around two or three classes, say a hundred students maximum, but on the other hand research may centre on one's own class of 20 to 30 students. Good dissertations (Lees-Rolfe, 2002) have also resulted from in-depth studies of just one student. What is not likely to happen (although I have had a few good MEd dissertations, against my advice, which have) is that research will be undertaken with hundreds of students or involve the collection of tens of thousands of pieces of data (Fan, 1998). Neither time nor access are usually available to allow this to be achieved and even if it does then the overall timescale for the research will almost invariably limit the analysis of it, which begs the question, 'Why was it collected in the first place?' (Bell and Opie, 2002).

Hopefully this last paragraph has shown that there is no definitive answer to the amount of data you might collect. This quantity, as it should be, will be determined by your research question, the methodology you choose to investigate it and the procedure(s) you select to gather the data to answer it. This may sound less than helpful but it reflects the realities of educational research. At the risk of being criticised by others more eminent in the field than myself, the following are guidelines based on my experiences with MEd students. Take them as guidelines though, as there are no hard and fast rules, and listen to your tutor's words of advice.

If you are asking closed questions (see Chapter 5) keep the total number of data items obtained to no more than 2,000. This will give you around 20 data items per student, for your three classes of 30. This should be more than sufficient if you have defined your research question well. However, if some of these questions are open ended you are well advised to reduce the total number asked.

If you are undertaking interviews you might consider limiting these to no more than six people (less is acceptable); with no more than ten questions being asked; and to take around 45 minutes to complete. This may seem very small but just transcribing a 45-minute interview will take you a good two to three hours and then you'll spend more time analysing your findings and collating views. Invariably your interview questions will have arisen from an analysis of a previous questionnaire so you have this data to analyse as well.

Results which can be generalised

Although there is *no need to try and provide results which can be generalised*, the findings may have important implications, either for personal practice or others working in similar areas. But, collecting large volumes of data in order that the educational research they stem from might provide useful generalisations is not necessary or, if one is really honest, even possible given the scale of research being addressed in this book. As Bassey notes, 'the study of single events is a more profitable form of research (judged by the criterion of usefulness to teachers), than searches for generalisations' (1984: 105).

Bassey draws a distinction between 'open' generalisations where 'there is confidence that it can be extrapolated beyond the observed results of the sets of events studied, to similar events' and 'closed' generalisations 'which refers to a specific set of events and without extrapolation to similar events' (1984: 111). He goes on to link the latter term with the 'relatability' (1984: 118) of a piece of educational research, that is how can it be related with what is happening in another classroom. Perhaps the most telling comments by Bassey are that although '"open" generalisations are the more useful in pedagogic practice, they also seem to be the more scarce' (1984: 103). Perhaps the merit of any educational research is 'the extent to which the details are sufficient and appropriate for a teacher working in a similar situation to relate his (or her) decision making to that described' (1984: 119). In short the relatability of the work is more important than its generalisability.

Hypothesis and undertaking of experiments

The third and fourth elements of our list of what research requires suggest the need to have a hypotheses and to undertake experimental work. These may seem essential to educational research, for as Walliman notes:

Does Studying a foreign language in high school increase students' verbal ability in English?

Julie obtains lists of all seniors in her high school that did and did not study a foreign language. Then she compares their scores on a standard test of English reading and grammar given to all seniors. The average score of the students who studied a foreign language is much higher than the average score of those who did not.

Does this observation show that studying another language builds skill in English?

Figure 1.2 Problems of experimental research

> A good hypothesis is a very useful aid to organising the research effort. It specifically limits the enquiry to the interaction of certain variables; it suggests the methods appropriate for collecting, analysing and interpreting the data; and the resultant confirmation or rejection of the hypothesis through empirical or experimental testing gives a clear indication of the extent of knowledge gained. (2001: 174)

However, this technique of educational research suggests that the action of people can be controlled or conditioned by external circumstances; that basically they are the products of the environment they find themselves in. In this case thoughts, personality, creativity and so on, are irrelevant. You may like to think about this latter point in terms of your own personal development, working environment and culture. In so doing ask yourself if you have been conditioned to think or perform in a particular way or have you been the controller of your destiny? It is unlikely that you will come up with just one view as in reality this is dependent on particular situations and as these change over time you are likely to pitch your personal answer somewhere in between these extremes.

Look at the example in Figure 1.2, adapted from (Moore, 1997: 94), and before glancing at the answer decide for yourself what you think it might be and discuss it with others if you have the opportunity.

The answer to the question in Figure 1.2 is that it does not. Students will (in most cases at least) have decided whether to study a foreign language that is, it is their *personal choice* to do so, and for many of them they will already be better at English than the average student. So, these students will differ in their average test scores for English but there can be no suggestion that studying a foreign language has caused this (see Chapter 3 for more about the issue of causality). Moore goes on to indicate how Julie might undertake such an experiment but then highlights the impracticality and unethical nature of doing so.

Objectivity rather than subjectivity

The terms objective and subjective are often used in everyday conversation and in general people understand what they mean when they use them. They both refer to the degree that personal feelings and opinions should have in any argument. From a purely objective standpoint such conscious perceptions have no place. Knowledge has to be built upon demonstrable facts or observations. A subjective stance takes an opposing view. Here knowledge is regarded as belonging to the individual as a result of his or her own consciousness and thoughts. In this way prominence is given to individual points of view and the need to have a collective opinion is of secondary importance. Perhaps there is no need to rehearse these definitions here but a clear appreciation of their differences, and how these influence educational research, is important. What is being considered here is the *epistemological* stance one takes: 'the very bases of knowledge, its nature and forms, how it can be acquired, and how communicated to other human beings' (Cohen et al., 2000: 6). Pat Sikes will develop these points in Chapter 2, and what is offered here is just a quick overview of the main issues. It needs to be noted though that what follows are not hard and fast rules and educational research almost inevitably ends up becoming a blend of research procedures.

To take a pure objectivist's standpoint requires some assumptions to be made. First, events have causes and these can be found – *determinism*. The aim then is to formulate laws to account for these events. For this, research of any phenomenon should result in outwardly measurable criteria; which originate from experience; can be verified by observation; and so used to derive a particular interpretation – *empiricism*. Such research clearly lends itself to the kind of hypothesis and experimental work noted previously and quantitative approaches in an attempt to lead to generalisability. All these are aspects of *positivism*, discussed later in this book, although further comprehensive discussion of this area is also provided by Cohen and colleagues (2000: 8–17).

We have already noted though that undertaking experimental work in educational research is fraught with difficulties and the extent to which generalisability of findings is attainable, scarce. This 'scientific' approach to research, although demonstrably successful in the field of natural and physical science, comes under justifiable attack, at least from a subjectivist's point of view, from a social science position in that it excludes '*notions of choice, freedom, individuality, and moral responsibility*' (Cohen et al., 2000: 17).

Table 1.1 Comparison of positivistic and anti-positivistic approaches to educational research

Positivistic approach	Anti-positivistic approach
Quantitative research techniques	Qualitative research techniques
Objective	Subjective
Experimental	Naturalistic
Pure	Applied
Outsider research	Insider research
Statistical analysis	Non-statistical analysis
Impersonal	Individual
Certain assumptions taken for granted	Taken for granted assumptions investigated
Macro concepts: society, institutions, norms, roles, positions	Micro concepts: individuals, personal constructs, negotiated meanings
Generalise from specific	Interpret the specific

◄─────────────────────   Continuum   ─────────────────────►

McMillan and Schumacher state this position quite clearly when they note that to the layperson 'objectivity means unbiased, open-minded, not subjective and as a procedure refers to data collection and analysis procedures from which only one meaning or interpretation can be made'. But they then go on to note that 'although objectivity is important in all research, it is more difficult in research on humans' (McMillan and Schumacher, 1984: 5).

Such criticism of *positivism* leads to an *'anti-positivist'* view where what is important are individuals' values and self-interpretation and representation of their experiences. In short, the characteristics that make humans human. Although Table 1.1 provides a comparison of these two views of educational research, as we shall see shortly, caution needs to be heeded in interpreting it as suggesting that educational research follows well-defined patterns falling squarely into one approach or another. As you will come to realise, actual research normally lies somewhere along the continuum between these two extremes.

Up to this point we have said nothing about qualitative and quantitative research procedures, preferring instead to begin to give the reader a feel for the kind of approaches to educational research that are possible. This is important as it is the approach taken which will largely determine the procedure(s) used although a particular approach does not negate the use of any particular procedure which probably leads to part of the reason for Wellington's comment that, 'Research can be messy, frustrating and unpredictable' (1996: 7).

To be a little more precise taking a positivistic approach to educational research will almost certainly lead to procedures, which result in the collection of quantitative data and testing of hypotheses, such as data from questionnaires and hard facts from experimental work. Conversely, research which seeks to obtain softer facts, and insights into how an individual creates, modifies and interprets the world in which they find themselves, an anti-positivistic approach, would employ qualitative techniques. In this case interviews and participant-observation would predominate.

To round off this section we have noted that educational research often does not follow well-defined patterns falling squarely into one approach or another. This is clearly discussed by Travers (2001) in the opening chapter of his book on qualitative research. Here, although discussing that from an interpretivist's (anti-positivistic) perspective that 'there are no benefits in working with large data sets, since these encourage a positivist mentality towards analysing interviews' (2001: 11), he discusses proponents of positivistic approaches to qualitative research, such as the British ethnographer Martyn Hammersley (1991), who he notes 'argues that all studies should be judged by a set of scientific criteria, which include reliability and representativeness (the same criteria used in quantitative research)' (2001: 10). Similarly a grounded theory approach to research (e.g. Glaser and Strauss, 1967; Strauss and Corbin, 1997) 'has taken on a positivist flavour, in the sense that it presents qualitative research as a scientific method' (2001: 21).

In short then, drawing a positivist and anti-positivist approach to educational research may seem to have little value. Indeed some might argue that it serves little purpose at all. However, it does provide something of a starting point for beginners, as trying to come to terms with the nuances of interpretation of research approaches can be problematic for short-term research such as that often associated with MEd work. Hopefully, what should be clear is that linking any procedure slavishly to any particular approach is wrong. The reality is of course that a range of procedures pertinent to the research at hand should be used rather than a resolute adherence to any deemed more appropriate. The important issue is to ensure that the research procedure(s) used is appropriate to the research question being asked and the research answers being sought and this is developed further in the next chapter.

Use of statistics

The mention of the word statistics to a group of people new to educational research is likely to give rise to, at the very least, some disquiet. To indicate that a working knowledge of statistics may be needed, will invariably turn this into a full-blown panic attack. Unfortunately, the significance attributed to the 'importance of including statistical evidence' in some cultures only adds to this problem.

Statistics have their rightful place and, used appropriately, are an important part of the armoury for educational research. Later (see Chapters 7 and 10) reference to the two aspects of statistics – *descriptive* and *inferential* – and the degree of their importance will be made. The reality is that the majority of educational research at MEd level need go no further than using straight-forward descriptive statistics with recourse to inferential statistics limited to a few specific areas, such as experimental research.

That something is proved

Many newcomers to educational research invariably feel they have to prove something. Whether this phenomenon, as with the presentation of statistical evidence, is a personal, cultural or political trait is in some senses immater-ial, but the fact is it does exist. The reality is that it is very difficult to 'prove' anything in educational research. We have already discussed the issues of relatability versus generalisability and indicated the view that the former, besides being achievable, is of far more importance to actual practice. We have also highlighted the problems of taking a positivistic (objective) approach to working with human beings. These points indicate the difficulty of 'proving' anything in educational research; yet this is often seen as the necessary outcome if it is to be of any value and taken seriously by others.

So, let's say your research question is:

> An investigation to prove that using a Chinese word-processing
> program helps students with writing in Chinese.

This question is not only fraught with difficulties but at MEd level, I would argue, not achievable. Over the six months typically available for your research, you might, over a few weeks observe a class or two seemingly enjoying using the program. Interviewing some of the students you observed might indicate that they felt it helped them with their writing skills. Tests on these students might even indicate there seems to be a general improvement in the number of and speed at which they can put Chinese sentences together correctly. Do these findings answer the research question?

No, what they actually do, and no more, is indicate that there appears to be some positive value in using a Chinese word-processor to help students with writing in Chinese. If you were going to try and obtain categorical proof for your research question, although it is doubtful if you ever could, you would be looking at issues such as working with hundreds of classes, catering for age, gender, race, social class, academic background, home and school environment, language use in the home, access to resources and so on, and carrying out a longitudinal study over several years. Clearly a research task not feasible within the timescale typically allotted to an MEd.

This may sound very discouraging but let us change the research question to:

An investigation to ascertain whether using a Chinese word-processing program helps students with writing in Chinese.

Now your MEd research can be influential. The evidence you collect can certainly answer this question and, depending on where it was carried out, over what timescale, with what age and gender students, and access to resources (although looking at all these aspects would not be appropriate) provide an indication to others whether it would be worth looking at your research in the context of their own teaching.

I'll leave you with a question. Which of the above two research questions would seem of most value in having an impact upon day-to-day educational practice and helping to inform wider considerations for the use of Chinese word-processors to help students with writing Chinese?

Specific expertise, as it is difficult

The commonly held view is that often research is 'done' by academics, who are specialists in their field, and who have the time and resources to do it. This view has achieved prominence as a result of where educational research takes place – in institutes of higher education. Such work is also, and I think unfairly in many cases, criticised for its lack of relevance to actual educational practical. The view that teachers can do educational research is not new. As Howard and Sharpe note:

> Most people associate the word 'research' with activities which are substantially removed from day-to-day life and which are pursued by outstandingly gifted persons with an unusual level of commitment ... we would argue that the pursuit is not restricted to this type of person and indeed can prove to be a stimulating and satisfying experience for many people (teachers included) with a trained and enquiring mind. (1983: 6)

It is also important to understand that teachers should do educational research as it is 'part of the teacher's professional role, so as to improve their self knowledge and practice' (Hitchcock and Hughes, 1989: 3–4). In this sense connections with practice do not disappear and it addresses relevant problems in their context.

The view that teachers can, and should, undertake educational research has received prominence over the years and indeed one of the most recent funding initiatives from the UK Department for Education and Skills (DfES, 2002), Best Practice in Research Scholarships (BPRS, 2002), squarely focuses the place of research on the practising teacher. How much this is a backlash against the universities – although teachers still have to work in conjunction with institutes of higher education using their expertise, for example, in research procedures – is not an issue for this book. What is evident is that teachers I have worked with have welcomed the opportunity to undertake classroom-based research, which is aimed at informing their own and/or their school's practice. Reports published on the DfES website are indicative of the kind of research which could form the basis of an MEd dissertation and help to dispel the notion that research requires specific expertise only found in institutes of higher education.

If anything a collaborative venture – the focus of MEd courses and relationships between students and tutors – is the crucial factor in any educational research venture.

Can I do educational research?

This question invariably brings up procedural terms such as questionnaires, interviews, surveys, data and experiments and we have addressed these above within the context of the purpose of educational research. Generic terms such as quantitative, qualitative and statistics have also been addressed in this latter context and hopefully by now you will have some idea of how these terms and the procedural ones are linked. You are beginning to understand that any fear you may have had of educational research and your ability to do it is based solely on the myth surrounding the need to understand complex terms and have specialist skills to undertake it.

This is not to minimise or denigrate the value of educational research, or the excellent work carried out in a whole host of settings such as higher education. It is, though, an attempt to try and demystify the area so that those of you new to it can build up the confidence and acceptance that you can do educational research. It is also to make you aware that although typically you will be undertaking your research over a short period of time it is nevertheless of value and, in terms of influencing personal practice, probably more so than any larger, longer research project.

The final types of terms that this second question invokes are ones of practicality: hard work, time consuming, problematic, difficult, requires expertise. There is no use denying that undertaking educational research is hard work. It needs careful planning and organisation if it is to be completed successfully within expected timescales and David Hyatt in Chapter 3 will raise these issues again. It will also be time consuming, and require commitment and sacrifices from yourself and others. There will be problems, but this is where regular contact with your tutor is so important and making sure your research is achievable, not only from a pragmatic viewpoint, but also in the timescale allotted. It does require expertise but again nothing you cannot acquire with the help of your tutor.

In short you can do educational research and the rest of this book provides you with additional information to help you to do so.

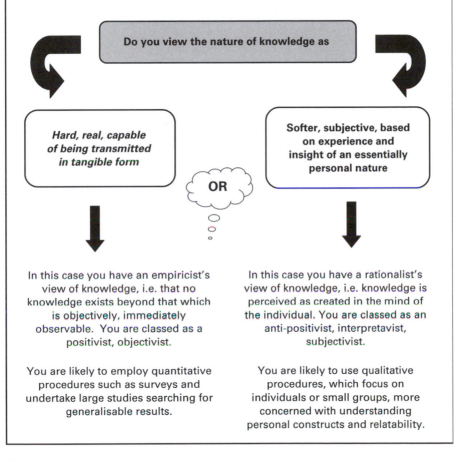

Research Paradigms

Your views of research will be dependent on a number of factors but perhaps the most significant is your epistemology. By this we mean your view of how knowledge is acquired and how it can be communicated to others. How you align yourself profoundly affects how you go about uncovering knowledge of social behaviour. The following tries to put this into some kind of structure for you.

Do you view the nature of knowledge as

Hard, real, capable of being transmitted in tangible form

Softer, subjective, based on experience and insight of an essentially personal nature

OR

In this case you have an empiricist's view of knowledge, i.e. that no knowledge exists beyond that which is objectively, immediately observable. You are classed as a positivist, objectivist.

You are likely to employ quantitative procedures such as surveys and undertake large studies searching for generalisable results.

In this case you have a rationalist's view of knowledge, i.e. knowledge is perceived as created in the mind of the individual. You are classed as an anti-positivist, interpretavist, subjectivist.

You are likely to use qualitative procedures, which focus on individuals or small groups, more concerned with understanding personal constructs and relatability.

Figure 1.3 An overview of research paradigms

Summary

This chapter has attempted to dispel some of the myths surrounding educational research. Its aim has been to show you that undertaking educational research is not the prerogative of a chosen few who make it the focus of their working life. Educational research is 'doable', albeit at different levels of depth and sophistication, by all interested in making a 'systematic, critical and self-critical enquiry which aims to contribute to the advancement of knowledge' (Bassey, 1990: 35) of the world around them.

It also begins to show you how a view of knowledge determines the type of research you would engage in and the procedures you might use, and this is indicated in Figure 1.3.

Thus, the overall intention of this chapter has been to begin to allay any fears you might have as a newcomer to educational research. You can do educational research.

2 Methodology, Procedures and Ethical Concerns

Pat Sikes

When you embark on a research project, having defined the focus and drafted research questions, decisions have to be made about how you are actually going to set about doing the research and about which methodology, or approach, you will adopt. More specifically, and for each and every research case, you have to decide what it is possible to find out which answers, or provides information that goes towards answering, the questions being asked. In other words, you, as the researcher, have to decide what is going to constitute 'valid' data, or evidence, and which procedures, or techniques, are going to be used to collect and analyse it. Sometimes these decisions may be relatively easy to make but as soon as you start asking questions that can be interpreted and, therefore answered, in various ways, then things become more difficult. In educational research, indeed in any research that involves people in social settings, multiple perspectives and interpretations are almost inevitable. A good rule is never to think that anything is straightforward and 'obvious', never to take anything for granted and never to leave any assumptions unquestioned.

In this chapter my aim is to follow this rule and to look, critically, at some of the issues and considerations that have to be borne in mind when selecting methodologies and procedures for a particular piece of research. As has already been explained, throughout this book the term 'procedure' is preferred to 'method', primarily in order to avoid the confusion that can arise when 'methodology' and 'method' are used interchangeably. They are not the same thing, and being aware of how they differ and, as a consequence, being able to address, discuss and offer a rationale for both methodology and procedure, is a necessary and crucial part of the research process – and should constitute a significant and substantial section of any research report, paper or dissertation that may eventually be produced!

An important methodological and procedural consideration is how people involved or touched, in any way, by a research project might be affected by their involvement. Researchers need to give attention to the ethical implications of their work and so, in the second part of the chapter, I will be raising some ethical issues that need to be addressed when doing educational research.

Working definitions

Before proceeding with the chapter, look at Figure 2.1.

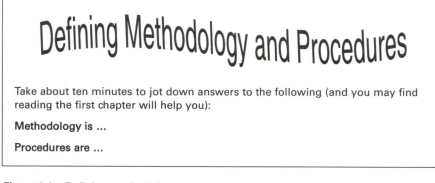

Take about ten minutes to jot down answers to the following (and you may find reading the first chapter will help you):

Methodology is ...

Procedures are ...

Figure 2.1   Defining methodology and procedures

The task of the researcher is to investigate, to find things out, to interpret findings and to make sense of the aspect(s) of the world they are focusing on. Their business is to get knowledge. *Methodology* refers to the theory of getting knowledge, to the consideration of the best ways, methods or procedures, by which data that will provide the evidence basis for the construction of knowledge about whatever it is that is being researched, is obtained. Methodology is concerned with the description and analysis of research methods rather than with the actual, practical use of those methods. Methodological work is, therefore, philosophical, thinking, work. A slight complication is introduced by the way in which the word, methodology, is also used to denote the overall approach to a particular research project, to the overarching strategy that is adopted. Thus, Case Study, Life History and Action Research are examples of methodological approaches.

Procedures – or, as they are often referred to, methods – on the other hand, are the specific research techniques that are used in order to collect and then analyse data. Thus, a Case Study (methodology) may involve interviews, questionnaires, observation and documentary analysis (procedures). Similarly, an Action Research project (methodology) will need to use procedures such as tests, questionnaires, and interviews, to collect information in order to evaluate the intervention that was its focus.

Selecting methodologies and procedures

Researchers have to be able to justify and argue a methodological case for their reasons for choosing a particular approach and specific procedures. It is on the match between methodology and procedures and research focus/topic/questions that the credibility of any findings, conclusions and claims depends, so the importance of getting it right cannot be overemphasized. Since different methodologies and procedures yield different types of evidence, selection of particular methodologies and procedures also, inevitably, involves ruling out forms of data that would have been obtained had other ones been used. Thus, methodology and procedures determine the nature of the findings of research. For example, it would be difficult, if not impossible, to make generalisations about the efficacy of a behaviour management strategy on the basis of an action research study which focused on one teacher using it with one class. Similarly, it would not be possible to make claims to represent teachers' pedagogical values and beliefs following a study that had used an interactional observation schedule, yielding numerical data, and had not solicited, either through interview or written communication, the views of teachers themselves.

Decisions about which methodologies and procedures will be used in any research project are usually influenced by: what can actually be done; what is practical and feasible; by situational factors of various kinds; and by personal predilections and interests. One of the very first tasks that researchers need to undertake is to think about the implications for their research design, conduct and reporting, of such considerations as:

- The physical, social, political and historical contexts in which their research project will be located.
- The reasons why they are doing the research.
- How they conceptualise the situation they are researching.
- The sorts of questions that they are seeking answers for.
- The type of information that their questions will produce.
- The scale of the research and the financial, personnel and other resources available to conduct it.
- The nature of the research population and the ability of informants to provide particular types of response.
- Ethical and moral issues relevant at the various stages of the research process.
- If applicable, what are the requirements and expectations of any organisation or body that is commissioning and/or funding the research?
- When, and over what timescale the research will be done.

Rarely is there only one way to go about things. To present research design as being a straightforward, technical matter of 'horses for courses', with researchers 'objectively' choosing the most appropriate, if not the only possible, methodology and procedures for a specific research project, would be misleading and even dishonest and immoral (Sikes and Goodson, 2003). To reiterate: multiple perspectives and interpretations of social situations are usually, if not always, possible. This means that most research topics could be approached from a range of different theoretical and philosophical positions and investigated by using most of the available methodologies and procedures. However, since, as has already been noted, methodologies and procedures, as a result of their differences, yield different types of information, they could well end up providing different bases on which different interpretations could be made leading, quite legitimately and logically, to different emphases and even conclusions. To admit this is not to say 'anything goes' but rather places the responsibility for justifying and constructing a rationale for their chosen methodology and procedures, and for demonstrating rigour in their theorising and practice, firmly on the shoulders of the researcher themselves.

Researcher positionality

Usually, the most significant factor that influences choice and use of methodology and procedures is 'where the researcher is coming from' in terms of their philosophical position and their fundamental assumptions concerning:

- social reality – their ontological assumptions;
- the nature of knowledge – their epistemological assumptions;
- human nature and agency – specifically their assumptions about the way in which human beings relate to and interact with their environment.

Assumptions of this nature are coloured by values and beliefs that are based in, for instance, political allegiance, religious faith, and experiences that are consequent upon social class, ethnicity, gender, sexuality, historical and geographical location, and so on. It seems to me (and here I am making a statement that has to be understood in the context of my own fundamental assumptions) that the way in which researchers are biographically situated, the consequent perspectives they hold and the assumptions which inform the sense they make of the world, inevitably have implications for their research related understandings, beliefs and values, for the research paradigms they feel most comfortable with, and, thereby, for their research practice.

Following Guba (1990: 17) and Denzin and Lincoln (2000: 19) I define paradigm as a basic set of beliefs that guides action. In the recent past, the two main paradigms that have influenced educational research are the scientific, positivist, objective, quantitative paradigm and the interpretative, naturalistic, subjective, qualitative paradigm (although it is important to remember that *all* research is interpretative in that it can only offer an interpretation, not an actual replica, of the world). The characteristics of these paradigms and some of the (negative) implications that the tendency towards a polarised conceptualisation of them has had for educational research and researchers were discussed in Chapter 1. There it was also pointed out that educational research projects frequently make use of procedures that have come to be associated with both paradigms and that, therefore, to some extent, the dichotomy is a false one, a framework for comprehension rather than an accurate representation of how things 'really are' (Pring, 2000). Nevertheless, even if people do mix and match and employ triangulation by using more than one procedure (Cohen et al., 2000), I believe that it is important for all researchers to spend some time thinking about how they are paradigmatically and philosophically positioned and for them to be aware of how their positioning – and the fundamental assumptions they hold – might influence their research related thinking and practice. This is about being a reflexive and reflective and, therefore, a rigorous researcher who is able to present their findings and interpretations in the confidence that they have thought about, acknowledged and been honest and explicit about their stance and the influence it has had upon their work. This is important given that a major criticism of much educational research is that it is biased and partisan (see, for example, Hargreaves, 1996; Tooley, 1998). It is also important in terms of ensuring a coherent, and hence justifiable, research design. Thus, in this section of the chapter I am going to look, briefly and in turn, at how assumptions about ontology, epistemology and the nature of human relations are intimately bound up with assumptions that impact upon educational researchers' decisions about methodology and procedures. For reasons of presentational clarity I shall be describing extreme positions (i.e. I will be saying people either see things in this way or they see them in that way – 'this' and 'that' being diametrically opposed). However, people's views and positions are frequently not as clear-cut as I may appear to be suggesting and readers should bear this caveat in mind.

So: How researchers approach research has a great deal to do with:

- ontological assumptions concerning the nature of social reality;
- epistemological assumptions concerning the bases of knowledge;
- assumptions concerning human nature and agency.

We will now consider these in turn.

Ontological assumptions concerning the nature of social reality

Ontology is concerned with the nature or essence of things so ontological assumptions about social reality will focus on whether a person sees social reality – or aspects of the social world – as external, independent, given and objectively real, or, instead, as socially constructed, subjectively experienced and the result of human thought as expressed through language. How, in these terms, they view the social world has implications for the sorts of methodologies and procedures they are likely to consider to be 'valid' means of collecting 'valid' data that can be used to make a 'valid' interpretation, thus creating 'valid' knowledge. Basically if the social world is seen as given and independent then it can be observed and accounted for through 'objective', quantifiable data. However, if a social constructivist position is taken it will be necessary to collect subjective accounts and perceptions that explain how the world is experienced and constructed by the people who live in it.

For example, and very simplistically, let us take research questions focusing on gender differences. The independent, given view of reality might be that any differences in intellectual ability and aptitude between boys and girls, men and women, are mainly the result of natural, biological, physiological and hormonal causes. These differences can therefore, be observed and may even be measured and quantified by an outside observer – that is, the researcher. A social constructivist view, however, might explain differences in terms of socialisation, as the outcome of different expectations, experiences and ways of being treated, which although they could, possibly, be observed by an outsider, would also need to be explained by the people involved in the situation.

I suspect that, these days at least, most people whose research focuses on gender difference take the view that both nature and nurture have a contribution to make but even so I also think it is likely that they will see one type of influence having the edge and being dominant. This will, inevitably, colour the interpretation they make and the conclusions they draw. It may also affect any action arising from their research. To put it at its most basic: if gender differences are believed to have biological origins then very little, if anything, can be done to improve and develop the performance of the lower achieving group whereas if how people are treated is seen to be significant then it may be possible to change behaviours and, thereby affect outcomes.

To those who are concerned with social justice issues, natural theories are, at the least, problematic, and at worst, dangerous in that they can be used to support inequality. The history of education (as is the history of the world) is littered with research-based justifications for treating particular groups of people (e.g. women, Blacks, Jews, the working classes) differently and usually, less favourably, than others. Clearly, researchers' ontological assumptions can have ethical consequences and I will be considering these in more detail later on. At this point though, it is worth pointing out the importance of thinking the implications through thoroughly at an early stage of research design.

Also important is the question of consistency and coherence, which means that researchers need to be sure that the methodologies and procedures they use are in accord with their ontological position. And they need to make a convincing case for their practice in the light of their fundamental ontological assumptions. They must be able to argue that the procedures they use collect the sort of data that legitimately and validly answers the questions they have posed. Equally important is that they make their position clear in any account they produce – be that a journal article, a dissertation, or a report to colleagues. To fail to do so would be to lay themselves open to criticisms of unacknowledged bias.

Epistemological assumptions concerning the bases of knowledge

> Many of the bitter arguments about the significance of research findings are founded in fundamental disagreements about knowledge and how to get it: these are precisely disagreements about methodology and epistemology. (Griffiths, 1998: 33)

Epistemology is the theory of knowledge, thus epistemological assumptions concern the nature of knowledge, what constitutes knowledge and what it is possible to know and understand and re-present. The reason for doing research is to get knowledge and to communicate that knowledge, often with the ultimate view of informing practice and/or policy and, thereby, improving things in some way. Consequently it is impossible to engage in research and not be concerned with epistemology and with epistemological questions and issues. Central to such concern is the notion of 'truth': truth in terms of how the data/evidence that research procedures obtain corresponds to and reflects the knowledge it is claimed that it does; and truth in terms of how the researcher communicates and re-presents the knowledge they get from their research. As Griffiths suggests, epistemology, and particularly the relationship between methodology and procedures and knowledge and truth, is a contentious and controversial area for researchers and consumers of research.

Basically the main focus for disagreement centres on whether:

> it is possible to identify and communicate the nature of knowledge as being hard, real and capable of being transmitted in a tangible form, or whether knowledge is of a softer, more subjective, spiritual or even transcendental kind, based on experience and insight of a unique and essentially personal nature. (Burrell and Morgan, 1979, quoted in Cohen et al., 2000: 6)

In terms of research design and choice of procedures, if the assumption is that knowledge is real, objective and out there in the world to be captured, researchers can observe, measure and quantify it. However, if it is assumed to be experiential, personal and subjective, they will have to ask questions of the people involved. These differences are much the same as those identified with regard to ontological assumptions.

Questions around truth, validity and accuracy can be posed of both fundamental positions – although it must be noted that contemporary thinking, sometimes although not always, influenced by postmodernism, is that absolute truth is (presently) unattainable. Even natural scientists, working out of the positivist tradition, frequently tend to the view that knowledge at any time is provisional and that it is only possible to claim to be able to make an interpretation based on what can be known given the available resources, knowledge and understandings. This is quite a different position from that taken by those who believe that all knowledge and truth is relative, which again can be different from the view that there are multiple realities, depending upon social positioning and life experiences.

The sorts of truth questions likely to be asked of research based on a hard view of knowledge tend to be about causality and the extent to which procedures yield the knowledge claimed. For example: is it possible to be confident that significant improvement in reading ages as evidenced by reading tests over a period of time, are the result of a new teaching approach? Or might it be to do with other things that the research procedures did not tap in to?

Research which proceeds from the epistemological assumption that knowledge is experiential and subjective will usually place considerable emphasis on the accounts given by informants – either verbally in interviews or written and in response to questionnaires. In this case the major truth challenge is likely to focus on whether or not informants have been honest. Sometimes informants do lie deliberately and their lies are detected, maybe as a result of using triangulation techniques or by happenstance. However, the question of what counts as 'truth' or 'lies' with regard to informants' accounts can rarely be answered simply or easily. This is because the whole issue of how words can actually reflect 'reality' and experience is, in itself, complex and problematic. Then it is also the case that such things as faulty memory, inadequate vocabulary, partial or erroneous knowledge, and a desire to tell the researcher what it's thought they want to hear, lead to an account which can be shown to be 'untrue' but was not given with the deliberate intention of deceiving (see Sikes, 2000, for an extended discussion of issues around truth and lies in informants' accounts).

Regardless of how they are positioned in terms of their epistemological assumptions it is crucial that researchers are clear in their own minds as to the implications of their stance, that they state their position explicitly, and that they are either able to substantiate any claims to knowledge on the basis of their research or are tentative and cautious in presenting their conclusions.

Assumptions concerning human nature and agency

Essentially, these assumptions are concerned with the way in which human beings are seen to act within the world. Do they respond in a mechanistic way to their environment and the things that happen to them or do they initiate action and make choices? Is their behaviour determined by innate instinctual forces or by external conditions and forces, or do they act voluntarily and out of their own free will? For researchers, who are themselves, human beings, this is an interesting area because whatever they decide inevitably applies to them as well as to their research population.

I have described two extreme positions and most people would probably plump for somewhere in the middle. Some things are done voluntarily and others because, for whatever reason, we have no choice. Of course, this is a complex area that highlights issues of social power and agency as well as raising questions about natural behaviours. Basically, the more social power you have, the more you can choose what to do. The scenario is further complicated by the way in which people may have power in certain social settings but not in others. In the section on ethics I shall be returning to questions of social power as they relate to educational researchers who are often working with children and others who, relative to them and in the research context, have much less power.

Assumptions about human nature and agency have clear implications for methodological and procedural choices. If people are believed to behave in a predetermined or reactive way, then observation and experiments will be appropriate techniques; if, however, they are felt to make decisions about what to do, procedures which seek explanations and understanding from their perspective will be needed. In this section my aim has been to demonstrate how researchers need to explore their fundamental assumptions relating to ontology, epistemology and human nature and agency because these have major implications for methodological and procedural choices. However, I have not intended to suggest that these assumptions are fixed once and for all and it may be that in the course of a research project, perhaps as a result of involvement in and experience of, particular research procedures and the sorts of information and knowledge they produce, people's thinking alters. It is not at all unusual for someone to start out using a particular methodology and set of procedures and end up with serious concerns about their appropriateness for the particular questions and situations being investigated. When this happens decisions have to be taken about whether to continue down the original route or whether to begin again. Of course, much will depend on what time is available and how strongly someone feels about writing up a study using an approach they are no longer happy with or confident about. An alternative strategy, and the one I would always advocate, is to build in a section that deals with why there has been this change of position. Researcher honesty is important and 'telling it as it was' can only be in the interest of good research practice.

To give you some practice of considering methodological issues consider the Figure 2.2. Spending time thinking about philosophical issues may seem to be a diversion when time is limited but research *is* a philosophical endeavour

Identifying Research Paradigms

Having discussed two research paradigms (Positivistic and Interpretative) decide which of the following research questions fits with which paradigm. Discuss how you have come to the decision you have? What implications does your selection have in terms of the procedures you might use?

1 Does more frequent use of textbooks increase student achievement?
2 How are texts used by teachers and students in the classroom?
3 What are students' and teacher's view on the instructional value of using interactive whiteboards?
4 Does the use of computer simulation software improve students' understanding of issues associated with population growth?
5 Has the implementation of Problem Based Learning helped students in developing group working?

Figure 2.2   Identifying research paradigms

and failure to attend to the thinking side of things will inevitably impoverish the enterprise as a whole. Also, it is my view that researchers who have examined and reflected upon their assumptions and consequent values and who are prepared to make their positionality explicit, provide themselves with a strong basis on which to design and conduct rigorous work that they can justify and which will stand up to scrutiny. They are also likely to be well aware of the ethical implications of their work because they will have considered their relationship vis-à-vis the people who may be touched by their research. This is important for much educational research is by, for or with people – be that students, teachers, parents, administrators or others – and educational researchers have a responsibility to act in an ethical manner. In the following section of this chapter the focus will be on some of the ethical issues and questions related to methodology and procedures that educational researchers need to consider before, during and after they embark on their work.

Ethical issues and questions

> Without adequate training and supervision, the neophyte researcher can unwittingly become an unguarded projectile bringing turbulence to the field, fostering personal trauma (for researcher and researched), and even causing damage to the discipline. (Punch, 1994: 93)

To people starting out on a small scale research project as part of a qualification, Maurice Punch's words might sound alarmist and extreme and unlikely to apply to them. Nevertheless, it is the case that any research that involves people has the potential to cause (usually unintentional) damage.

'Ethics has to do with the application of moral principles to prevent harming or wronging others, to promote the good, to be respectful and to be fair' (Sieber, 1993: 14). This definition does, I believe, make it clear why all researchers need to be concerned with ethics. Various professional bodies, organisations and institutions (e.g. the British Educational Research Association, the British Psychological Society, individual universities) have their own codes of research ethics and these are very useful. However, on their own they may not be enough to prevent harm and hurt because the unique characteristics of each instance of research have to be considered in their own right. A useful acid test when considering methodologies and procedures is to ask yourself how you would personally feel if you or your children or your friends were 'researched' by means of them? If you have any qualms whatsoever then you need to think very carefully about the morality of subjecting anyone else to them.

Ethical considerations apply throughout the research process and I am now going to move on to look at, and raise questions concerning what I believe are the major issues at each stage. The headings I am using are not meant to be seen as definitive or totally inclusive, nor are they neat and tidy, but are, rather, offered as a framework to inform thinking and planning towards ethical research.

Research design

- What exactly do you want to know and why do you want to know it? Can you justify your interest?

Research comes into the lives of people who are the focus in various ways, taking up their time, involving them in activities they wouldn't otherwise have been involved in, providing researchers with privileged knowledge about them – and therefore, potentially, power over them. If the research is simply to confirm a personal theory, satisfy curiosity or help the researcher get a qualification and there are no benefits for anyone else, then maybe it is unethical to proceed. It is possible to conceive of research that feeds prurient interest – such as, finding out details about pupils' home backgrounds, or research that touches on sexual matters – and which therefore, is questionable. Research that seeks to 'prove' the superiority of people possessing particular characteristics may also be dubious.

- If you are intending to do anything that is in any way 'experimental' what are the implications for the people who will be involved? If you are using a 'control group' will people assigned to it miss out on anything that you suspect will be beneficial? Can it be justified?

The key ethical issue here centres on differential treatment. If it becomes clear, before the research as originally designed is finished, that a 'treatment' is either having positive or negative effects, will the researcher be prepared to abandon their plans?

- Insofar as you are able, have you thought about potential unintended or unexpected consequences either to the people directly involved in the research or as a result of what you might find out?

Obviously, unintended outcomes or consequences cannot be anticipated, however a careful risk assessment can be undertaken. Researchers need to think carefully about the consequences of being involved in research that adopts particular methodologies and procedures. For instance: how might being case studied affect a child? What might be the consequences of reflecting on past negative experiences for a teacher involved in a life history study? Then there are considerations about how people other than the researcher might use findings and how this use might have far-reaching implications.

- If you are intending to do covert research of some kind, can you justify it?

As I am using the term here, 'covert' research refers to all instances where researchers are not straightforwardly honest about what they are doing. This may involve simply not saying that any research is taking place. In such cases the researcher doesn't reveal that they are a researcher and participates in the social setting concerned under another identity. This may be the identity by which they are usually known, for example a teacher doing research in their own classroom just carries on as normal. In other instances people may say that they are doing research but conceal the true focus of their interest, either because they wouldn't be permitted to study what they were really interested in or because it is felt that people would try to change their behaviours if they knew these were the ones that were being investigated. Covert research of this kind has often focused on such topics and issues as: prejudice and discrimination of various kinds; behaviours and practices which are widely regarded as socially unacceptable, illegal or taboo; secret organisations; powerful groups. In some cases strong justifications for covert research can be made because findings from it can lead to positive improvements and wider social justice. For instance, within the scope of educational research, studies of racist and sexist behaviour and practices have been covertly undertaken, which the researchers felt was to the benefit of the greater good. This is an area where the limitations of ethical codes are highlighted.

- How do you regard the people you are going to be 'researching'?

It is important to think about how you as the researcher conceive of, and are going to refer to, the members of the research population. Talking about 'subjects' can be understood to carry some unfortunate connotations. 'Subject' can suggest that these people are 'othered' and their humanity neglected: this is unethical. I prefer to use the term 'informants' and while this might be more obviously appropriate in the case of research that collects verbal accounts, it is relevant to other types of research too in that, essentially, it is the members of the research population who provide the information. Language is critical and the language that we use reflects our fundamental assumptions, understandings and beliefs. In thinking and talking about and designing research considerable attention has to be paid to the words that are used because of the meanings they carry.

Access

- How are you going to access your research population? If you choose to do your research with people who don't possess much social power (e.g. children, captive populations, your own students) can you justify why? And are you exploiting their 'weakness'?

Accessing research populations raises a number of ethical issues, mainly focusing on questions of social power. Traditionally quite a bit of research has been done with people who were not in a position to say 'no'. Of course, this means that findings from research with such populations, are specific but this is not always acknowledged. John Bowlby's work on maternal deprivation, for instance, was based on research done with boys in Borstal and yet, although this was not made explicit, findings were extrapolated to the wider population. Gaining the permission of 'gatekeepers', head teachers, or parents for example, may be appropriate in some cases, but not in others. It is also possible that informants' responses may be influenced when they know that a researcher has been given access to them by, for instance, their head or their teacher. Of course, the more people you ask for permission the more chances there are that it will not be granted. In the interests of ethical practice this is probably a risk that has to be taken.

Procedures of data collection

- Are you asking people things you wouldn't want to be asked?
- Are you asking people to do things you wouldn't want to be asked to do?

As I noted earlier, an acid test when it comes to deciding whether procedures are ethical, is whether or not the researcher would feel comfortable if they or people close to them, were the 'researched'. There is also the question of whether it is ethical to ask people to do things that they normally wouldn't do, and which may be detrimental to them. The example that is often cited with respect to this issue is that of Milgram's (in)famous (1963) research into obedience to authority in which people were instructed to give electric shocks – of lethal potential – to others. Unbeknown to them the 'shocks' were administered to actors.

Milgram's work was contrary to the notion of 'informed consent'. This notion arose out of the Nuremberg Nazi trials following the second World War. Horrendous experiments of all kinds were conducted on people under the auspices of the third Reich leading to the drawing up of a code for scientists, the key demands of which can be summarised as follows: that,

- all known aspects of the research are disclosed to all those involved;
- information about the research is given in a form that potential participants can understand;
- the individuals involved are capable of making an informed decision to
  participate;
- agreement to participate is essential.

Such requirements raise issues for researchers working with young children and those with learning disabilities because others may have to take the decision to participate on their behalf. Even so, and when appropriate circumstances pertain, these considerations can be a useful guide. Indeed in recent years it has become common for researchers to seek written informed consent from the people they work with. However, as Fine and colleagues (2000) point out, such consent may be seen as having the effect of absolving the researcher of their moral and ethical responsibility:

> The consent form sits at the contradictory base of the institutionalisation of research. Although the aim of informed consent is presumably to protect respondents, informing them of the possibility of harm in advance and inviting them to withdraw if they so desire, it also effectively releases the institution or funding agency from any liability and gives control of the research process to the researcher. (Fine et al., 2000: 113)

When choosing and designing research procedures it is also significant in terms of respect for respondents, to think about the amount of time that participating in the research will take. Time is precious and many of us have experienced the frustration of starting out to complete someone's research questionnaire and of feeling increasingly fed up as we turn yet another page and address yet another question! Often such questionnaires end up in the bin and as researchers we should remember this!

Research relationships

- You have a basic human moral responsibility towards the people you are working with. Are you sure that you are doing as you would be done by?

It is important to remember that research relationships are two-sided and that the people who are being 'researched' will make their own interpretations of what is going on, regardless of researchers' intentions. It may be the case that informants are not interested in having any more involvement in a research project than answering a questionnaire or taking part in an interview – as researchers who have sought respondent validation have sometimes found to their disappointment. However, it is ethical practice to ensure that they are given as much information as possible and as they require.

- Could you be accused of 'rape research'?

Patti Lather talks about 'rape research' (1986). This is research where the researcher goes into the research setting, gets what they want and then leaves, never to return and giving nothing in return. By and large, this has been the traditional approach to research and not only is it disrespectful of informants, it can limit dissemination of findings and potential positive outcomes. Researchers should think about what they can give back, about what's 'in it' for their informants and seek to find some sort of reciprocity. Even so, the chances are that the greater benefit will be to the researcher, who must ensure that they properly express their gratitude.

- Are you manipulating people and relationships in order to get 'good' data?

People who use various types of interviewing in their research, myself included (see particularly Measor and Sikes, 1992, and Sikes, Measor and Woods, 1985), have often talked about the need to establish good relationships with informants because this will mean that they are more likely to want to help you. Researchers have to remember though that, as well as being in possession of information that they require, their informants are people with emotions and feelings. Care must be taken to avoid leaving people feeling that they have been instrumentally and cynically manipulated. Coffey (1999) provides an eloquent and moving discussion of research relationships.

- Are you sensitive to the implications of any differences in terms of social power between researcher and 'researched'.

It often seems to be assumed that the balance of power between researcher and researched is always in favour of the researcher. This is not the case. Sometimes researchers do have more power. For instance they may be older, in possession of more knowledge, be in social or organisational positions that give them greater influence or possess characteristics (e.g. their sex or 'race') that carry greater weight. When they are more powerful they should be mindful to use that power responsibly and ethically. And they should do well to remember that it is the informant who, at the end of the day, has the information that they want and people who think that they have been 'used' or badly treated may well 'lie'.

Researchers who claim to be engaged in emancipatory or empowering research should think carefully about how this positions them vis-à-vis their informants – and should heed Barry Troyna's (1994) warning that such claims are frequently grandiose and at best naïve.

Interpretation and analysis

- Do you acknowledge any theoretical frameworks or value systems that may influence your interpretations and analysis?

If researchers have been reflective and reflexive about their stance and, insofar as they are able, have considered and made explicit the fundamental assumptions underlying their choices of methodology and procedure then they will be aware of potential influences upon their interpretations and analysis. To fail to do this would be unethical.

Writing up

- Do you 'own' your research in your writing up.

A number of ethical questions and issues arise at the writing up stage of the research process. As Tony Carroll notes:

> The reflexive handling of the report poses for the reader the challenge of considering how well the researcher has acquitted him or herself on issues such as:
> - where the researcher stands;
> - what positions are taken up, and
> - what political and ethical stances are attached to those positions (rather than on the question of verisimilitude to an out there world).

and in much educational writing,

> there is a strong tendency for the research text not to draw attention to itself as a text … writing is seen as a neutral vehicle for transporting the truth. Thus

'textuality' of research falls away with writing appearing as simply an unmediating means for communicating a reality that is outside the text (Usher, 1996, quoted in Carroll, 2001: 102)

Research writing is not neutral. The language that is used and the information that is communicated are all significant. To hide behind text is unethical. One issue that I feel strongly about, but which I am aware is controversial, is the use of 'I' when writing about the research process in papers or dissertations. In my view using such phrases as 'the researcher' or 'the author' is a distancing strategy. Researchers should be prepared to 'own' their work and the most immediate and obvious way of doing so is to say 'I'.

- Do you make the research process appear to be neat and unproblematic?

Researchers have an ethical responsibility to other researchers following after them. Traditionally accounts of research make the process appear to be neat and unproblematic. Rarely is research like this. Things can and do go wrong at all stages and failure to 'tell it like it was' is both dishonest and unethical in terms of the impression that is presented. New researchers who have only read traditional accounts can easily come to the conclusion that they are the only person to experience difficulty and may give up or feel inadequate. Researchers should share their problems, difficulties and the things that they learn, through 'honest' accounts of how it was for them. Often, it is the things that are left out that are the most significant!

- Are informants sufficiently protected in written accounts?

Usually, informants involved in research projects are offered assurances of confidentiality and anonymity. In small-scale research this is sometimes difficult but it would be unethical to make promises that cannot be kept.

Another issue concerns how informants are presented in research accounts. Researchers should guard against portraying informants in any way that might damage their self-esteem. This may mean such things as editing out 'ums' and 'ers' from reported speech if people feel that literal transcription makes them appear incoherent (even if they are anonymised!). Once again, the acid test looms large and applies in the vast majority of cases: do as you would be done by.

Data dissemination

- Are my informants sufficiently protected when it comes to data dissemination?

Much of what was said under the heading of writing up applies here. Researchers submitting dissertations to university libraries should be aware that it is usually possible to place their work under an embargo, limiting general release for a specified period of time. However, it requires particular commitment and awareness that few people are likely to have to seek out a thesis in the first place. Researchers should be cautious when it comes to dissemination and consider the implications for their informants.

Avoiding harm/Doing wrong

- The aim is not to harm anyone or do any moral wrong (and not to queer the pitch for other researchers either). This isn't simple because one can never know what the unintended outcomes will be.
- Do the ends ultimately justify the means?

Researchers must do all that they can to think through eventualities and possibilities and feel confident that insofar as they are able, they have taken all possible precautions to avoid harming and doing wrong to anyone touched by their research. This is not a simple and straightforward matter and there are no answers that are applicable in all situations either.

Summary

This chapter has discussed the importance of considering methodological issues, when undertaking any kind of research project. It has highlighted the fact that sharing research plans and decisions and choices about methodologies and procedures with supervisors and critical friends is essential, but perhaps most important is being aware that research is inherently a political activity in that it affects people's lives, however lightly and tangentially. Accepting and acknowledging this will go some way to ensuring that research is ethical, rigorous and can be justified.

As a conclusion to this chapter consider the ethical issues set out in Figure 2.3 and discuss your views with others.

Exploring the Ethics of Research
What would you do?

	YOUR SITUATION
1	You are talking with a colleague about the problem you are having with part of your study. Your colleague offers to write the section of the study for you. What do you say?
2	You know a person in another school, who is happy to be interviewed for an important part of your study. The Principal of that school cannot be contacted for permission for this person to be involved. What do you do?
3	You have daily access to staff files, which contain information helpful to your study. You could count the numbers of staff in each of your categories and report the figures without naming any individual. No one would know how you got the information. Do you do this?
4	You want to conduct a study, which involves collecting a significant amount of numerical data. You want to perform statistical tests on this data but do not know which tests to use or how to do it. A friend says he/she will do it for you. Do you use their help?
5	You want to observe some lessons taught by each of four members of your department in a school in order to collect some data for your research. Two of your staff are eager to help, the other two are not. You are the head of that department and could insist they help. What do you do?
6	You tape an interview in which a member of staff makes allegations of professional wrongdoing by a senior member of staff. This wrongdoing has no relevance to your study or the purpose of the interview. What do you do with this information?
7	You are conducting a study into the effectiveness of your leadership style within your department. You want to tape record department meetings, with a view to examining only your own performance. If you tell your department you know that half the group will object to the meetings being taped. What do you do?
8	You have conducted a study into your college's management style and have included views of close colleagues. They have made frank and open comments to you during interviews. However, you get another job in another country and so have to submit your study after you have left the college. You want to write a conclusion very critical of the college management, based largely on the views of your past colleagues who still work there. The question is what do you do?

Figure 2.3   Exploring the ethics of research

3 Writing Research?

David Hyatt

For many students embarking upon a Masters level course, this will entail the first piece of academic writing that they have been required to do for ten years or more, as the majority of those taking such courses tend to be mid-career professionals. For most MEd students, perhaps the greatest concern they feel when starting a new course is to know exactly what is expected of them in terms of their assignments and also what is this mysterious thing we call 'academic writing'. In this chapter my aim is to explore some of the usual requirements of such courses, to consider the conventions of such courses, to look at the possible process, to consider the importance of feedback, to offer a number of tips, and to conclude by returning to the issues that you will raise in the following activity.

Expected requirements for student academic writing

I'd like to start this chapter by asking you to reflect on your thinking about your own perceptions on the area of academic literacy. Consider your own responses to the questions in Figure 3.1 – you might find it useful to make a few notes on these questions and then refer back to them as you work your way through this chapter.

To begin with I'd like to consider the usual requirements of student academic writing. While the exact requirement will differ from institution to institution the following is meant to cover areas that in my experience appear to be common ground. It is important to check with your own course tutors and documentation exactly what is required. It is also interesting to note that such requirements can change as you move through your career. Robin Lakoff (1990) describes the need to conform to requirements as a Bell Curve, beginning with low formality in writing at an early age and moving to a peak at the stage of students completing Masters courses and holding

What are your views of Academic Writing?

○   *What are the purposes of academic writing?*
○   *What are the features of good academic writing?*
○   *What are the features of bad academic writing?*

Figure 3.1   Views of academic writing

untenured teaching positions at university. This is the stage where they need to prove themselves as members of the discourse community and so the pressure of being in a relatively low status position is most acute. Later with tenure and moving on to professorships and higher status within the discourse community, academics move down the curve and in a position to flaunt the requirements and conventions to suit their own ends as they no longer have to stake their claim. However, not all academics choose to do this and many still eschew the crucial traits of clarity and conciseness.

Using a range of sources

The critical evaluation of a range of sources is crucial to a credible piece of academic writing. This means that you need to examine issues from a range of perspectives and not simply and unquestioningly accept the opinions of authors, no matter how prestigious they may be. You need to problematise the key issues and the literature you refer to – what are the alternatives to or criticisms of any position and especially what are the implications implied within these perspectives? You can hold any position you want but you must weigh up the argument before coming to a judgement, the conclusion you arrive at must relate to this problematisation of the key issues. You need to undertake a critical examination of theoretical issues raised – again look at a range of theoretical and conceptual standpoints, look for strengths weaknesses and implications in these positions and relate the literature to this criticism. You will also need to show awareness of limitations of the literature and of your own research/analysis and conclusions. This is a strength not a weakness. It shows you are reflecting on your work and thought. It shows you are making critical and self-critical judgements about the issues.

Criticality

Criticality is a key word that appears again and again in assessment criteria and academic journals but what does this mean? In a recent small scale survey I conducted with colleagues and students the following key elements of criticality emerged and terms such as analysis, variety of sources, synthesis, substantiation (either through literature or experience) and reflection were raised.

COMPOSITION

> We might interpret it as the quality of being able to view arguments critically – analysing, synthesising points of view and so forth. (Student 1)

> It implies the ability to understand, analyse and appraise the ideas, views and findings expressed in a variety of source materials. The student's opinions must be substantiated in some way, for example, by reference to other materials or the student's own experience. (Student 2)

> In this regard a narrow interpretation might be to show awareness of the *range* of literature on an issue and to try to assess the validity of approaches from a position of detachment. (Student 3)

> The possible criteria are: is there a central thesis? Is it supported by evidence? (Student 5)

REFLECTION

> In my particular context as an MEd student, criticality also implies a reflective cycle involving the appraisal of my own work and working context in the light of current theory and accepted practice, and vice versa. (Student 2)

CONTEXT

> In essence criticality for me is the understanding that ideas and positions do not occur in a vacuum, they are socially derived and can never be 'objective'. Likewise the critic can never be objective. The value of such an understanding then lies in the opening up of debate and examining one's own position and prejudices in turn. (Student 3)

TRANSPARENCY

> Criticality is concerned with making things explicit and open to scrutiny and challengeable. In this regard it is perhaps the opposite of an implicit and commonsensical view. If things are held to be commonsense they are considered unquestionable. (Student 3)

ENQUIRY

> Maintaining a 'vigorously questioning attitude' to all the materials I read, in the spirit of open-minded enquiry. (Student 4)

> A keen willingness on the part of the student to question every aspect of the course on which they are following. (Student 6)

HEALTHY SCEPTICISM

> Things cannot be taken for granted just because they have been published and so on. ... With regard to my own studies via the Internet, I would say that critical-ity was never needed more than in such a context: as a long-suffering subscriber to numerous 'discussion lists' I have no doubts as to the speciousness and crass tendentiousness of much that is put out on the Web. (Student 4)

POSITIVENESS

> Criticality should be constructive in spirit: flaws in research procedures, inadmis-sible conclusions drawn from inadequate data and other such failings can be indicated without the need to resort to ridicule and insult. ... A critical reading (with positive orientation) of everything is essential. (Student 4)

> Criticality does not imply a negative approach. It allows me to look and comment holistically (on myself or others). It allows me to compare and contrast, support or not a particular argument or line of thinking, it allows me to stand back and be an academic. (Student 7)

> I also think of it as having something to say about an issue which can be posi-tive yet meaningful, negative or somewhere in between. (Student 8)

THE INEVITABILITY OF DEVELOPMENT/EVOLUTION IN ANALYSIS

> It is not just allowable but desirable that arguments should be open to modifica-tion and that positions may be redefined. ... Criticality to me also needs to acknowledge that the accepted wisdom of today may be overturned at a later date, which is to say that the process is relative rather than absolute. (Student 4)

SELF-CRITICALITY

> It means I need to look at my own work and the writing of others. (Student 7)

IMPLICATIONS FOR TEACHER DEVELOPMENT

> I think that criticality is a difficult skill to develop; it implies making the leap from just accepting and describing what is written by well known authors to having the confidence to express your own opinions on the subject matter. Perhaps it needs to be actively 'taught' and practised on higher education courses prior to the writ-ing of assignments. (Student 2)

INSTRUMENTAL VALUE FOR HE STUDENTS

In generic terms for studies at this level:

> Criticality is a skill which students on higher education courses are required to develop and demonstrate in their course work/assignments/sessions. (Student 2)

> As a higher education student this is something that I need to be more aware of than as an undergraduate. (Student 7)

and in specific ones for individual courses:

> Criticality is one of the marking criteria for the present course. (Student 3)

There were also both instrumental and cultural implications for overseas students:

> As far as I'm concerned, it's a valuable part of our own academic tradition (of higher education, that is) but not by any means one, which is universally valued. The concept of criticality is one, which I am trying to get across to my group of postgraduates from Taiwan and Japan. It seems to be a concept, which is embedded in our own culture but is in opposition to other academic traditions (e.g. Confucianism). (Student 9)

Instrumentally, students from other cultures may wish to adopt this approach in order to meet the requirements of their particular course of study. If Student 9 is correct in her analysis, there is a clear tension for students in adopting a critical approach where it contrasts with their own academic traditions, where the critical approach could be perceived as Western academic (or even learning) imperialism. Similarly a tension for the lecturer would exist in the promotion of a critical approach, which could be viewed as ethnocentric and methodologically dogmatic. Issues surrounding ethnocentricity in English Language teacher education have been researched (Liu, 1998; Sridhar, 1994) yet there appears to be little research on the methodological demands of international higher education students. While there is a danger of oversimplifying and stereotyping cultures and their approaches to learning and teaching, such issues of methodological prescription, dogma and imposition need to be engaged with.

One of the problems that arises is that tutors may tend to use words such as criticality, reflexivity, problematisation, reflective practice and so on, without having engaged with students as to their understanding of these terms. Such terms are often contested and contestable, and their meaning can vary from context to context, from individual to individual. It is crucial that you discuss with tutors both your and their understandings of such key terms as a mismatch between personal definitions is one of the main causes of, from a tutor's viewpoint, a piece of work seeming to lack credibility.

Evidence

A key criticism of some student work that appears regularly in feedback is an apparent lack of evidence to support assertions. You need to provide supporting evidence for all your assertions, and this usually takes the form of reference to the research literature, to your own research or your own practice and experience. You should not make unsubstantiated claims.

Synthesise theory and practice and research

Links between theory and practice – what effects theory can have on pedagogy? Remember all the literature should be analysed critically (showing strengths, weaknesses and implications, as well as how various perspectives relate to one another and where they diverge). Remember all the way through the dissertation you should try whenever possible to relate theory to practice – reflecting on practice by relating it to theory and also evaluate theory by showing how it relates to practical applications.

Make your own point

Quotations are useful tools for providing supporting evidence for your claims but you should not rely on quotations to do the job of argumentation for you. You need to make your point yourself and then use the quote to support your argument, and not the other way around. Many writers feel that using a quote from an eminent authority will add to the credibility, but this can often result in the feeling that the writer is making spurious claims of credibility for that work. Use quotes only when they make a point strongly and clearly – too many can ruin the flow, and beware the temptation to use quotations out of context, particularly where a quote seems to fit your work perfectly but you are aware that your point of argument is different from that of the writer you are quoting.

Presentation

First impressions are indeed formative, if not lasting, impressions. Good quality presentation implies the author has taken care over the work and has fully appraised him/herself of the requirements of the task in hand. This means clarity, conciseness, organisation, structure, coherence, cohesion, proofreading, referencing and formatting. Most courses would now expect assessed work to be word-processed and if you are not yet word-processor literate then this can be viewed not as a difficulty but the opportunity to acquire a new, valuable and lifelong skill.

Plagiarism

Samuel Johnson is famously quoted as saying *'Your manuscript is both good and original, but the part that is good is not original and the part that is original is not good.'* Plagiarism is a complex issue with many cultural and social implications. Pennycook (1994) has problematised the issue which is regularly evaluated as an unproblematic, negative aspect of writing. He raises the issues of textual ownership, memory, intertextuality and the ways in which different cultures and subcultures view textual borrowing. For Masters students the main problem comes with using the work of others and claiming it as your own. On most courses this is an unacceptable practice and can lead to failure. It is essential to always acknowledge where the work of others has impacted on your own work either directly or indirectly. This acknowledgement again can be viewed as a strength and part of the process of outlining your positionality or the inevitable agendas that you bring to your writing as a result of your beliefs, values and experiences. On a pragmatic note, it is very likely that your tutors will know if you do attempt to use the work of others without giving credit. Tutors are likely to be familiar with the content and also inconsistencies in style, grammar and organisation can be much easier for a reader to spot than for a writer.

Why take the risk when acknowledging the sources of your work is viewed as a strength? A final point to be noted here is that of 'self-plagiarism'. This is where you use your own work from previous assignments verbatim for later assignments or a dissertation. Many external examiners view this as unacceptable practice as in effect you are claiming credit for the same work twice. However, most Masters courses are viewed as developmental processes and so you would be actually encouraged to relate current work to previous work and hopefully to build upon previous assignments. The problem comes with a word-for-word re-use of previous work and so don't avoid previous topics but work on them again from the start and try and build upon your previous critical evaluation. Perhaps the most useful and succinct advice comes from a 1980s song (Morrissey and Marr, 1986) which cautions against the temptation of plagiarism:

> If you must write prose or poems
> The words you choose should be your own
> Don't plagiarise or take 'on loan'
> There's always someone, somewhere
> With a big nose, who knows
> Who'll trip you up and laugh when you fall.

A consideration of academic writing conventions

Conventionally in western academic communities academic writing still displays a traditional 'objective' authoritative style. Conventions are changing regarding formality and the moves towards the use of narrative, life history, personalisation, emancipatory discourse in academic writing are changing the potential approaches. It would be wrong to give you a strict set of rules that must be followed at all costs – the danger of not doing so is thought to offer no guidance at all. All your writing is context dependent – it will differ depending on topic, approach, literature and many other factors. A valuable insight into the different approaches to academic writing can be found in Woods (1999).

There are many conventions that have a purpose. Referencing and quotation conventions are not academic nit-picking but the way you clearly delineate your work from that of others and show that you acknowledge where the thinking of others has impacted on your work. It is likely any course of study will provide you with a reference guide, which will reflect its particular requirements. Various guidelines can usually be found on the web pages of university libraries and those at the University of Sheffield (2002) and Manchester Metropolitan University (2002) are two such examples.

Conventions are also changing regarding how writers identify themselves in their writing (e.g. increased use of 'I' and 'We') and the debate has moved beyond one of objectivity versus subjectivity. It is probably appropriate to use the first person form when talking about issues that you have been personally involved with – say an introduction or an account of the process of your research – though less appropriate in other more detached sections – such as a literature review. As Bailey and Ochsner (1983) put it, 'Why depersonalise the personal?' Before you can try to impose your own style on academic writing, I think it's important to understand the traditional approach to style and organisation. According to the fascinating paper by Lakoff (1990), referred to earlier, there seems to be a convention that the more senior and respected an academic is the more personal and engaging their style may be – though not all academics take advantage of this convention! However, at the early stages of your writing at MEd level it may be best to err on the side of following the traditional conventions, and to make the decision whether or not to challenge, subvert and change these at a later stage. Discuss these issues with your tutor as understanding your audience is crucial in any act of risk assessment, and challenging existing conventions and power structures, while often fundamental to development, is a risk. Please don't take this advice as a prescriptive, mechanical set of rules to be followed at all times but as an indicative guide to the conventions in writing that have prevailed.

Specific points to consider

WHEN TO USE 'I', 'WE', 'YOU' ETC

It might be appropriate to use such pronouns when referring to your own experiences and context, but less appropriate when trying to critically analyse and evaluate the work of others. So avoid expressions like 'I think Chomsky was wrong when he said …'. The point is to give your work a voice, and yet to avoid mere unsubstantiated anecdote. Alistair Pennycook (1994) has written a thought-provoking article in which he considers the 'politics of pronouns' and how their use helps to position the reader and the writer.

WHEN AND WHY USE OF THE PASSIVE VOICE IS APPROPRIATE

Consider when you do or don't want the agents of the process you are describing to be revealed. Transformations of active constructions into passive forms can be motivated by the desire to elide agency and therefore systematically background responsibility for actions in some instances or to foreground responsibility in others. The manipulation of agency transparency serves to construct a world of various responsibilities and power, such as 'The present perfect is used to …'. By removing the agent, the use of a particular grammatical form is given an unquestionable, universal function, in spite of its context of use and the political dimensions I am raising here. Such an analysis is almost always absent from textbooks and grammar reference books using such definitions. Again consider an example from the IATEFL Teacher Trainers and Educators SIG newsletter:

> These trainees will also be entering a profession where peer observation is considered a valuable developmental tool. (IATEFL, 2001: 29)

The passivisation of the consideration of peer observation here elides and suppresses any agency, and in doing so effects an implied authority to the proposition – one that is shared by all 'right minded' members of the discourse community, perhaps. Simpson describes such passivisation as 'the "doer" has been excised completely from the process, fending off the awkward who by? question' (1993: 87). Similarly the activisation of passive may be a selection made where the author wishes to emphasise the agency of a process, particularly where the agent is to be evaluated with strong praise or condemnation. This may raise ethical issues though in the transparency and honesty of your writing.

AVOID DIRECT CLAIMS

Not 'Carter (1995) is right when he says …' but 'Carter (1995) may be right when he says …' and then seek to provide appropriate evidence for that claim.

USE 'TENTATIVE', 'DISTANCING' ATTITUDINAL MODALITY

For example, 'possibly', 'it could be seen that …', 'it could appear that …', 'it might seem that …' and so on. By hedging to avoid commitment and distancing yourself from the truth-value of the propositions you are making prevents you from being too closely aligned with any one particular viewpoint. Distancing yourself from the argument creates the 'feel' of objectivity. Being too 'close' to your claims gives the feeling of subjectivity. There is a caveat, though, and that is that writers who distance themselves too much may find their work lacks credibility, and so, as with much of what is suggested in this book, a balance is needed.

AVOID 'OBLIGATING' MODALITY

Terms such as 'must', 'should' and so on, are best avoided. They are acceptable in the conclusion, the best place to make recommendations and suggestions – but then only with evidence to support them.

AVOID DIRECT ATTITUDINAL MODALITY

Terms such as 'certainly', 'undoubtedly', 'obviously' and 'clearly' suggest you are only considering one possible viewpoint. An example might be 'My research clearly meets my aims', a dangerous claim to make for any researcher.

THE USE OF NOMINALISATION AS OPPOSED TO VERBALISATION

This means presenting something in the form of a noun when it is perhaps more realistically described in other ways. For example when we say 'the *university* has decided …' we represent the university as a 'thing' that can make decisions and so suggest it is a coherent, unequivocating whole, rather than the sum of various groups of people. It creates a view of the university that may in some ways not be a wholly accurate picture. The noun is the lexical realisation of an idea and so nominalisation has been seen as 'the language of thought' – the verb is the lexical realisation of an action or a process and so has been viewed as 'the language of action' – it seems likely that the language of thought is more appropriate than the language of action in an academic context – for example, the phrase 'their education' has a more academic feel to it than the phrase 'what they have learned/been taught', though they both mean largely the same. They may mean the same but the former is a nominalised version of the second. Nominalisation is also a feature of the written word as opposed to the spoken word and academic literacy is more frequently encountered as a written medium.

I am not suggesting that you nominalise your work unnecessarily to give it credibility, but it is a feature of much academic writing and you will meet it in the writing of others. You need to view these nominalized forms with criticality and caution. Good academic writing has the virtues of being clear and concise.

Other problems

AVOID OVERGENERALISATIONS

Take care with danger words such as 'all', 'none', 'always' and 'never'. Also avoid over-general words like 'nice', 'good' and 'useful'. Phrases such as 'most', 'seldom', 'often' and 'as is widely known' are also problematic as they are designed to persuade the reader without providing adequate evidence.

AVOID UNSUBSTANTIATED CLAIMS

Everything must be supported with evidence. Also do not misuse quotations out of context to give an impression that the writer(s) did not intend. This also goes for using unnecessary references to give your work a spurious air of authority, and also using terms that have become hackneyed through overuse (e.g. 'reflection'), and without critical engagement. It's fine to talk about 'reflection' but what does that mean and what are the different and contested perspectives on this. You need to avoid taking things for granted.

BE CAREFUL WITH RHETORICAL QUESTIONS

These can imply the writer's commitment to the position taken. For example the writer who asks the question 'So where do we go from here?' and then proceeds to give the reader one such possible direction runs the risk of pre-supposing that the answer given is the only possible option and so can diminish the criticality of the work.

BE SPECIFIC

Avoid using statements like 'and so on', 'Carter (1992) and others have suggested …'. Name all your sources and any points you wish to make. If it's relevant include it in the text of your work, if it's not, leave it out.

USE SUBJECT SPECIFIC LEXIS

It is important to begin to be aware of and use the specific language of the subject area you are working in. John Swales (1990) introduced the concept of a discourse community, meaning a group of people who shared a similar, and specific way of talking related to their professional interests, such as lawyers, medical professionals, education professionals and so on. Part of the reason for undertaking study at this level is to become part of such a discourse community and understanding and using the specific language is part of this process. However, you need to take care because terms such as criticality and reflexivity may be used differently by different authors and theorists, so again, the need for weighing up and discussing the way you are using such terms is crucial.

AVOID DRAMATIC/LOADED LANGUAGE

This refers to terms such as 'best', 'incredible', 'stupid' and 'pointless'. Also avoid judgemental pseudonyms: Mr Megaphone in Woods (1999) example from a study by Beynon (1985), is a judgemental reference to a loud teacher. Such pejorative evaluation of individuals is inappropriate within academic writing.

DON'T OVERCLAIM OR UNDERCLAIM

Only state what can fairly be drawn from the evidence. Don't get carried away with your claims but don't be falsely modest either. A colleague's MEd student made quite detailed claims with respect to, amongst other things, the age, gender and academic ability of students who would benefit from the use of a Chinese word-processor in developing their use of the Chinese written language. On analysis it was revealed the evidence for his claims was based on that of 12 boys using the word-processor all of whom were from a quite prestigious local school. All the MEd student could legitimately write was that his evidence seemed to show that with these specific pupils there appeared to be some benefit in using the Chinese word-processor to develop their competence in Chinese written language – a very different outcome!

AVOID SEXIST OR GENDER STEREOTYPING LANGUAGE

This is completely unacceptable in academic writing. Not all head teachers are males, not all school secretaries are females! Use strategies such as '(s)he', 'he/she', and 'they' when referring to mixed gender populations or to generic groups, such as students and teachers.

The use of these conventions is in no way meant to be a substitute for the critical thought and evaluation required at Master's level. Presenting a range of sources, critically evaluating the authors' claims, critically examining the theoretical and conceptual issues raised in the piece of writing, showing awareness of criticisms and limitations of the literature and your conclusions, supporting evidence for all assertions made … these are all key elements of successful writing at this level. Appropriate academic style complements and enhances a piece of writing but should not be seen as a substitute for the preceding elements.

Also this discussion of conventions is not meant as a suggestion that your writing should be overly dense, turgid and impenetrable. The most effective academic writing has the virtues of being both clear and concise.

Audience in academic writing

Earlier in this chapter I said that advice on appropriacy needs to be context-dependent too. A key player in decisions about appropriacy is audience. Some academics demand the traditional objective approach whereas others openly reject and are irritated by its use. Find out your tutor's stances and tailor your work accordingly. The whole notion of audience is a confusing and contested one. There appears to be a duality of audience – to use a term coined by Alwin Fill (1986) there is a 'divided illocution' – the message is being directed at two discrete audiences. You are clearly writing for us – as experts in the field of Education, but you are also writing for display, to show us what you know and understand. Your writing is projected as if to an interested, 'educated', aware lay-person – you need to define your purposes, terms, concepts, ideas to show us (and potentially the external examiner) that you really understand them. Don't take things for granted, but take care not to patronise us. Avoid examples like this where the writer was discussing two well-known figures in the world of ELT/Applied Linguistics: 'Swain 1985, not to be confused with Swan 1985, claimed that …'.

Feedback

It is perhaps essential to conceptualise academic writing on a Masters course as part of a developmental process. Your writing at the end of the course will have improved significantly as a result of the reflection, drafting and adjustment that you will have undergone. A crucial aspect of this is tutor feedback. Tutor feedback is a central element of the teaching that takes place on a Masters course and this is even truer on distance education courses. It is essential to be clear about what a tutor means by his/her comments and never be afraid to follow up on any points that are unclear or confusing. A recent study of a corpus of tutor feedback (Hyatt, 2000) showed that feedback tended to fall into a range of different categories, dependent on their function. It may seem strange to focus on these areas but they are indicative of the kind of feedback you could expect to receive and as such should inform the development of any future writing you undertake. As noted earlier, an understanding of audience is central to any type of writing and reflecting on the type of comments your tutors may make could help you to focus your writing at an early stage. The following is a list of comment types that may be included.

Categories of comment types

PHATIC
These refer to comments whose purpose is the establishment and maintenance of a good academic and social relationship between the tutor and the student. They are divided into two types:

- *Comment* – Where the tutor comments generally on the content indicating an interest, surprise, and so on, at what has been written.
- *Encouragement* – Where the tutor offers comments that are intended to encourage the student in future work.

DEVELOPMENTAL
These refer to comments made by the tutor with the intention of aiding the student with subsequent work in relation to the current assignment. Again, there are several types:

- *Alternatives* – The tutor offers alternatives, suggestions and recommendations in place of what the student has written or points out omissions in the student's work.
- *Future* – These are comments on how the student needs to address a point directly in subsequent work.
- *Reflective questions* – Here the tutor poses a question, as opposed to making a direct point, for the student to reflectively consider.
- *Informational comment* – Here the tutor offers a direct comment on a related and complementary topic, with the intention of offering the student additional academic insight into the topic under discussion.

STRUCTURAL

These comments refer to the structural organisation of the assignment, either as a whole or in sections, and can include the following types:

- *Discourse level* – These comments consider the organisation of the assignment as a whole in terms of the constituent sections, such as introduction, literature review, and conclusion. These comments may consider how each of these constituent sections may be put together, in terms of rhetorical moves, or how they themselves may fit together to give a structure to the overall assignment (coherence).
- *Sentence level* – These comments look at the organisation of individual sentences, in terms of length, relations to other sentences (cohesion).
- *Stylistic* – These comments consider the use and presentation of the academic literacy within the assignment. Areas under consideration include:

  - punctuation
  - lexis
  - syntax/word order/grammar
  - proofreading/spelling
  - referencing/citation/quotation/bibliography
  - presentation: page numbering, subtitling, figures, tables, captions, footnotes, endnotes, contents pages, word length, acronyms, etc.
  - register: the appropriate language within a context of situation (what, who and how of a text); this would include such aspects as voice, audience and purpose of the text.

CONTENT

This section includes comments on the content of the assignment in terms of their appropriateness/accuracy or their inappropriateness/inaccuracy. These divide into three categories:

- *Positive evaluation* – Here comments on the strengths of the assignment are noted and tend to include features such as synthesis of literature, theory and practice; appropriate synthesis of personal experience; clear argumentation and reflection.
- *Negative evaluation* – Comments here are noted on weaknesses of the assignment, which may include a deficit in the above features as well as problems relating to the provision of evidence, lack of clarity or the need for clarification, or a lack of criticality in the work.
- *Non-evaluative summary* – Comments here unevaluatively offer a summary of aspects of the assignment.

METHODOLOGICAL

This section only applies to research based assignments, where the presence or absence of appropriate discussion on aspects of the research design and analysis are discussed.

- *Approach* – Here comments may be made on the philosophical and epistemological positions of the research, and how these relate to the research paradigm through which the enquiry is approached, and the researcher's consideration of positionality.
- *Methods* – Here comments are made on the practical aspects of the research design, the collection and analysis of the data, the sample, recording and so on, including the researcher's criticality in these discussions.
- *Process* – Here comments are made on the process, timeframe and practicality of the conduct of the research and might include issues such as piloting, distribution, non-response, problems encountered, including the researcher's criticality in these discussions.
- *Administrative* – Comments that relate to administrative procedure of the course.

It is important to understand the types of comments you are receiving so that you can act upon them appropriately. Remember, at Masters level, you are free to disagree with the tutor's comments, though given the collaborative nature of this work, and the fact that the tutor will be grading your work, you would be advised to do this diplomatically. Most courses have systems by which you can recommend a second marker if you are unhappy with the first one, though in my experience, there is rarely a major difference in markers' perception, as they have undergone a range of moderation procedures. The bottom line is that feedback is there to help you – make sure you understand the recommendations, the reason for the recommendations and that you act on them.

Structure of Research Writing

Abstract
Introduction
Literature review
Methodology and procedures
Results
Analysis
Conclusion
Bibliography
Appendices

Figure 3.2   A possible structure to research writing

Structuring your research-based assignment

Let's move now to consider the structuring of your research-based work. The following again is meant to be a guide to thought rather than a prescriptive model that must be slavishly followed. Each piece of work will have its own requirements due to its contextual nature and this needs to be borne in mind when considering which elements of the following can be included and which are inappropriate. Figure 3.2 shows the elements in the structure of research writing.

You start with an abstract, which provides an overview of the research and, crucially, its main findings. It is generally quite short, 200–300 words or so, and its purpose is to give the reader an overview of what they will find in the main body of the dissertation. Figure 3.3 is a particularly good example taken from an MEd dissertation (Shukor, 2001).

The introduction then follows the abstract. Structurally an introduction needs to bridge the gap between the relevance of your topic to the general world of education and your particular project, and so moves from the more general to the more specific. A useful structural approach would include the functional sections shown in Figure 3.4.

The functional sections of an introduction are now expanded:

- *General setting* – How your work is relevant to the world of education.
- *Aspects previously studied* – A brief outline of the topics and contexts of previous studies in this area. By describing these and then moving on to describe your particular project and context, and how this is different from previous work, you establish a niche and a justification for your own work.
- *Research questions* – What you hope your research will answer.

ABSTRACT

Small-group discussions are a key activity during problem-based learning (PBL). This is when students discuss the learning issues, exchange ideas, engage in peer teaching and decide on the solution as a group. What exactly do students think during these discussions? Do they engage in active thinking of the subject under discussion, or are they simply listening passively? How are their thoughts in the PBL small-group discussions compared to their thoughts in the conventional tutorial discussions? This study aims to answer these questions. It is an extension of a study done in Maastricht by Geerligs (1995) on students' thoughts during the PBL small-group discussions. The students' thoughts in this study were obtained using the 'thought-sampling' method. During these discussions, students report their thoughts at random times at the signal of a bell. The thought reports were classified into the following categories: content-related (passive), content-related (non-passive), procedure-related, metacognitive-related, off-task, and miscellaneous.

The study shows that students are inclined towards content-related (non-passive) thoughts during both the conventional tutorial discussions as well as during the PBL small-group discussions. There is a comparable pattern of thoughts during the conventional tutorials, whereby the content-related (passive) and (non-passive) thoughts were prominently high for all the four weeks. However, students' thoughts in small-group PBL discussions are mixed. The content-related (non-passive), procedure-related, and off-task thoughts show relatively high percentages during the PBL small-group discussions. It seems that students' thoughts during the PBL discussions ensue the various stages of the PBL process.

The dissertation further discusses the implications of the findings towards the management of the PBL process, as well as the importance of good management of the hidden curriculum. It is advocated that structured PBL process leads to better students' learning, and the hidden curriculum in terms of the PBL tutors' skills, the assessment components within the PBL process, and even students' perception of the new approach, determines the success or failure of the process. The dissertation further recommends that similar study could be conducted in order to affirm the current findings, or a case study could be conducted on a smaller group of students using the stimulated recall procedure.

(Shukor, 2001)

Figure 3.3 An example of a dissertation abstract

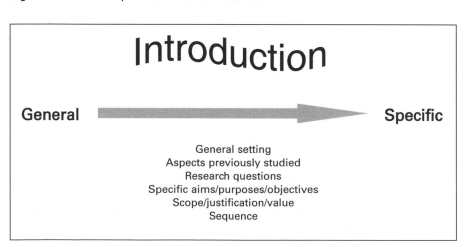

Figure 3.4 Possible functional sections of an introduction

- *Aims and objectives* – A detailed discussion of those you intend to use in tackling these research questions including a statement of the value/ relevance of this work, bearing in mind that the aims need to be stated in a way that is likely to lead to evidence that will illuminate the issues under consideration.
- *Scope and justification* – A statement of your dissertation: what you can cover within the word limit and what you can't from this topic; what you have chosen to focus on and why, as well as what you are not focusing on and why. The latter section shows that you are aware of the other complementary issues surrounding this topic that you don't have the space to consider in depth.
- *Sequence* – A good way to end the introduction is to offer a statement of what you intend to follow – this acts as an advance organiser and improves the readability of the assignment.

This is not the only acceptable format for an introduction but should give you some ideas about what to include.

Then you would move to a critical literature review, offering perspectives on the topic from a range of standpoints. This literature must not simply be descriptively reported but analysed in terms of its strengths, weaknesses, implications and interpretations. You need to weigh up the evidence for and against different interpretations by examining the theoretical and conceptual issues raised, looking at alternative interpretations, critically examine the evidence base for assertions made, and by showing an awareness of the limitations of interpretations. In the critical appraisal of the literature it is crucial not to simply accept the opinions of authors, particularly where they are not supported by the evidence. Remember you cannot include all the literature on a topic due to space restraints and so you need to select literature which is relevant to your topic and argument and not other literature that may be interesting but beyond the scope of your work. The literature can help to give coherence to your argument and the work as a whole and there needs to be a clear link between the literature you appraise and the aims outlined in your introduction.

The next section is likely to be one on methodology and you may recall that a definition of this has been raised by Pat Sikes in Chapter 2. In the first instance you should address how you conceive the work in terms of the various orientations to research, and the way your work is conceptualised in epistemological and ontological terms. You can find help with the range of potential orientations in the research methodology literature and a few books that might be particularly helpful are Cohen, Manion and Morrison, (2000), McDonough and McDonough (1997) and Wellington (2000).

You need to demonstrate the way in which your methodology is appropriate to your aims, taking into account possible alternative approaches. Then you need to move on to a detailed description of the process and

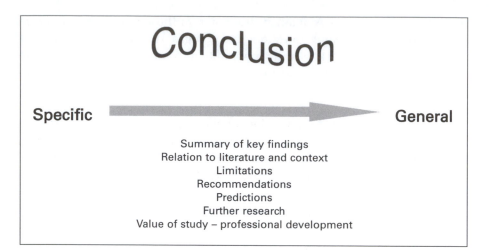

Figure 3.5 Possible functional sections of a conclusion

procedures of your research. What you did, who you did it with and why you did it this way. Limitations of your research as well as the justification are crucially important to include.

The next section would include the results and analysis, and could be either through a statistical analysis for purely quantitative data (see Chapter 7) or through a categorical analysis for more qualitative data. This involves preparing the data, for instance transcribing the interviews and then identifying and indexing it in terms of the context of its collection date, location and participants (see Chapters 8 and 9). The findings can then be organised around themes or keywords, both themes that you consider might be important before you conduct the research such as implications for pedagogy; implications for teacher development; implications for management; and so on, as well as other themes that emerge from the data and have developed as you see significant patterns emerging. The data can then be pulled out and collated under these various and developing categories.

You should link to previous/other findings and the literature to triangulate the research. This type of approach can help to avoid the feeling of a mechanistic list, that is sometimes the effect of a question-by-question analysis. The findings often feel better with some quotes from your transcripts to bring them to life.

The final step of your dissertation is the conclusion. As with the introduction a useful structural approach would include the functional sections described in Figure 3.5, although in this case one would move from your particular project to the general world of education.

An appropriate structure for the conclusion is to begin with a summary of the key findings (note this is only the most significant outcomes!), then relate this back to the literature you reviewed (did you come to the same conclusions or not) and to your context (this may be the reason for any differences). You can also create an overall cohesion for the assignment by relating back to your original questions and discussion if you have answered them and if not why not (there may be a perfectly justifiable reason!). Next you could move on to the limitations that have constrained your research. These are inevitable, and admitting them does not suggest a weakness in your work, rather it illustrates that you are thinking about your work critically. A key aspect of your conclusion should be any implications or recommendations that you can make on the basis of your research – these could be pedagogic, curricular, managerial or teacher-developmental. Depending on the context of your work you may be able to make some predictions on how your research topic may be affected by other change (e.g. any potential changes in the attitude of the Chinese administration to teaching medium in Hong Kong). Finally, a good way to end the conclusion is to point out any directions for future complementary research that your work has suggested – dissertations often raise many new questions as well as answering the ones you set out to look at. This brings the dissertation back out to the general world of education from the specifics of your research and so, in bringing you back to where you started from to create an overall coherence to your work.

Remember the drafting process is crucial. Your tutor would probably like to see drafts of each section, not just the finished assignment. Supervisors like to see your questionnaires/interview schedules before you use them. Often another person's suggestions can save a lot of time and effort.

Process

Again processes for working towards a dissertation will vary from individual to individual though the structure may be worth considering. Figure 3.6 gives a possible approach to the research process.

Some advice I've been given (or wish I'd been given!)

Time management

A useful exercise is to make a 7-day, 24-hour timetable for a typical week in your life. Blank off all the activities you do including watching television and sleeping. You will see that your life, in fact everyone's life, is full. It stands to reason then that some activity will have to be dropped to provide the 8–10 hours a week that most Masters study requires. A PhD student from Hong Kong pointed out to me her philosophy was 'In order to gain something, you have to give something up' and I have found these to be very wise words to

A possible approach to the Research Process

- Choose a topic that interests you.
- Clarify your topic by organising the work into key areas and themes. Don't worry too much about order at this stage; stay flexible and open to new ideas.
- Consider the ways these topics and themes interrelate and how to present these in a systematic way.
- Attempt to present the above in terms of a dissertation plan or outline and discuss this with your tutor to ensure you are on the right lines.
- Focus your research question tightly.
- Think about your aims and what you'll need to do to achieve them in terms of covering various topics and themes. Make sure your aims are consistent with the title of the work you are addressing.
- Read widely around the topic.
- Start making notes, summaries and analyses of your reading; the sooner you start writing, however informally, the easier it becomes.
- Consider the links between your own experience, the literature, theoretical perspectives and the research of yourself and others.
- Decide on the methodological approach to use and why.
- Within this framework, decide what data you will collect and how you will collect it.
- Work out how you will analyse your data (before you collect it and check it fits in with your methodology). Look at the conclusions the data analysis leads you to and what constraints or limitations there are on this.
- Produce a first draft as advised by your tutor, although with a dissertation this is often chapter-by-chapter, and take note of the feedback offered.
- Act on this feedback as appropriate and redraft this into a revised draft.
- Proofread (and get a critical friend to do so too) for errors, coherence, cohesion, credibility, presentation and formatting.
- Submit your final work.

Figure 3.6   A possible research process

apply to study and writing. You are the only person who can decide what goes and stays, but remember something has to go! On the other hand remember to give yourself and the people close to you time to do other things – they will give up, and put up with, a lot to support your study so make sure they and you have enough 'time out'. Feeling guilty can be highly counterproductive.

You can make the most of your time though – try to avoid 'displacement' or 'study-avoidance' activities – mine are tidying my desk, making coffee and answering e-mail – be aware of your own! Give yourself a cut off point for reading – there will always be another article, or book to look at. Decide how much time you can allocate to this, and make sure you start writing. Writer's block can often come because of the fear of being judged on less than perfect work. Don't worry in the early stages about perfection, get the main ideas down and polish at the end of the first draft. Drafting is essential to good academic writing (a former colleague once told me each article he wrote went through at least 30 drafts) and drafting is, by definition, imperfect. It is however, the key to learning how to improve your writing.

Space management

Make sure that you try to find a comfort zone to work in – somewhere quiet, well lit, airy and comfortable, with plenty of space is ideal. Don't forget the value of disturbance gatekeepers, such as the answer phone, to avoid distracting interruptions.

Referencing as you go

There is nothing worse than finishing your assignment and then having to spend days and days searching the library, your notes and various databases for the one reference you forgot to note down. Keep details of every reference and make sure they include name, initials, date, title, publisher and page numbers. Remember to keep more than one copy of this as things can go wrong – in the six years in my present job students have had fires in the office and at home, crashed computers, stolen briefcases, but I am still waiting for the first assignment to be eaten by the family pet! I now keep references as I go on a separate word-processing file, which enables me to build these up alphabetically and simply paste into my work when I finish. I have also found keeping a quotations book very useful – every time I come across a quotation that interests me or strikes a chord it goes into the book (with full reference details) and countless of these quotes have come in useful in subsequent writing (including a number in this chapter!).

Proofreading

A high standard of presentation is expected at Masters level and one of the keys to this is careful proofreading, in order to avoid spelling, grammatical and other errors, which can create an unfairly pejorative impression of the care with which you have conducted your work. This includes the use of appropriate referencing systems. A detailed consideration of this is probably beyond the scope of this paper, particularly given the growth in citation from new information and communication technologies such as the internet, but useful further guidance can be found on the following websites:

- www.unn.ac.uk/central/isd/cite/
- www.bournemouth.ac.uk/using_the_library/html/harvard_system.html

Proofreading needs to be done personally, despite the time-consuming nature of this activity. Spell-checkers on computers can be very useful, but can lead to unseen problems as the following example shows.

I was marking an assignment from a student based in Hong Kong who was writing about the change of sovereignty in that country and who wrote: 'There will undoubtedly be pedagogical and curricular implications with the *hangover* of power'. I know there was a big party to mark the occasion but this student was unaware that handover didn't appear on her spell-checker.

The value of a critical friend

Often though we can be too close to our own work to judge it critically and hence the value of a critical friend to read through your work and to offer constructive comment on it. The critical friend can be a colleague, family member or friend whose opinion you value. The term 'critical friendship', coined by Stenhouse (1975), has been defined by Hatton and Smith (1995) as 'to engage with another person in a way which encourages talking with, questioning, and even confronting, the trusted other, in order to examine planning for teaching, implementation and its evaluation' (1995: 41). While this definition is focused on the role of critical friendship as a part of teacher development, it can equally be applied to such a collaborative relationship within the writing process.

You can prime your critical friend with pre-questions, as you might do with a pilot study, by asking them to note anything that is unclear, ambiguous, offensive, unsupported by evidence, anecdotal or poorly presented.

Conclusion

In conclusion, my questions at the outset of this chapter have been answered in the course of the chapter. The purpose of academic writing is to meet the aims of the writer and so it is logical that the writer needs a clear understanding of his/her aims at the outset. Good academic writing is clear, concise, critical, credible, evidenced, well structured and well presented. Bad academic writing does not display these features. The great danger in trying to write a chapter such as this one is in appearing prescriptive. Each piece of academic writing is contextually unique and so there cannot be one fixed and definitive approach. The way to develop one's writing skills is to read the writing of others, to practise, to take advice and to experiment. Be aware that writing is a process rather than a 'one off' activity. Crème and Lea (1997) have categorised writers in different ways:

- 'patchwork' writers who knit together different elements of the writing;
- 'diver' writers who plunge straight in;
- 'grand plan' writers who use carefully thought out plans to work from;
- and 'architect' writers who construct the edifice in advance.

It is important to think about which type of writer you are and which one you would like to be, as well as the implications of these different approaches.

My final piece of advice would be to remember to enjoy your writing. Rather than subscribing to the view of Robert Heinlein, who said: 'Writing is not necessarily something to be ashamed of, but do it in private and wash your hands afterwards'; instead try to embrace the view of Goethe who claimed 'The most original authors are not so because they advance what is new, but because they put what they have to say as if it had never been said before.'

Summary

For most people, even experienced practitioners in the field, embarking upon a piece of academic writing is not an easy task. So for those students whose last venture into such territory occurred a number of years in the past, their concerns and worries are likely to be significantly heightened. Experience suggests that what these students need is an insight into the nuances of academic writing and practical guidelines for its completion. My intention has been that this chapter provides such information. It discusses issues such as academic audience and general concerns of content, which need to be considered, for example using a range of sources, criticality and plagiarism as well as those of academic writing conventions. This material is then complemented with suggested guidelines for an appropriate structure for completion of a piece of research work, based on my experiences of working with MEd students over the past ten years or so. Although this material in itself provides comprehensive support for anyone coming back to academic writing after a lengthy time gap from such activity I have supplemented it with two further sections. One on the type of feedback a student might expect on his or her writing and another whereby I have reflected on advice I was given (or wish I had been given) with my own writing. Whether my intention to provide a valuable guide to academic writing has been successful will be up to you the reader to decide.

4   Reliability, Validity and Credibility

Jon Scaife

This chapter is about a particular kind of writing, namely research writing. Research writing is the writing that new researchers do in their final year projects or Masters dissertations. It is also writing for doctoral degrees, and writing for chapters and articles. The chapter does not focus on important technical issues, such as detailed distinctions between different types of validity, as there are already many published accounts of such things. Neither does it discuss different styles of writing (this has already been covered in Chapter 3) that may accompany distinct research methods, such as writing up a scientific method as opposed to a personal narrative account. The chapter focuses on the quality of the communication between the writer and the reader. In case it appears that 'quality of communication' is light-weight or lacking substance, it is worth noting that this very thing is at the heart of the reader's judgement of written material. The reader's judgement plays out in many ways. It influences assessors' and examiners' grading of projects, dissertations and theses; it shapes referees' recommendations about submissions for publication, and it propagates through the wider, continuing impact that the writing has on the thoughts and actions of readers.

I believe that central to the quality of communication between writer and reader is the reader's sense of trust in the writing. This chapter aims to help new research writers to write so as to gain the trust and confidence of the reader. It also aims to help the reader to be critical, that is, to read research writing critically. To be a critical reader is to expect a writer to earn one's trust and confidence.

The need to discuss ideas of trustworthiness and confidence in research writing comes largely from my experiences of supporting and assessing the project and higher degree writing of postgraduate students. While it has been easy enough to point student writers towards references on methods and techniques, we – the students and I – have regularly and repeatedly struggled with notions of credibility and criticality in writing and reading.

And so this chapter aims to help researchers to increase their understanding about how to construct credible accounts of their research, how to make appropriate claims and how to gain and maintain the confidence of their readers.

The chapter addresses the following themes:

- making statements in research writing;
- discussing connections and relationships in research writing;
- using the ideas of reliability, validity and trustworthiness in research writing.

Examples and practical questions will be used to help to bring these abstract ideas to life.

Statements

Writing up research is an act of communication. There may be a time delay between the researcher's writing and anyone else's reading of the research, but it is always assumed that the writer will have readers. Indeed, one of the purposes of writing up research is to communicate it, and this applies just as much to a new researcher as to a Nobel laureate. There are very many ways in which people communicate with each other and only some of those ways are appropriate in research (not that this is fixed forever – what is 'appropriate' tends to evolve with time).

Before we consider various kinds of statements, here is a word to consider: Brazil. Could I ask you to think about Brazil for a couple of seconds? If you've dwelt on 'Brazil' for a moment you can probably complete this statement: 'When I thought of Brazil I thought of …'. When I did this myself I came up with several things: football, bossa nova, rain forests, nuts. Here, then, is a factual statement: when I thought of Brazil I thought of football. It is also a subjective statement, because it is expressive of, and particular to, my own thoughts. I have no grounds whatever for extending the statement into this: when you thought of Brazil you thought of football. People sometimes ask me whether it is acceptable to include subjective statements in research writing. My view is that it is certainly acceptable, as long as it is clear that the statement *is* subjective. Consider this claim: 'children born in the second half of the school year tend to make more friends than those born in the first half of the school year'. Taken on its own, this claim is unwarranted. However, if it were preceded by this: 'From my experience as a teacher I believe that …' then the claim becomes explicitly subjective and indisputable. In fact hunches like that one can provide a fruitful lead into interesting research, opening up the possibility that the claim might be reasonably extended beyond its subjective origin.

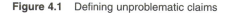

Which would you regard as unproblematic?

1   Girls tend to do better than boys in school.
2   Being illiterate is a disadvantage in industrialised countries.
3   Smaller classes result in better educational experiences.
4   Problem-based learning (PBL) is a valuable educational approach.

Figure 4.1   Defining unproblematic claims

Here is a different kind of statement: 'School children sometimes turn up to class without their pens'. This is not a subjective claim; it is much wider in scope than that. Nobody would blink at this claim in everyday conversation but would it be appropriate in an account of research? After all, no support has been offered to back it up.

In my view, such a claim can be made in research because it is reasonable to assume that if a large number of teachers (relevant judges) were asked about their subjective experiences of this issue, there would be widespread agreement with the statement. The decision about whether to risk using an unsupported, non-subjective claim hinges on whether the writer judges the claim to be 'unproblematic', which in this context is roughly equivalent to self-evident or 'generally accepted'. If the reader agrees, all is well. Look at the further examples in Figure 4.1 and try and answer them before you look at my comments.

Although it is somewhat artificial to make the judgements in Figure 4.1 out of a specific written context, I would not make claim 1 or claim 3. Neither would I make claim 4, though I agree with it, because I would not count on it being unproblematic to the reader. I would, however, venture claim 2 without support, because I judge it to be unproblematic. Perhaps some would disagree, but I would be willing to take the risk.

If you are fairly new to educational researching you may prefer not to venture any risky assertions. It is different if you have an international track record of research – you can expect to 'get away with' making unsupported claims on the basis that if they proved groundless, your professional reputation would suffer. In fact, as a professional researcher you would be *expected* to venture forth into the land of intuition, imagination and judgement.

Let us turn to statements that are neither subjective nor unproblematic. In order to maintain the reader's confidence in your account, which is surely a desired aim, such statements should be supported. Here is an illustration: 'Girls' performance in school science can be improved by creating girls-only classes'. On its own, this statement would stretch the critical reader's trust in the writer too far, as it is certainly not self-evident. Realising that this would be the case, the writer might add, 'according to Scaife (1998: 75)'. By quoting a source in support of the claim the writer gives the reader grounds for confidence. Some sources 'count' in this respect and some don't. If, for instance, you had a neighbour, called Lee, who happened to utter the statement above, you would be on very shaky ground if you wrote in support '(Lee, 2002)'. The strongest support comes from sources that have been refereed before they were accepted for publication, such as academic books and journal articles. Many internet sources are not refereed so if you are looking for strong support for a claim it would be worth being carefully selective if you use internet sources.

Another way to support a claim is to draw on your own research. If you have gathered and analysed data, you will almost certainly want to report your findings. Possible approaches to this are to construct interpretations, draw conclusions or offer answers to research questions. All of these involve making claims, support for which comes from your own data. This is sometimes referred to as an 'evidence-based' process.

There is a further way to support claims that you want to make, and that is by the use of argument. Argument may, of course, be based on research data, but it is also possible to use argument without drawing on data. In mathematics, claims may be based on argument from logic. In the arts, argument flows from critical judgement. Argument may also be based on metaphor or other parallels, or on an appeal to values such as social justice. In the field of education we are not confined to a scientific approach, that is, arguing from data. We may want to make use of argument from interpretation and other products of our critical judgement. We may even appeal to logic. However we choose to elicit support, it is important to be aware of the need to safeguard the reader's confidence in us. Imagine that someone has chosen to write a Masters dissertation about the relationship between teachers and learners in a distance education programme. As a basis for the exposition of their views they might decide to quote Paulo Freire:

> In cultural synthesis, the actors who come from 'another world' to the world of the people do so not as invaders. They do not come to teach or to transmit or to give anything, but rather to learn, with the people, about the people's world. (Freire, 1972: 147)

This passage could be used as the basis for an argument, or a series of claims. It is part of an 'argument-based', as distinct from an evidence-based, process.

One final point about statements in research is this: what if you have a statement in your head that is neither subjectively framed, nor unproblematic, nor supported – but it won't go away from your thoughts! What can be done with it? One answer is to restate it, not as a claim but as an hypothesis or a question, or as a problematic statement: in short, as a research topic!

Connections

Many interesting statements in research refer to connections between things. This is particularly so when data are involved. There are distinct types of connections or relationships between things. The aims of this section are to clarify and distinguish two familiar types and to help the researcher to avoid the trap of confusing the two. Some cases are included for readers to consider and to check their ideas against mine.

Causality

There is a causal relationship between two things if the incidence or existence of one thing guarantees the incidence of the other, all else being equal. For example, 'pressing the power switch causes the monitor to turn off', and 'the force of gravity causes things to fall'. In everyday speech the word 'cause' is used more informally, such as 'high winds cause roof damage'. But the language that is used in research tends to have sharper precision than everyday speech. The use of the word 'cause' to imply certainty in research is a case in point. However, note the word 'tends' in that last-but-one sentence. Is there such thing as an absolute, guaranteed certainty in the world? Life tends to be complex and resistant to description by tidy laws, so if research is to be informative about the messy everyday world in which we live, as opposed to some ideal or model world, then there has to be some flexibility in the use of language. In practice, the word 'causality' in research tends to imply that for all practical purposes the incidence of one thing brings about the incidence of another thing. (Readers interested in thinking further about the nature of causality might find the ideas of the eighteenth-century empiricist philosopher David Hume rewarding. In *A Treatise of Human Nature*, Hume (1992) argued that causality could not be assumed to reflect some underlying lawfulness of nature but is simply a shorthand way we have of expressing that certain things or events tend to follow others, and that we expect them to continue to do so.)

Correlation

Correlation concerns the extent to which there is an association between two things. If there is a 100% association between two things (we'll call them A and B), then B is invariably associated with A and the 'correlation coefficient' between A and B is 1. In the opposite situation, that is if B is never associated with A, the correlation coefficient is −1. These are the extreme cases. If B is sometimes associated with A the correlation coefficient is between −1 and 1. Note that the closer the correlation coefficient is to −1 or to 1, the stronger the correlation and the more predictable the relationship between A and B.

Strong correlation is not causality!

Sometimes, strong correlation is taken to indicate causality. Beware! An association is not the same as a causal relationship. Strong correlation is a description of a tendency, not a certainty. Even a 100% association between two things doesn't guarantee a causal relationship (as some of the cases below should illustrate). You'll be on very shaky ground if you claim that strong correlation *proves* the existence of a causal relationship – but it may be perfectly reasonable to *hypothesise* some kind of causal process. Sometimes there may be a strong correlation but no suspicion whatsoever of any possible causal link between two things. This could be because the two things in question are each separately related to a third thing. Or it may just be a coincidence. Cases are offered in Figure 4.2, but again could I recommend that you don't read on until you've given some thought to them.

Consideration of relationships

In each of the cases that follow you are invited to consider whether there is, or may be, a relationship between two named things. In each case, what would you say is the nature of any such relationship (e.g. causal; positive or negative correlation; reasonable to hypothesise causality; coincidence; common relationship with a third party; association but no causal link; etc.)?

1   Brake applied/car slows down
2   Better qualifications/higher pay
3   Age/quality of eyesight
4   City centre crime/number of CCTV (closed-circuit television) cameras in operation in the city centre
5   Number of CCTV cameras in operation in the city centre/city centre crime
6   Length of left arm/length of right arm
7   Day/night
8   Birth-rate in Britain between 1875 and 1920/production of pig-iron in the USA between 1875 and 1920
9   Class size/effectiveness of teaching
10 Teaching/learning

Figure 4.2   Consideration of relationships

Discussion of the cases

Having given some thought to the cases in Figure 4.2, the following are my comments on them:

1   This would be regarded as a causal relationship in everyday life – and in most research contexts. (But vehicle safety researchers might view this differently. Why might that be?)
2   A positive correlation – but not a causal relationship!

3 A negative correlation. Note the use of the word 'negative' to mean that when one thing increases the other one tends to go down.

4 When city centre crime increased, more CCTV cameras were installed, so there's a positive correlation – isn't there? …

5 …but on the other hand when more CCTV cameras were installed, city centre crime went down, so there's a negative correlation – isn't there?

Cases 4 and 5 show how statements about correlation (even if they are based on careful quantitative analysis) don't do the work of interpreting what's going on – that's an additional task for the researcher.

6 Although there's a very strong correlation there is no suggestion of a causal link. The association comes from a common link to a third factor – both arms are joined to the same body!

7 This is similar to item 6. Note that even though in this case there is a 100% association, there is not a causal link between day and night.

8 If you suspected a relationship between these two things then I would love to know how you came to think so! Most people would surely regard these things as utterly unrelated, yet the correlation coefficient between them is −0.98 (Wiseman, 1966). (What does the value −0.98 indicate?) This case is included as an example of a striking coincidence.

9 Many teachers feel intuitively that there is some kind of a negative correlation. On the other hand, people responsible for educational budgeting have been known to argue that 'class size doesn't matter'. (Note that teachers sometimes say that although large classes are undesirable, they don't like classes that are too small. So it would be imprecise to claim simply that 'teachers believe that class size correlates negatively with effective teaching'.)

10 One of the Big Questions in education. If it turns out that there is no positive correlation then what are we doing?! However, it is no simple matter to examine whether there is a positive correlation; we would first need to clarify what we meant by 'teaching' and by 'learning'. We might then ask: what aspects of learning are desirable (that's a massive debate in itself) and then: what aspects of teaching correlate positively with these aspects of learning? Who said educational research was simple?

The quality of statements and relationships: reliability, validity and credibility

You may have come across occasions when a piece of research has been described as bad, particularly when someone is arguing in opposition to the implications of the research. For instance: 'Minister, Smith and Tan (2002) have shown that there are enormous advantages to be gained from teaching science in junior schools.' 'Oh, that was a bad piece of research!' On what grounds might it be justifiable to describe research as good or bad? In this section we consider some indicators of 'goodness' of research.

Thought experiment

First, take a look at Figure 4.3. After a little discussion, what would probably emerge would not be an answer, but dissatisfaction with the question. The problem would be that people would have quite separate understandings of the word 'best' in this context. The question is badly defined because it uses a criterion that is too vague. Suppose that, in view of this, the group decided that the problem needed to be reworded, starting with a refinement of the criteria to be used to judge the pens. (Sharpening up the way a research question or topic is posed is a normal stage early on in the research process.) Let's suppose that some members of the group came up with some specific features, to replace the vague term 'best'. Here are the attributes that they decided to use to assess pens: cost of pen, running costs, colour, ease of use, style, durability and maker's name. Continuing with our thought experiment, members of the group were invited to imagine that they were going to select a new pen for their own personal use. Each individual was asked to judge the importance to herself or himself of the attributes above, for the purpose of choosing a pen. They were asked to rank the attributes in a list from the most to the least important. Let's call the set of lists produced by the individuals in the group 'S1'.

The research process in this illustration has so far involved:

- refinement of the statement of the problem;
- identification of a procedure for collecting data;
- data collection.

What would you say if you were asked at this point: Is the data set S1 reliable?

Reliability

Reliability is an important consideration, in that it may be useful as an indicator of 'goodness' or quality in research. Unfortunately for the new researcher, reliability is used in the literature in a number of different ways, as Hammersley (1987) has shown. Amongst the differences, however, there are some commonly occurring features, principal among which are repetition and consistency. Wellington takes reliability to indicate: 'The extent to which a test, a method or a tool gives consistent results across a range of

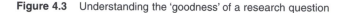

Pen Exercise
The Research Question

Imagine that this question was put to a group of researchers:

'Which of your pens is the best?'

Discuss what you understand by this research question and whether you see it as problematic. If you do find it problematic note down why this is. What do you need to know/do to make it less problematic?

Figure 4.3   Understanding the 'goodness' of a research question

settings, and if used by a range of researchers' (2000: 200). Bell adopts a similar definition: 'The extent to which a test or procedure produces similar results under constant conditions on all occasions' (1999: 103).

In some research settings this is fairly unproblematic. In a carefully controlled scientific experiment, for instance, conditions are tightly specified so that, in principle, any researcher in the field could replicate a particular data gathering process and expect to obtain the same data as any other researcher. Following Wellington, Bell and others I would describe this by saying that *the data-gathering process* is reliable. (Others might say that it is the *data* that is reliable. I prefer to regard reliability as a property of the whole process of data gathering, rather than a property solely of the results.) In a setting such as a classroom, a researcher may quite reasonably choose to use a research approach (or 'paradigm', if you prefer) that is not 'scientific'. Some conditions in the classroom may be entirely beyond the researcher's control, and yet may be of interest to the researcher. Repetition of observed circumstances, or 'constant conditions', to use Bell's words, may be largely a matter of luck and in such circumstances it would not make sense to expect replicable results from the use of a data-gathering procedure. As a result, reliability would not be a useful criterion to use to assess the goodness of that particular research.

Before one comments on whether a process is reliable it makes sense to decide whether it is reasonable to judge the process in that way. If it does make sense, as in the scientific example above, then reliability should be used to judge goodness. If it doesn't, as in some classroom-based research, for example, then reliability should not be a yardstick. So – to return to our thought experiment, with Figure 4.4.

My answer to the question in Figure 4.4 would be that first I can't comment yet because nothing has been repeated, and second, in any case, I would use reliability to judge the *process* of data gathering, not the product. So let us just

Pen Exercise
The issue of reliability

What would you say to the question:

'Is the set of data S1 reliable?'

Before you read on, you may find it fruitful to consider your own response to this question.

Figure 4.4   Considering the issue of reliability

carry the thought experiment a little further. Suppose that the data-gathering procedure were repeated by the group a week later, and that someone else agreed to administer it another week after that, each time with the same subjects. That would give us two more datasets, S2 and S3. The reliability of the data-gathering process could now be judged by the closeness of S1, S2 and S3.

Although in the field of education there are research procedures in which reliability is not a useful criterion, there are many occasions in which it does make sense to judge data-gathering processes in terms of reliability, and to design research procedures so as to achieve a high degree of reliability. One way to do this is to use a 'test–retest' procedure, in which an instrument is used and then used again with the same subjects, and the sets of results are compared. The retest could involve the same researcher or someone else. The comparison of datasets S1, S2 and S3 is an illustration of the test–retest procedure (in fact this is test–retest–retest). The time interval between test and retest may be an important consideration in deciding whether to use this procedure. If the interval is too short, subjects' memories of the test may influence the retest. If it is too long, the subjects' beliefs, behaviours and so on may have changed. Because of these hazards, test–retest should be used with care. Another way to check reliability is to use an 'equivalent forms' procedure. As the name suggests, two equivalent versions of a data-gathering instrument are used with the same subjects and the results are compared. A third approach is the 'split-half' procedure. Here, a single instrument is used. The resulting dataset is split into two halves and the two half-sets are compared. On an instrument that consisted of, say, one hundred short items, one way to use the split-half procedure would be to compare the score on the odd numbered items with those on the even ones. This would tend to avoid problems arising from familiarity or fatigue.

You may have noticed that I have been discussing reliability using examples in which data-gathering procedures have been repeated with the same subjects. The reason for specifying the same subjects is as follows: I am using the word reliability to describe the extent to which a data-gathering process produces similar results in similar conditions. If the subjects changed then the conditions would not normally be similar. If we got different results by using the same procedure with different subjects, would that tell us that the procedure was unreliable? That is clearly not the only possibility. Only if we were confident, through some independent means of judging, that in relevant respects one sample of subjects closely resembled another might we conclude that different results meant that the procedure was unreliable. Fortunately, most researchers – and probably all new researchers – in education are engaged in small-scale or case study research, rather than large-scale surveys, and so if reliability is a consideration the researcher can focus on achieving it with her or his actual subjects.

Validity

In our imaginary scenario can we say anything about validity? Validity is a word that is as overworked as reliability, to judge from Hammersley's survey (Hammersley, 1987). Wellington's application of the word validity is appealing on account of its practicality and conciseness: 'Validity refers to the degree to which a method, a test or a research tool actually measures what it is supposed to measure' (Wellington, 2000: 201).

However, things are not always as straightforward as they seem. In Wellington's definition there is an instrument (a method, test or tool), there are the results of the use of the instrument (actual measurements), and there are the intentions or claims of the researcher (what is supposed to be measured). All of these ingredients are essential to Wellington's formulation, the implication being that the term validity refers to them collectively, not separately. I find that it makes sense to think of the validity of the *relationship* between a claim and the result of a data-gathering process, rather than the validity of these things on their own. To make things a little more concrete, consider four possible claims that might conceivably be made on the basis of the datasets S1, S2 and S3, as set out in Figure 4.5.

Here are my views on Figure 4.5. It is valid to make claim 1, because the claim is compatible with the data. It is not valid to make claim 2, because we don't know how stable the data are over time. Without knowing about that, we are not justified in generalising the data from the current time. People can change their minds, after all. It is not valid to make claim 3, because we have no grounds for generalising from our sample of respondents to people as a whole. And neither is it valid to make claim 4. Can you see why this is so? It is because, in Wellington's terms, the data are not what they are claimed to be. Respondents were not asked to name the features that were important to them as individuals, they were asked to rank features that had already been selected.

Pen Exercise
The issue of validity

1   The data represent what the respondents currently think about the importance of the named attributes in selecting a pen.
2   The data represent what the respondents think about the importance of the named attributes in selecting a pen.
3   The data represent what people currently think about the importance of the named attributes in selecting a pen.
4   The data represent what the respondents currently think are the important attributes in selecting a pen.

We can now ask about validity in a different and, in my view, more useful way. For each of the claims 1 to 4 we can ask: 'In view of the results of the data gathering process that was used, is it valid to make this claim?' You may like to pause for a moment to form your opinions on each of the four claims.

Figure 4.5   Considering the issue of validity

Instead of writing that 'it isn't valid to make claim X', you may prefer the more concise statement: 'claim X isn't valid'. The economy of the second statement is appealing but it could easily be taken to imply that validity is a property of a claim on its own. It would be helpful for the researcher to regard such a statement as shorthand for: 'it isn't valid to make claim X on the basis of the data-gathering process that has been used to support it'. As long as the researcher has a coherent understanding of the way he or she is using the concept of validity, pitfalls should be avoidable.

Note that claims 2 to 4 lack validity, but not because they are obviously false. In fact we cannot tell whether or not they are false without further research. The issue of validity concerns the relationship between the claim and the accompanying process of data gathering. If suitable data were obtained, each of claims 2 to 4 could then be argued to be valid.

Researchers are involved not only with their own data but also, through the literature, with other people's data. In view of this it would be helpful to be able to use the term validity to characterise the relationship between a claim and any data-gathering process that is used as grounds for the claim. This broader application incorporates the use made of validity in the examples above. In addition it allows for a judgement of the 'goodness' of claims made on the basis of other people's research. In short, if I make a claim on the basis of someone's (my own or other people's) research data and you regard my claim as warranted by that data – that is, you believe that the data is saying what I claim it is saying – then you would judge my claim to be valid.

There are several types of validity referred to in the educational methodology literature. One of the common distinctions is between 'internal' and 'external validity' (see, for example, Cohen and Manion, 1994: Ch. 8). An idea of the difference can be gained by revisiting our thought experiment. Let's assume that the datasets S1, S2 and S3 were sufficiently close for us to be confident that the data-gathering procedure was adequately reliable. We can then make the valid claim that the data represent what the respondents currently thought about the importance of the named attributes in selecting a pen. Suppose that the data revealed that the two most important attributes for the group were cost and style. As an outcome of the research, therefore, we could publish the claim: 'amongst the given criteria, cost and style were paramount for the group'. If someone else then scrutinised the study and reached the conclusion that our account was self-consistent and reasonable, they would regard our claim as being internally valid. It is internally valid because it is a valid claim about the contents of the research study. Internal validity is all very well – in fact it is essential whenever validity is an applicable consideration – but a study is potentially more interesting if its findings can be applied beyond its own research content. 'External validity' is an indicator of the extent to which this is reasonable. Suppose, for example, we used the outcome of our imaginary study above to claim that cost and style are the two key factors when people select pens. We should certainly expect the retort that the claim lacks external validity. We would be on slightly better ground if we made the more modest claim that researchers prioritise cost and style. It could be said that this second claim has more external validity. Do you find it reasonable that external validity can arise by degrees, rather than be all-or-nothing? I see this as inevitable since, by definition, any generalisation ventures into territory that is beyond the content of the study in question. There is always some element of the unknown, and so hundred per cent external validity is unachievable.

Reliability and validity have been discussed as indicators of goodness, respectively, of data-gathering processes and of the relationship between claims and data-gathering processes. These are potentially very useful considerations in the design of a research study. In the final section of this chapter we consider the notion of trustworthiness and credibility, which some people regard as holistic indicators of goodness in research.

Trustworthiness and credibility

> The basic issue in relation to trustworthiness is simple: How can an inquirer persuade his or her audiences (including self) that the findings of an inquiry are worth paying attention to, worth taking account of? What arguments can be mounted, what criteria invoked, what questions asked, that would be persuasive on this issue? (Lincoln and Guba, 1985: 290)

The criteria that have conventionally been used to judge goodness in research are validity, reliability and 'objectivity'. (Note that 'objectivity' is used in the literature in distinct ways. In its 'strongest' form it is associated with absolute truth, while in its 'weak' form it implies a consensus amongst informed observers.) Lincoln and Guba (1985) have questioned whether these three criteria are universally useful. They have suggested that a more appropriate indicator might be the *trustworthiness* of the research. Before you throw your hands up in dismay at having engaged with the contents of this chapter so far, only to be urged to disregard them, please be reassured! I do not intend to promote trustworthiness as a replacement for what has gone before. If your understanding of the use of statements and relationships in research has developed during the reading of this chapter, then you will be much better placed to consider the additional, and valuable, idea of trust-worthiness and its close relative, credibility.

Trustworthiness, according to Lincoln and Guba involves credibility, transferability, dependability and confirmability. These four concepts are extensions, or adaptations, of the 'traditional' categories of internal validity, external validity, reliability and objectivity. Sturman (1999) emphasises the value of the first, credibility, as a useful indicator of goodness in case study research. I will focus on credibility here, since much educational research conducted by new researchers comes into the category of case studies. Readers who are interested in exploring the broader notion of trustworthi-ness in research could refer to Lincoln and Guba (1985) or to Bassey's short-ened, simplified account (Bassey, 1999).

Sturman (1999) lists several strategies that can enhance the credibility of case study research. You may find it interesting when looking at these strate-gies to imagine yourself reading two research accounts, one of which has made use of the strategy in question and the other of which has not, and to ask yourself how you would feel about the two accounts:

1 Data-gathering procedures are explained.
2 Data is presented transparently and in ways that enable ready re-analysis.
3 'Negative instances' are reported. (This doesn't mean that the researcher should invent some spurious data to gain credibility! It means that data are included whether or not they fit the beliefs or intentions of the researcher.)
4 Biases are acknowledged.
5 Fieldwork analyses (that is, the ways in which data have been handled when first obtained) are explained.
6 The relationships between claims and supporting evidence are clearly expressed.
7 Primary data (the researcher's own) is distinguished from secondary data (other people's).

8 Interpretation is distinguished from description (for instance, the researcher hasn't tried to pass off a problematic statement as an established fact).

9 A diary or a log is used to track what took place during the study.

10 Procedures are used to check the quality of the data.

Regarding the final point, some procedures for checking data quality have been discussed earlier in this chapter. An additional procedure that can contribute to the credibility of a research account is 'triangulation'. This is where data-gathering procedures are applied separately – or preferably independently – to the same subjects (or system). As a result, statements can be made about the subjects that are separately warranted. We had an example of triangulation in the 'pens' thought experiment above: when a new researcher was employed to obtain dataset S3, we had 'triangulation by researchers', because the new data were obtained from the same subjects, using the same procedure but using a different researcher. If, on the other hand, we had changed the procedure, while keeping the subjects of study and the researcher unchanged, we would have had 'triangulation by procedures'. Here is an everyday parallel: suppose that someone told you some surprising fact that you found rather implausible. And shortly afterwards, someone else who was wholly unconnected with the first person called you and independently told you the same fact. The impact of hearing the same fact from two unconnected sources is much greater than if there had been only one. The word 'triangulation' is a helpful metaphor here, derived from the practice of surveying; a better map of a landscape can be obtained if one uses more than one line of sight.

Summary

This chapter has examined various types of statements and considered their suitability for use in research writing. It has distinguished subjective statements, statements that can be taken as unproblematic, and statements that need support from data or argument if they are to be used in research.

Two particular forms of relationship have been examined: correlation and causality. Indicators of 'goodness' in research have been considered. Practical strategies have been discussed for evaluating and enhancing reliability, validity and credibility in small-scale research.

5 Research Approaches

Clive Opie

If you have read the preface to this book you will be clear as to its focus and that by concentrating on MEd dissertations it intentionally aims to limit discussion of research procedures to those which are 'doable' within the timescale typically associated with these postgraduate qualifications. There is no suggestion that other research procedures not included here are in any way less valid, for example ethnographic study, but just that they are likely to be impractical. As Jan Gray, a university lecturer in Australia who completed a PhD thesis in this area, and which was awarded a prize for 'outstanding scholarship in postgraduate research' notes:

> I would tell any of my Master students it would be impossible to achieve the degree of immersion necessary (for an ethnographic study) in the time allowed for a Masters degree in order to be able to develop an understanding of how a culture works. (Bell and Opie, 2002: 170)

By a similar token it has been suggested that taking a grounded theory approach is likely to be impractical due to the time needed to become conversant with this research approach and, once understood, the time for transcription and analysis of findings. The latter is not, in fact, completely true and some good MEd dissertations have resulted in employment of such an approach. In addition commercial computer software (e.g. ATLAS.ti and NUD·IST) is now readily available to help with such analysis and although necessarily time consuming it is still achievable and the chapters by Ann-Marie Bathmaker and Mike Pomerantz show this. This chapter will therefore confine itself to detail on Case Study and Action Research approaches as these will undoubtedly form the mainstay of MEd work. It will also refer to Experiments and Grounded Theory as approaches as these are possible but, as each require particular skills and time, and in the case of Experiments significant ethical issues arise, they are not so straightforward to implement within the constraints of an MEd.

Case study

The two typical questions often asked by MEd research students is 'What constitutes a case study?' and 'How many people do we need for a case study?' The first questions arise simply from uncertainty of this approach while the second results from a view that as research needs to result in some generalisable outcome then clearly numbers of participants will be important. We have in fact addressed the answer to this second question earlier (p. 5) where we noted that for the type of research likely to be undertaken over the timescale of an MEd it is the relatability of the findings to similar settings, rather than its generalisability, which should be considered as the important outcome.

Rather than just to appear to dismiss the answer to the second question we can provide a more satisfactory answer to both questions if we start from a general statement of the term case study.

> a specific instance that is frequently designed to illustrate a more general principle. (Nisbet and Watt, 1984: 72)

> the focus is ... one unit of analysis. (McMillan and Schumacher, 1984: 322)

> concentration upon a particular instance in order to reveal the ways in which events come together to create particular kinds of outcomes. (Hitchcock and Hughes, 1989: 214)

> an opportunity for one aspect of a problem to be studied in some depth within a limited timescale. (Bell, 1999: 10)

In other words a case study can be viewed as an in-depth study of interactions of a single instance in an enclosed system. The issue of numbers for a case study is therefore meaningless. It could involve a single person, a group of people within a setting, a whole class, a department within a school, a school. We will stop here as you can see that the size of the case study in terms of numbers is increasing and as continually expressed throughout this text limiting this quantity will be essential for MEd work.

As with all research the important thing about a case study is that it is methodically prepared and the collection of evidence is systematically undertaken. Crucially the focus of a case study is on a real situation, with real people in an environment often familiar to the researcher. Its aim then is to provide a picture of a certain feature of social behaviour or activity in a particular setting and the factors influencing this situation. In this way the interactions of events, human relationships and other factors are studied in a unique location. To try and get a better understanding of a case study approach let us consider a number of examples and the research procedures (see Chapter 6) used in them.

Example 1   A study of one student's use of the internet for self-study in science

This case study involved a mother and daughter with the mother carrying out observational research as a participant observer (Chapter 6, p. 128) on her daughter using the internet to see how much she could teach herself about various aspects of science (Lees-Rolfe, 2002). One might baulk at this research and you would be right to be concerned about all sorts of issues such as the reliability and validity of the findings to say nothing about the possible social damage such research could do to a mother–daughter relationship. These, and other concerns, were constructively addressed and presented in the thesis. Although the research resulted in initial difficulties the final outcome was a most illuminating and rewarding (for both mother and daughter) piece of research as perhaps the following extract helps to show:

> She [daughter] asked why acids are soluble. When I didn't give her an answer she tried to go to a heading on one internet site that wasn't a link and got a bit irritated with it not being a link.
>
> She went to another site.
>
> D. 'So anything that gives off a proton is an acid and everything that takes a proton is a base?'
>
> She carried on reading and then
>
> D. 'Bases dissociate? What is dissociate?'
>
> I told her to go to the glossary I gave her and she refused and went to a dictionary on Yahoo.
>
> D. 'Separate – It would have been quicker for you to have told me.'
>
> M. 'This is supposed to see whether you can learn from the internet without a teacher.'
>
> D. 'It is easy to use the internet for learning for what they have on it but something like that it is quicker for you to tell me.'

Here we see a clear delineation on the part of the daughter as to the value of the internet versus a teacher and this issue was raised on several other occasions.

You might also like to know mother and daughter relationships were not damaged by this research. They did start from a strong base and the agreement was made that if there were any signs to indicate that their relationship was deteriorating the research would stop.

Example 2   How well are visually impaired students integrated into a mainstream secondary school?

This thesis described a case study undertaken with visually impaired pupils and their specific resource teachers; non-visually impaired pupils; and general teachers of one school (Samuel, 2002). It set out to document, through observational research as a non-participant and the use of semi-structured interviews, the various views of integration of visually impaired pupils into mainstream education from these perspective groups. The case study paints a very poignant, but balanced, picture of the issues as the following comments hopefully show.

The following comment would seem to be quite damning:

> an honest confession by the staff is that at times there is a need to 'move on and not wait for the visually impaired' during lessons in order to meet the needs of the regular peers, and meet the deadlines of completing the syllabus.

However, when taken into consideration with the following comment:

> Teachers agreeing that they may not be adequately prepared in terms of training and support to give to the visually impaired students the best education or similar to the normal peers. However, they urged me not to doubt their compassion and care for the visually impaired students. They said, 'these students are for real and we will continue to help them in whatever way we can'. One teacher commented that when serving students with disabilities one needs to be 'empathetic' and render 'service from the heart'.

This is much more indicative not of a non-caring attitude amongst general teachers but one of frustration that they had not had the opportunity to have training to better equip them with an understanding of how to work with visually impaired students and the resources they would need to do so.

Similarly the following would seem to indicate fellow pupils care little for their visually impaired peers:

> From data gathered from interaction with these visually impaired students and observation, I found that the level of participation appeared to be minimal for at least five of these students. Penny seems to have better participation in class. She actively contributes during group discussions, and at times spearheads the discussions. Moreover, she participates in class dramas, and joins the rest of her peers in outings and excursions. The other five students seldom participate in such activities. Arun participates occasionally. However, he stated that he ends up getting so frustrated that peers tend to forget his presence in the midst of their conversation while on such outings. A sense of being left out always hinders him from joining such activities. Yani said that she can 'sense' that her regular peers see her as a 'burden when placed in their group'. According to Yani, she feels left out as they normally do not consult or ask for her opinions.

This has to be balanced though with support that is given through designated 'buddies' which did work well and of an appointed resource teacher:

All students seemed to be happy with the provision of a resource teacher. She being visually impaired, students felt that she is in a position to understand them better.

Example 3   A study of the implementation of programme-based learning (PBL) in a department in a polytechnic

The basis for this case study (Shukor, 2001) was that her polytechnic had set a mandate to its staff to implement PBL into their teaching and although many lecturers were in the process of modifying their teaching to include PBL, she felt that:

> having an insight into the contents of students' thoughts could help understand students' learning, design good problems, and also influence some of the operational issues of PBL. For example, if the lecturers knew that students' thoughts were inclined towards more reflective thinking in PBL small-group discussions, as compared to during the conventional tutorial discussions, the lecturer could extend the usage of the PBL small-group to promote this form of thinking within the discussions in their modules. Therefore, the practical objective of this case study is to understand students' thoughts and help in any way to improve the PBL process.

Several questions were raised in the mind of the researcher. What exactly do students think during these discussions? Do they engage in active thinking of the subject under discussion, or are they simply listening passively? How do their thoughts in the PBL small-group discussions compare with their thoughts in conventional tutorial discussions?

The researcher worked with three teaching groups over eight weeks extending a case study done by Geerligs (1995) on students' thoughts during PBL small-group discussions. The students' thoughts in this latter study were obtained using a 'thought-sampling' method. During the small-group discussions, students reported their thoughts at random times at the signal of a bell. The thought reports were classified into six categories: content-related (passive), content-related (non-passive), procedure-related, metacognitive-related, off-task and miscellaneous. The findings of her case study suggested that:

> Within the PBL environment the study showed that the different stages of the process resulted in a variety of students' thoughts patterns. Although the patterns as shown may still need reinforcement in terms of greater empirical evidence, the initial findings from this study are an encouraging start for PBL practitioners to reflect on the importance of good implementation issues, as well as the role of each PBL stage in meeting the overall objective of the PBL approach. The high percentages of off-tasks thoughts in all the four weeks of the small group PBL discussions are somewhat disturbing and may need to be addressed by PBL practitioners.

Example 4   Ascertaining the views of students
of their Diploma in Nursing course

The Diploma in Nursing course in question was set up with the aim of providing an educational and experiential foundation for students to function effectively as registered nurses at a beginning level when they graduated and to address known problems of nursing education such as a decline in student enrolment in nursing programmes; the low status of nursing which was believed to have contributed to poor recruitment; and the high attrition rates/shortage of nurses. This exploratory case study (Fan, 1998) was carried out to help enhance the understanding of these pertinent problems and to examine whether the new Diploma in Nursing programme might help in addressing them.

The study involved the use of a lengthy, detailed and carefully structured questionnaire (Bell and Opie, 2002) of the entire first 234-student cohort to complete the diploma course. There is not space to go into all details of design of the questionnaire but its inclusion here reflects a case study at the very upper levels of that doable at MEd level. Fan was an extremely dedicated student and although producing a commendable dissertation there is little doubt the length of time he spent producing his thesis would not typically be available to most MEd students. High dedication resulted in the findings of his case study being quite far-reaching and although the overall view was that

> All in all, from analysis of students' responses in the study, it would be fair to summarise their view by concluding that the majority had found the diploma programme to be both educational and useful.

With 'Nearly all (97.8%) of the students believing that the polytechnic diploma would improve the image of nursing.' These needed to be taken in connection with other findings showing that students were:

> less contented with the amount of time spent at work-placement (due to time required at college for theoretical studies) though they felt that they had learned much from it. Likewise, they were also less contented with the amount of clinical supervision given during their work-placements.

Hopefully these examples have shown that a case study can cover a multitude of areas involving a range of procedures and that the question of numbers is, in many respects, irrelevant. What they do highlight is the nature of a case study being an in-depth study of interactions of a single instance in an enclosed system.

What a case study does not do is set out to implement any changes as a result of its findings. Although findings from a case study may influence practice, or result in recommendations for change, this is somewhat secondary to this research approach and is certainly not part of the research process. Once completed and detailed it is arguable that a case study is 'done and dusted'. There are though various occasions where the main focus of the research approach is to purposefully and positively influence practice through implementation of some form of change – this is the process of action research.

Action research

Action research offers a means of providing an understanding to a problematic situation and whether this situation concerns people or procedures is immaterial. Although typically action research will concern itself with practitioner issues (Carr and Kemmis, 1986) the essence of action research is that it enables a reflective cyclic process to be brought to bear on the understanding of the problem at hand. This reflective cycle starts with an analysis of the problem and if we stick with our practitioner example this might revolve around, the implementation of a new teaching method or learning strategy; attempting to encourage more positive work attitudes; or studying the efficiency of administrative procedures. From this analysis identification of a suitable, often small-scale, systematic intervention aimed at achieving a more desirable outcome will evolve. This intervention will then be implemented and monitored using a variety of research procedures (e.g. questionnaires, interviews, observations). The findings will then be analysed, evaluated and reflected upon with the aim of providing further modifications to, or redefinition of, the original intervention. These changes will then be implemented and the whole cyclic process commences again. This process is diagrammatically expressed in Figure 5.1.

You may recall that our opening comments about research noted that it involved a 'systematic process' overcoming more 'common-sense knowing'. Keeping this in mind Kemmis and McTaggart encapsulate this notion, and the points in Figure 5.1, in their view of action research:

> to do action research is to plan, act, observe and reflect more carefully, more systematically, and more rigorously than one usually does in everyday life. (1992: 10)

There is not space in this text for a detailed analysis of the issues pertaining to action research and for this the reader is referred to further reading (Cohen et al., 2000). What will be presented here are the general types of action research, the characteristics of it with respect to a practitioner-based approach to educational research and a series of starting points for commencing action research.

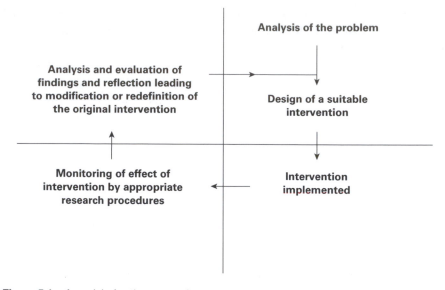

Figure 5.1 A model of action research

Main types of action research

Although we have noted the general process of action research this nevertheless allows for variations in styles of action research. These styles reflect the level at which they take into consideration the social and political factors which influence practice and, interestingly, can be seen to have similarities with forms of reflective practice discussed by Schön (1987), Cruickshank (1987) and Zeichner and Liston (1987). The styles of action research are detailed in Table 5.1.

Of the styles of action research shown in Table 5.1 it is just worth noting that the 'critical' variant of emancipatory action research has come in for considerable criticism inasmuch as it is seen to: 'wrest action research away from practitioners and into the hands of theorists and the academic research community only and ...undermines the significance of the individual in favour of groups' (Cohen et al., 2001: 233). The reader is recommended to read the chapter on action research by Cohen and colleagues (2001) for much fuller discussion of the critique of 'critical' action research. Although criticising a particular style of action research the overall value of it as an approach to research is not denied and perhaps the most powerful aspect is it's ability, as stated by Somekh (1995) 'to bridge the gap between research and practice'.

Main characteristics of action research

If we focus on practitioner-based action research then we can consider the main characteristics of it (Kemmis and McTaggart, 1992; McKernan, 1991; Zuber-Skerritt, 1996) as:

Table 5.1   Styles of action research

Action research	Design
Technical	This merely aims to undertake action research to render an existing situation more efficient and effective. What it does not do is to seek to challenge the legitimacy of the situation nor the wider social and political factors, which may have given rise to it. This is representative of Schön's (1987) notion of 'reflection-in-action'.
Practical	Here consideration is given to understanding and interpreting the social factors, which have led to a particular situation. In other words the wider factors, which influence a teacher's practice are given consideration. Understanding and interpreting social situations that teachers find themselves in, with a view to improving them, is crucial to this design of action research and identifies with Cruickshank's (1987) notion of reflective practice.
Emancipatory	This has as its agenda the development of an understanding of illegitimate structural and interpersonal constraints (Grundy, 1987), which thwart the empowerment of individuals and social groups. In this case action research is designed with a political agenda of improvement towards a more just, egalitarian society. Zeichner and Liston's (1987) view of reflective practice in teaching mimics this idea of action research although they use the term 'critical' reflective practice. The term 'critical' is used to describe a variant of emancipatory action research where rather than focusing on individuals there is a broader agenda of changing education, changing schooling and changing society (Kemmis, 1997).

- enabling practical problem solving;
- collaborative and participatory;
- seeking to understand social systems and the processes of change within them;
- being undertaken *in situ*;
- focusing on problems that are of immediate concern;
- offering formative feedback such that aims and methodology are open to variation;
- seeking to deliver usable and sharable outcomes;
- involving critical analysis and reflection on situations;
- providing defensible justification for any educational work being undertaken.

These characteristics are not exclusive as for example the view that action research should always be collaborative is seen by some as restrictive, seemingly ignoring the individualistic approach of 'teacher-as-researcher' (Stenhouse, 1975; Whitehead, 1985).

Personal points to consider when commencing action research

The following are adapted from Kemmis and McTaggart (1992) who when considering undertaking action research suggest these personal considerations:

- involve yourself in the action research;
- be organised;
- start small;
- ensure supportive work-in-progress discussions are planned for;
- be tolerant and supportive throughout the process;
- be persistent about monitoring;
- be prepared to work hard to ensure sharing of responsibility for the whole process;
- be open to changing how you think about things;
- register progress with all interested parties not just those involved directly;
- ensure time to write up your work;
- be explicit about what you have achieved;
- continually question yourself if your work is actually helping you.

As you can see this list takes us back to the comment by Somekh earlier, which indicated that action research is a means of forging links between practical and theoretical concerns.

What follows now is another example, from one of my MEd students, of a piece of action research exploring attitudes to mathematics by a particular group of students they had to teach.

Example

As part of her mathematics timetable Lily Soh (2001) had been given the job of teaching a particular group of students known as 'repeat students'. These students had failed various exams first time around and now, as their name indicates, had to repeat various parts of their course in order to resit them. The term 'repeat students' carried with it various negative connotations which, whether true or not, were perceived by various other teaching colleagues to have some credence. These resulted in a perception that 'repeat' students were lazy, academically weak, problematic, awkward and troublesome. Lily was of the opinion that although some of these views may have had some validity a 'labelling syndrome' surrounded the 'repeat' students making the position far worse than it actually was. She therefore decided to undertake a piece of action research to first ascertain the causes why these particular students had ended up having to repeat their studies in mathematics, then second, acting upon these findings, for example, by modifying her teaching, and finally ascertaining the impact of the changes she had implemented with a view to further action as necessary.

By interviewing her set of 'repeat' students, using a semi-structured interview procedure, she was able to show that they felt that the main factors for them not doing well in mathematics in a previous semester were that:

(i)   the module was too difficult;

(ii)   there was too much material to learn;

(iii) they had made insufficient personal effort;

(iv)   the lecturer was boring, unfriendly and impatient;

(v)   the lecturer taught at a very fast pace;

(vi)   they were not motivated;

(vii) no one helped them when faced with problems.

Lily interpreted these results as indicating that:

> the students attributed their failure mainly to external factors [see (i), (ii), (iv), (v) & (vii)] and one controllable factor [(iii)]. The student or the teacher can influence almost all of these factors. For instance, students can increase the amount of effort to be expended since they find that they did not work hard enough in the last semester. On my part, I can help them to overcome factors (i) and (ii) by breaking the materials into smaller chunks before presenting to them. In addition, I have control over the delivery pace [factor (v)] and my rapport [factor (iv)] with my students.

On probing further she found that it appeared that many of their difficulties stemmed from their lectures and that they found lecturing an ineffective teaching method. Interestingly these same students initially faced similar motivational problems with some of their engineering modules, but then the laboratory lessons and hands-on experiments, which supplemented them helped them to understand those materials that they could not grasp during the lectures. As a result Lily decided she would: 'conduct my lessons in small tutorial groups and do away with lectures. When I announced my intentions, the students expressed much enthusiasm in the new arrangement.'

To improve their understanding of mathematics, the majority of the students also suggested that the lecturer 'uses examples to illustrate concepts', 'explains solutions clearly step-by-step', 'summarises what is learned' and 'informs them why they are learning the subjects'. A few students also proposed that the lecturer should 'allow students to work on assignments together' and 'provide a way for feedback when they encounter problems'. Interestingly, though the students 'favoured the conventional method of teaching, whereby their teachers "passes" knowledge to them', which was something initially Lily wanted to change, she was determined not to impose her own style and so all of the points above were taken on board by Lily in her lessons:

> As I have chosen direct instruction as the main approach in delivery, I am afraid that students might become passive learners and depend totally on me for information. I decided to inject a little difference by planning for students to work in groups for tutorial assignments. The aim of arranging for group work is to allow for interaction and collaboration in class. The assignments are also based on application problems that require the students to understand the material before

they could apply it. In this way, I hoped to encourage the students to participate more actively in their learning.

In aiming to help her students' understanding she noted that:

> Since most students have feedback that they are confused by the many formulae and applications of 'Differentiation and Integration', I created a simple summary sheet and gave it a sophisticated name, the 'advance organiser'. This idea was borrowed from Ausubel (1963) who believes that a person can learn new material more meaningfully when the new material can be subsumed under their existing concepts.

She also decided:

> to introduce in class a 'How am I doing?' diary which the students could use to express in writing about their progress. This is to provide a channel for the students to communicate their problems to me. I have previously experienced cases whereby a particular student appeared to be progressing fine but in fact he/she was struggling to keep up, and I did not notice the problem until too near the examination, which was a little too late to provide help. Hence, the purpose of the 'How am I doing?' diary is also to help me identify students who are facing difficulties so that I could render assistance immediately. The students are required to write the 'How am I doing?' diary weekly. Eventually, the 'How am I doing?' diary could also serve as the students' journal with the record of their own progress.

At this point Lily had completed the first part of her action research and moved into the second part, implementing the changes she had decided upon. It is worth recalling our earlier comments in this chapter about her research style. Although Lily did talk with her teaching colleagues and they knew of her research she basically followed an individualistic approach of 'teacher-as-researcher' as proffered by others such as Stenhouse (1975) and Whitehead (1985) while identifying with the personal considerations (see p. 81) for undertaking action research outlined by Kemmis and McTaggart (1992). Lily implemented her changes over a 14-week period and, as all good action researchers should be, she was systematic in her approach to the collection of details and analysis of the impact of the changes that her work produced.

Lily had no choice about when her lessons should run. The times allocated – 3 pm to 5 pm on a Wednesday afternoon, when other students were undertaking extra curricular activities, such as sports, and 9 am to 11 am on a Saturday – would not strike many as the most conducive to achieving successful outcomes. However, her personal drive and enthusiasm to do the best for her students and to stick with the findings from her initial data collection paid dividends. She noted that during lessons:

> the students asked me questions frequently to clarify their doubts and when I posed questions, they were always eager to volunteer their answers.

> When given questions to solve in class, I noticed that they would concentrate and stay with a single task, paying attention to details until it was completed.

Even more positive in her eyes was the fact that:

> when they got back their marked homework, instead of comparing grades, they were more interested in exploring their mistakes and making amendments. I interpreted this as showing that the students' focus has shifted from getting the right answer to learning *how* to get the right answer. I could sense that they are more concerned about the accuracy of their work rather than how well they have done compared to their classmates.

In addition she noted her students attended classes more punctually, paid attention, asked questions regularly, completed their homework promptly and produced good quality work. She was also of the opinion that feedback, which was concise, accurate and informative had also played a part in this success and constantly reminded herself to ensure this continued.

A positive response to the use of an 'advance organiser' also materialised. It was common to hear students mention things like 'I can't remember, let me look at the advance organiser' or 'let's refer to the advance organiser before we proceed further'. Interestingly some students found her format of 'advance organiser' very dull and one created his own format which ended up resembling a mind map. Although he felt it was 'messy' Lily suggested that he shared it with the class. He willingly agreed to do so and this sparked off further exciting activity that the students appeared to enjoy. As Lily noted:

> I could not believe that what started off as a routine exercise of summarising had evolved into. I could also see from this activity that different students learn in different ways. The feedback received on the use of 'advance organiser' and then the 'mind map' has been positive. I think the students realised that summarising the material learned, regardless of the methods used to do the summary, is one good way to help them review their materials.

The 'How am I doing?' diary was though much less well received. After a few weeks, many students, for variety of reasons – for example, 'it is a waste of time; it's faster if I tell you my problems' and 'not an effective way of tracking my progress' – requested to stop writing the diary. Considering it was not achieving its aim and not wanting to pressurise her students into doing something they disliked, she decided to give them the freedom to decide whether to continue with it or not. Eventually, all students chose not to write the diary. Here we see Lily being open to change as her work progressed, another important consideration of action research (see p. 82).

Another positive development was the willingness and desire of students to work in pairs to solve problems and generate their own for other pairs to solve. You may work in an educational culture where such activity is commonplace but Lily did not and as she noted it threw up several surprises:

> The first surprise came when I saw that the questions submitted for the first quiz and subsequent quiz to be appropriate and required very little editing. I had expected them to make many mistakes while formulating the questions. The second surprise was when I observed that my students had typed and printed their questions based on the format for the previous quiz. I had assumed that the questions would be hand-written. The third surprise was that they did not only attempt to solve one quiz, but also requested for the questions of different groups. Beyond these pleasant surprises, I observed many benefits that were induced by allowing the students to formulate questions. The most obvious being that constructing questions to some extent ensures students' understanding of concepts. I could also see that students were learning and understanding most of the materials. Moreover, it is not common for students to work in pairs when learning Mathematics. While attempting the questions in pairs, the students tended to have endless discussions on how to tackle the problems. Sometimes, conflicts arose but somehow they reached a consensus, either by compromise or by trying the different approaches one at a time. Watching them argue over conflicting ideas and resolving them allowed me to observe the changes in their train of thoughts. It reminded me that my students were able to solve their own problems and could make their own choices and decisions.

Space does not permit a full discussion of Lily's action research but her reflections on it are reproduced here, as they are in my view indicative of the potential of this approach in bringing about real and positive change.

> When I was assigned to teach this group of repeating students, my initial feelings were one of misfortunate. I have heard often enough from other lecturers on the lack of motivation, low abilities and bad attitude of repeating students towards learning. However, I was also curious to know why the repeating students lacked the motivation to learn and how I could help them.
>
> I started by reading various literatures on motivation. From there, I realised that no student is unmotivated to learn. If we would observe carefully the students in the class, we will definitely see those who are not motivated to learn Mathematics but are motivated to learn other things. Hence, I wanted to identify what motivates these repeating students and provide them with an environment that will challenge them based on their perceptions of what motivates them. First though, I had to stop differentiating them from the other students and assumed they all had the potential and ability to learn Mathematics. I initiated some 'brain washing' for myself by practising 'mental rehearsal'. I repeatedly told myself that I should not be prejudiced against these students and I have to change my mind-set if I want them to learn successfully. The feeling was strange but it helped me to be more aware of my attitude towards them. I also wanted to instil in the students the importance of diligence. As such, I placed a lot of emphasis on making learning as a process rather than a product. I also encouraged them to focus on making good effort, being responsible and to ask for help whenever necessary. In addition, I chose to give comments and feedback based on their understanding of the materials and level of effort as perceived by me. When sloppy work was submitted, I reminded myself not to criticise but instead to feedback in

writing or speak to the student individually to identify the cause. I think the students knew that I was giving them an equal chance to learn by not stereotyping them. They responded by putting in more effort in their work. In the process, I learned not to underestimate the students' capabilities. There were times where their suggestions were better. If I had been very rigid and not allowing changes in my class, I would not have come to observe the different ways students learn, understand and work together to formulate quiz problems. It is really inspiring to see them being so highly motivated in the class. However, to achieve this kind of excellence requires special understanding and extra time and effort.

This study is one of the most valuable rewards for me in my teaching career. Most of the time, I am so concerned about completing the syllabus and maintaining the students' performance that I overlooked the aspect of students' motivation. In the process of doing the research, I paused and asked myself why I chose teaching as a career. I thought about it for some time and I realised that I want to do more than help my students obtain good grades. I want to have a hand in moulding them into responsible, independent and self-motivated individuals.

Experiments

In Chapter 1 we made passing reference to the difficulty of undertaking experiments in educational research. In particular that it

> suggests that the action of people can be controlled or conditioned by external circumstances; that basically they are the products of the environment they find themselves in. In this case thoughts, personality, creativity and so on, are irrelevant. (see p. 6)

This raises considerable ethical dilemmas and moral questions, which were discussed in further detail by Pat Sikes (Chapter 2). Despite these concerns it is possible to undertake experimental work but as the British Psychological Society detail on their website:

> In all circumstances, investigators must consider the ethical implications and psychological consequences for the participants in their research. The essential principle is that the investigation should be considered from the standpoint of all participants; foreseeable threats to their psychological wellbeing, health, values or dignity should be eliminated. Investigators should recognise that, in our multi-cultural and multi-ethnic society and where investigations involve individuals of different ages, gender and social background, the investigators may not have sufficient knowledge of the implications of any investigation for the participants. It should be borne in mind that the best judge of whether an investigation will cause offence may be members of the population from which the participants in the research are to be drawn. (BPS, 2002)

If we are as sure as we can be that any ethical issues have been addressed then there are a series of reasonably well-defined stages of experimental work which need to be followed. These are outlined here and then followed by an example of an MEd thesis (Lim, 1997) which employed this approach.

Words and phrases printed in bold italics are described in the Glossary in chapter 10.

Stages to experimental work

STAGE **1** AN ANALYSIS OF THE THEORY RELATED TO THE RESEARCH

This is, of course, an essential stage for any research but here it enables one to select the *independent* and *dependent variables*, which will be considered in the experimental research being proposed.

STAGE **2** FORMULATION OF A HYPOTHESIS AND SETTING AN APPROPRIATE LEVEL AT WHICH TO TEST IT

The first stage will lead to the premise for any hypothesis about the relationship between two or more variables being tested, for example, that introducing a new teaching method (the *independent variable*) will have an effect on test results (the *dependent variable*). Although it may sound odd what is actually tested is the *null hypothesis* (see the Glossary for further details on this) as one should always try in *inferential statistics* to disprove a hypothesis. In our case this would lead us to a *null hypothesis*, which stated that introducing a new teaching method would have no effect on test results. This book is not intended to provide in-depth detail of statistical methods and you may recall that it was noted earlier in Chapter 1 (p. 10) that recourse to *inferential statistics* was limited to a few specific areas, and experimental research is one such area. The other aspect to this stage is setting what is known as a *level of significance (p)*. This is the number of times the result obtained might have occurred by chance and is usually cautiously set at $p = 0.05$ meaning that only 5 times out of 100 is the result likely to have occurred by chance. So, if the findings show it less than this value of p this is indicative that the *null hypothesis* is false or in our case the introduction of a new teaching method did have an effect on test results.

STAGE **3** TAKING ACCOUNT OF YOUR POPULATION AND DRAWING A SAMPLE FROM IT

A population is the entire cohort of subjects that a researcher is interested in. Defining a specific population is the prerogative of the researcher but it needs to be realised that however this is done the findings can only be safely generalised to that specific population. Typically populations involve large numbers of subjects and so there will be a need to take a representative sample from it. Ways of taking samples will be discussed in Chapter 6, (p. 100) and further notes are detailed in the Glossary (p. 220).

STAGE **4** PILOTING YOUR EXPERIMENTAL PROCEDURES

Ideally piloting any actual experimental work should precede commencement of it in order to identify any issues to do with it. The example used later did not do this but nevertheless the importance of piloting should be seen as a crucial feature of all procedures and this will be discussed in more detail in the next chapter.

STAGE 5   ASSIGNING SUBJECTS TO AN EXPERIMENTAL OR CONTROL GROUPS

This might seem easy. A simple measure of the dependent variable, which in the example we have used so far, would be looking at past test results. From these results matched pairs could be produced and then one person from each pair assigned randomly to a control or experimental group. Yes, easy, isn't it? Yet because it is critical that as close a match of both experimental and control groups is made prior to the commencement of any experiment, this single measure, although important, is unlikely to achieve this end. What will also be required is access to other variables, which might be deemed to affect the outcome of the study, and a further matching of these made. In this way controlling for the effects of extraneous variables can be made. Lim (1998) gave careful thought to 'other' extraneous variables and we will detail what these were shortly. Trying to cater for a variety of variables is not without its own problem as Borg and Gall note:

> matching on a number of variables that correlate with the dependent variable is more likely to reduce errors than matching on a single variable. The problem, of course, is that the greater the number of variables that have to be matched, the harder it is actually to find the sample of people who are matched. Hence the balance must be struck between having too few variables such that error can occur, and having so many variables that it is impossible to draw a sample. (1996: 547)

STAGE 6   CARRYING OUT THE TREATMENT ON THE EXPERIMENTAL GROUP

If the previous stages have been carefully followed then this one ought to be quite straightforward with the key point being that the control group should not be subject to the treatment. At this stage the length of the experiment will be crucial as the longer it proceeds the more chance there will be that 'extraneous effects' will impinge upon the outcome. There is no ideal length for experimental work and as has been noted elsewhere the important point is for the researcher to recognise the possible failings of his or her work and to ensure these are discussed in their thesis.

STAGE 7   COMPARING THE EXPERIMENTAL AND CONTROL GROUPS AND TESTING FOR A CAUSAL RELATIONSHIP

This invariably looks at differences in mean results and uses *inferential statistics* to decide whether the observed differences are due to the independent variable or could have occurred just by chance.

Types of experiments

Before looking at an actual example of an experiment actually carried out for an MEd thesis (Lim, 1997) it is worth just noting the possible designs in experimental work. These are expressed using symbols and conventions from Campbell and Stanley (1963). Put very simply O represents the observation, X the treatment and R indicates whether random assignment to groups was made.

ONE GROUP PRETEST–POSTTEST
This can be illustrated as:

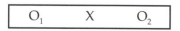

$$O_1 \qquad X \qquad O_2$$

A group O_1 are measured on some dependent variable, then given an experimental treatment X, and then measured again O_2. A major concern here is that, unlike a scientific experiment extraneous variables outside the researcher's control, could have, and in fact often are likely to have, an influence on any difference found. This concern should not lead to an outright denigration of this design but if it is used the researcher needs to make clear the implications it has for the validity of the research.

PRETEST–POSTTEST CONTROL GROUP DESIGN – 'TRUE' EXPERIMENTAL
This can be represented as:

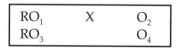

$$RO_1 \qquad X \qquad O_2$$
$$RO_3 \qquad\qquad O_4$$

Here the experimental design uses randomisation (R) so as to try and ensure a greater chance of equivalence of the groups being looked at. In other words an attempt to minimise the differences between the characteristics of the subjects in the groups has been made so as to limit the effect of these on the variable being looked at by the researcher in his or her experiment.

NON-EQUIVALENT CONTROL GROUP DESIGN – 'QUASI' EXPERIMENTAL
Educational research often does not allow for the kind of randomisation noted for 'true' experiments. The best, which can be achieved, is a compromise where groups being studied are as equivalent as possible. This design is designated by:

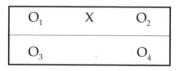

$$O_1 \qquad X \qquad O_2$$
$$O_3 \qquad\qquad O_4$$

Where the dashed line indicates that the groups have not been equated by randomisation.

Fuller details of experiments are beyond the scope of this text but further examples can be found elsewhere (Cohen et al., 2000). What is perhaps useful to conclude this section with is an actual example of an experiment conducted for an MEd thesis.

Example of a 'quasi' experiment

The MEd thesis by Lim (1997) detailed the work he undertook to gain a better understanding as to how a particular computer based learning (CBL) package WinEcon could be used to best benefit his students' learning of economics and to ascertain if its use could result in a statistically significant increase in examination scores – the experimental section of his thesis. It is probably easiest to describe his experimental work in the context of the stages that we have outlined above.

STAGE 1   AN ANALYSIS OF THE THEORY RELATED TO THE RESEARCH
This was thorough and detailed. It covered generic issues of students, details of the value of CBL packages in supporting learning as well as certain specific comments to do with WinEcon

STAGE 2   FORMULATION OF A HYPOTHESIS AND SETTING AN APPROPRIATE LEVEL AT WHICH TO TEST IT
Lim's *null-hypothesis* was that: 'The students in the experimental group improve by the same amount or less than the students in the control group' (1998: 46). His analysis was subjected to a *t-test* and as his hypothesis predicted the students in the experimental group would improve more than the students in the control group he subjected his results to a *one-tailed* test. He also set his level of significance at $p = 0.01$, which is lower than that typically employed, and which meant that only 1 time out of 100 would his result have been likely to have occurred by chance. Setting such a level of significance has implications for what are known as *Type I and Type II* errors and these are discussed further in the Glossary (p. 227).

STAGE 3   TAKING ACCOUNT OF YOUR POPULATION AND DRAWING A SAMPLE FROM IT
Lim worked with the complete cohort of two groups of students (N = 9 and N = 11) and so as he noted: 'As random selection of subjects was not possible, a variety of demographic and aptitude comparisons were made to determine if the control and experimental groups were similar' (1998: 39). Demographic details included average household income and whether any of the students employed a private tutor or sought additional help in other

ways while aptitude, based on the mean of past examinations, showed there was no significant difference between the two groups.

STAGE 4   PILOTING YOUR EXPERIMENTAL PROCEDURES

Due to the fact that he was limited as to the groups he had to work with Lim was unable to undertake any piloting. He was though fully aware of the limitations of the WinEcon package and the use of CBL per se and this provided a satisfactory substitute.

STAGE 5   ASSIGNING SUBJECTS TO AN EXPERIMENTAL OR CONTROL GROUPS

Lim's groups were defined by the access he had to students and his decision was to have his group (N = 9) as the experimental group and his colleague's group (N = 11) as the control group.

STAGE 6   CARRYING OUT THE TREATMENT ON THE EXPERIMENTAL GROUP

The experimental group used the CBL package twice weekly for one hour over a period of 28 weeks. While undertaking his experiment Lim was conscious of the ethical issues we have already raised earlier in this chapter. He raised the question as to whether it was 'fair to potentially advantage one set of students at the expense of another?' (1998: 44) and the arguments he put forward in his thesis show he thought carefully about such issues and that on balance his research should proceed.

STAGE 7   COMPARING THE EXPERIMENTAL AND CONTROL GROUPS AND TESTING FOR A CAUSAL RELATIONSHIP

His findings actually disproved his *null hypothesis* and he viewed this as indicating that the students in the experimental group using the CBL program performed better in economics than the control group using the traditional remedial program.

It is important to remind ourselves that his experiment was just part of his thesis. Detailed structured interviews with the students using the CBL package about their views of the value of it and how it impinged upon their learning styles and non-participant observation of their use of the CBL package by himself added to the richness and depth of his findings and discussion of them.

In conclusion to this section it is probably worth rehearsing the ethical issue concerning the psychological impact that experimental research may have on participants. All went well with Lim's research and there is no suggestion that any psychological damage has occurred to any of those students working with him. You might like to ask yourself, although Lim's literature review clearly indicated this would be highly unlikely, what would have been your reaction had the experimental group done worse?

Grounded theory

Grounded theory as an approach to educational research has already been mentioned in Chapter 1 (p. 9) in terms of recognising that research procedures can be associated with more than one research approach. We noted that it 'presents qualitative research as a scientific method' but saying this belies the significance that should be attributed to grounded theory.

Grounded theory, developed by Glaser and Strauss (1967), was based on the view that 'the study of human beings should be scientific, in the way understood by quantitative researchers' (Travers, 2001: 42). Although this view was strongly contested by interpretivists such as Blumer (1969) whose position was that the complexity of human life could not be interpreted by quantitative analysis, grounded theory has developed with writers such as Denzin (1997: 16) calling it 'the most influential paradigm for qualitative research in the social sciences today'.

The key aspect to grounded theory lies in the attention it gives to objectivity within qualitative research, an aspect regarded as lacking in ethnographic studies, which simply sought to produce detailed descriptions. In short grounded theory has as its foundation the production of theory, defined in the words of Glaser and Strauss as:

> a strategy for handling data in research, providing models of conceptuization for describing and explaining. The theory should provide clear enough categories and hypotheses so that crucial ones can be verified in present and future research: they must be clear enough to be readily operationalized in quantitative studies when these are appropriate. (1967: 3)

This seems simple and clear enough. Collect a range of qualitative data and then undertake an analysis of it to provide categories (a theory), which describe or explain any observed phenomena. Nothing could be further from the truth. Grounded theory follows a set of systematic procedures for collecting and analysing data and anyone using it does so only after working through a manual (Strauss and Corbin, 1998) and 'with a research group in a series of structured workshops' (Travers, 2001: 43). There is then nothing simple about employing a grounded theory approach to educational research. Its use requires a systematic rigour and much more careful consideration than this text can provide (see Patton, 2002).

The complexities of employing grounded theory means, not surprisingly, that it is unlikely to be an approach which will find wide use by students involved with Masters work. However, where access to a tutor well versed in its operation is available and time permits, the power of grounded theory deserves respect and should not just be disregarded out of hand. This is even truer, as this section concludes, if you are competent at working with computer technology.

One of the most important procedures used in grounded theory is the organisation of data into a set of themes or codes. Computer software analysis packages such as NUD•IST and ATLAS.ti lend themselves to the analysis of qualitative data and their use can enable the generation of theoretical categories from very small amounts of data (Dey, 1993). Ann-Marie Bathmaker (Chapter 8) and Mike Pomerantz (Chapter 9) provide an insight into the use of these packages from the perspective of their own research and these hopefully will help the inexperienced to decide if Grounded Theory and the use of computer software analysis is for them.

Summary

The purpose of this chapter has been to discuss the research approaches viewed as applicable and doable to those undertaking MEd work. These have centred around the Case Study, Action Research and Experimental work although the latter was premised on the need to consider very carefully the ethical dilemmas and moral questions which it inevitably generates before it is employed. In order to give some insight into the potential application each of these approaches was supported with examples of their use from actual MEd research work. Hopefully these will provide the newcomer to MEd research with the beginnings of a framework for applying each of the approaches to their own needs. The chapter finished with a brief account of the potential of another approach to educational research, Grounded Theory. This approach however, though of significant importance to the research world, requires considerable time to become conversant with and this, it is suggested, is unlikely to be forthcoming for the MEd student.

6 Research Procedures

Clive Opie

The previous chapter detailed those research approaches seen as practically appropriate to Masters work. As we have noted earlier (see Chapter 2) the research approach taken does not negate any particular research procedure being applied to it although certain procedures are more appropriate to certain approaches than others, and whichever is used stems from your methodological stance. This chapter discusses those procedures most relevant at Masters level: questionnaires, interviews and classroom observation.

Questionnaires

For many good reasons the questionnaire is the most widely used procedure for obtaining information. It is relatively economical, respondents in distant locations can be reached, the questions are standardised, anonymity can be assured, and questions can be written for specific purposes. The justification for its use, as with all research procedures, is that there is no other more reliable and valid method which could be used. However, as we shall see using questionnaires is not problem free but perhaps the most important limitation is that they:

> Can provide answers to the questions What? Where? When? and How?, but it is not so easy to find out Why? Causal relationships can rarely if ever be proved by a questionnaire. The main emphasis in on fact-finding. (Bell, 1999: 14)

Accepting this limitation, questionnaires are a useful procedure. However, designing a good questionnaire is not, as some foolhardy people would have you think, easy. There are important considerations to be made and we will look at these now (see Figure 6.1).

Main issues in questionnaire design

Layout
Question ordering
Sampling
Pilot study
Distribution and return

Figure 6.1 Main issues for consideration in questionnaire design

Layout

Look at Version 1 of a questionnaire (Figure 6.2). Do not worry too much about the actual questions, although you will undoubtedly raise some issues with them and these should be noted, but focus primarily on its presentation and completion. Jot down all the issues it raises for you in these contexts before you look at Version 2 (Figure 6.3) given later in this chapter.

You will undoubtedly have raised a number of issues with the example questionnaire. The first might be what is this questionnaire all about. Others though will probably include poor layout; inadequate spacing to answer questions; instructions where necessary on how to answer questions; uncertainty as to what is wanted; acknowledgement for taking part – you should always thank respondents for taking part in any research you ask them to be part of. Considering these issues:

- Try and make an overall impression with your layout which invites the respondent to want to read and answer it. Make sure response boxes are in a line and if possible vertically over each other for different questions.
- Give clear instructions of how you want it filling in, e.g. please tick the appropriate box, or circle your replies, etc.
- Ensure suitable spacing between questions and suitable space to answer 'open' type questions.
- Be very careful with the ordering of your questions, and we will look at this issue in more detail later.
- Thank your respondents for being prepared to take part.
- Although irrelevant here, make sure you have it typed. There is nothing worse than an illegible questionnaire. Few of us are that neat at writing not to warrant the use of a word-processor and the use of this technology will in turn enable any editing required after a pilot study to be easily achieved.

As I have noted, the first version of this questionnaire may have raised other issues for you so make sure you discuss them with other peers or a tutor as you feel appropriate. The second version of this questionnaire tries to

Questionnaire – Version 1

<u>Information and Communications Technology in Initial Teacher Education</u>

Name ————————————————— Subject —————————————

		Very good	Good	Poor	Hopeless
1	In your view:				

(a) What was the overall access to computing resources in **your classrooms** like?

(b) What was the overall access to computing resources in **your school** like?

(c) How did you find the general support from school teachers in your use of ICT in **your teaching**?

(d) What is your overall view to the attitude of your school's subject department to using ICT (and this may be very different from the support they can actually give)?

2   What did you feel about

(a) the overall support, in your school, for using ICT?

(b) if you felt the support for ICT was poor or worse can you offer reasons why?

3   If you made **no** use of ICT in your School Experience 1 teaching please move on to Question 3

How many times did you use ICT in your teaching in school?
How many times was your use of ICT in a specialised computer room?
How many times was your use of ICT, encouraged by the normal class teacher?
How many times was your use of ICT instigated solely by you?

Would you please give me an insight into the kind of ICT you used

CD-ROM____Databases____Data-logging____ DTP____Email____Internet____
spreadsheets____WP____

4   ANY OTHER COMMENTS

Would you please let me know of any other issues which you feel are important and constructive in the development of the use of ICT in the school where you had your first teaching practice.

Figure 6.2 A problem questionnaire

address the above issues, although the confines of this book has not permitted appropriate spacing for answering questions 2, 3 and 4, but you may see other room for improvement (see Figure 6.3).

The solution in Figure 6.3 is not likely to have answered all the issues you may have raised with the first version of the questionnaire and it introduces others. For instance in both cases the respondent's name has been asked for.

Questionnaire – Version 2

Information and Communications Technology in Initial Teacher Education
Student survey for School Experience 1

Dear ITE students,

I have been given the responsibility for coordinating the overall use of ICT during your ITE course. Your own tutors have been introducing you to the use of ICT during your University session and may I say I have been very impressed with what I have seen going on. You will be asked to evaluate this element of your ICT use later in the course.

The study of ICT will continue throughout your course and also as part of your school experiences. This short questionnaire is to help me keep a record of what is going on during your school experiences in our partnership schools. This information will be invaluable in that it will enable good practice to be shared and, hopefully, where, if it is deemed weaknesses exist in a school, for more support to be offered. The questionnaire does not ask for your school as with your name and subject I can work out which school you have been to. This will enable some security, over what could be delicate information, to be kept. For simplicity I have also assumed ICT is synonymous with computers although I realise this may not be so.

Thank you

Dr Clive Opie (ICT in ITE coordinator)

Name ————————————————— Subject ————————————

1   ACCESSIBILITY and ATTITUDE to the use of ICT

Please tick an appropriate box for each of the following answers

In your view:

	Very good	Good	Poor	Very Poor
(a) What was the overall access to computing resources in **your classrooms** like?	☐	☐	☐	☐
(b) What was the overall access to computing resources in **your school** like?	☐	☐	☐	☐
(c) How did you find the general support from school teachers in your use of ICT in **your teaching**?	☐	☐	☐	☐
(d) What is your overall view to the attitude of your school's subject department to using ICT (and this may be very different from the support they can actually give)?	☐	☐	☐	☐

---

2   ACTUAL use of ICT

If you made **no** use of ICT in your School Experience 1 teaching please move on to Question 3

(a)   How many times did you use ICT in your teaching in school?   _____

(b)   How many times was your use of ICT in a specialised computer room? _____

(c)   How many times was your use of ICT encouraged by the normal class teacher? _____

(d)   How many times was your use of ICT instigated solely by you?   _____

Would you please give me an insight into the kind of ICT you used by ticking any of the following, which are appropriate and then expanding where necessary underneath this list.

CD-ROM ____   Databases ____   Data-logging ____   Desktop Publishing ____

Email ____   Internet ____   Spreadsheets ____   Word-processing ____

Further details (e.g. specific CD-ROM, purpose of Email etc.)

3   OVERALL VIEW OF SCHOOL SUPPORT FOR ICT

I realise these comments may be quite subjective. If you have the opportunity, please discuss your views with your school partner before putting anything down, but if this is not possible then please give me your views.

(a)   What did you feel about the overall support, in your school, for your using ICT?

(b)   If you felt support for ICT was poor, or very poor, can you offer reasons why? For example keen interest by staff but lack of ICT resources; lack of interest in using ICT form teachers whose classes you had. Please be as constructive as you can in your answers.

4   ANY OTHER COMMENTS

Would you please let me know of any other issues, which you feel are important and constructive in the development of the use of ICT in the school where you had your first teaching practice.

THANK YOU FOR TAKING THE TIME TO FILL THIS QUESTIONNAIRE IN

Figure 6.3   Possible solution to the problem questionnaire

Many texts will tell you that you should leave asking for a person's name, if you ask for it all, until the end of a questionnaire and then ask for it only if they are happy to give it and to be contacted later about anything they have answered. In some cultures asking for such information could spell its death's knell so you need to take this issue into account.

The second version is now two pages instead of one and yet advice (for costs and increasing the chance of completion) is to minimise its length. There is no 'right' answer and you might like to think about which of the two versions you would be more inclined to fill in. The question order has also altered in the second version going from closed to open rather than mixed as in the first version. Again you will find arguments for and against such ordering although the common sequence is as in the second version and this issue is addressed more fully in the second section of this chapter.

As a final point, if you wanted to get further insights to the answers given to the questionnaire, what other procedure(s) would you think of using?

Question ordering

There would appear to be no hard and fast rule here. Some researchers wishing to avoid putting ideas into a respondent's mind would want to start with open questions and leave more structured or pre-coded questions to a later stage. This is sometimes known as a *funnel approach*. Others would start with factual, multiple choice questions about the respondent's own habits and so on, and then follow these with more open questions to elicit attitudes. However, what is generally accepted is that

> it is better to put demographic questions i.e. those on age, marital status, occupation etc. towards the end. This is partly because they are uninteresting and partly, being sensitive, they may be resented. Other sensitive questions on areas such as sexual orientation, health, income, professional status etc. should also not come near the beginning of a questionnaire. (Sapsford and Jupp, 1996: 105)

How an individual researcher decides to structure their questionnaire will be a combination of personal preference and cultural acceptance but nevertheless, so far, care over the layout of it and the ordering of the questions in it are two important crucial considerations.

Sampling

'How many students do I need to give my questionnaire to?'; 'Is just my class of 30 enough?'; 'How do I take a sample?' Not unfamiliar questions from beginning researchers and ones which, as with all research, are dependent on what it is one is aiming to do. It has already been noted in Chapter 1 (p. 10) that in most cases there is unlikely to be the need to undertake detailed *inferential* statistical analysis, that is, a requirement for further investigation of the data through appropriate statistical analysis. More often than not there is only likely to be the requirement of *descriptive* statistical analysis, that is, just reporting how many students said yes or no to an answer, with this perhaps split further into gender and/or age. Understanding the difference between these two forms of statistical analysis is crucial in terms of sampling size. As Cohen and colleagues note:

> There is, of course, no clear cut answer, for the correct sample size depends upon the purpose of the study and the nature of the population under scrutiny.

However, it is possible to give some advice on this matter. Thus a sample size of thirty is held by many to be the minimum number of cases if researchers plan to use some form of statistical analysis on their data. Of more import is the need for researchers to think out in advance of any data collection the sorts of relationships that they wish to explore within the subgroups of their eventual sample. The number of variables researchers set out to control in their analyses and the types of statistical tests they wish to make must inform their decisions about sample size prior to the actual research being undertaken. (2000: 93)

For *inferential* statistics sample sizes have to be carefully considered, and indeed be calculated (Cohen et al., 2000: 93–8) depending on the type of analysis being undertaken and the *level of significance* being sought. The simple reason for this is that the intention is to infer from the *sample* the characteristics of the whole population from which the *sample* was taken. In this case getting your sample size correct is critical.

With *descriptive* statistics the issues of sample size are not so critical although one has to be careful about how statistics are quoted. Here again 30 is a sort of *sample* number at which one shifts from quoting actual numbers to quoting percentages. To understand what this means look at this statement:

80% of University students felt that student fees should be abolished.

Ignoring the fact that the question asked to achieve this answer is likely to have been somewhat loaded (see below, p. 110) and so a poor question, ask yourself what *sample* size does it conjure up in your mind? It would be surprising if you were not thinking at least in the hundreds perhaps thousands even, if the research were done in just one university given the typically large student cohort size in most universities. Now ask yourself what is the minimum number of students the statement could refer to? The answer is of course 4 out of a total of 5. If this were the actual number of students asked you would quite rightly be critical of the findings in terms of validity. Of course the *sample size* should always be quoted in any research, although you might be amazed how many students forget to include this vital piece of information, but hopefully you will see why a line needs to be drawn somewhere in terms of quoting results. In addition to *sample size* there is also the issue of the representativeness of the sample.

Read the article – 'High art: "bald men with cellos"' – in Figure 6.4 carefully, and from it consider how representative do you feel the sample is. You may like to know that the sample is further split into two age ranges, five geographical locations, three areas of education, three levels of attendance at concerts (High, Medium and Low) and only three of those interviewed were non-white (Harland and Kinder, 1999: 64–5). Having done this read the reply to it which follows – it appeared about a month later than the original article, again in the *Times Education Supplement*. How valid do you find the comments made in this response?

'Classical' research

High art: 'bald men with cellos'

CLASSICAL music concerts are 'baggy and sad', art galleries are 'quiet and boring', ballet is 'pointless' and historic buildings are 'not for young people'. The findings of a new study on teenage attitudes to high culture will make depressing, if predictable, reading for arts professionals and educationists alike.

Launching the report, Trevor Nunn, artistic director of the Royal National Theatre, said: 'This is the strongest evidence yet of the challenge that we in the arts face.' He called on the Government to provide more funding for youth access projects. Twenty teenagers aged 14 to 18, from widely differing backgrounds were asked by researchers from the National Foundation for Educational Research what they thought about art galleries, theatre, dance, classical concerts, historic buildings and museums.

Only theatre generated any enthusiasm while the most commonly-used word to describe other forms of art was 'boring'. Many were seen as the preserve of the old and the rich. Only one of the 20 teenagers was positive about classical music. One 14-year-old girl said that at the theatre: 'You are looked down on by the old people, like "oh, you are not meant to be in here".'

Of classical concerts, another teenager said: 'You have to sit for ages in an uncomfortable seat, with the tiniest pair of binoculars, viewing some bald fellow with a cello.' The authors acknowledge that half of the battle for arts organisations is getting teenagers to a venue in the first place. Only three interviewees had been to a classical concert and 14 to the theatre in the past year. But of those most had ended up enjoying it.

The teenagers suggested venues could make themselves more attractive by staging shorter performances or laying on facilities like coffee bars. Among solutions offered in the report **'Crossing the line: extending young people's access to cultural venues'**, commissioned by the arts awarding body the Gulbenkian Foundation and the Arts Council, are 'arts mentors': older people who would accompany teenagers to events.

(*Times Education Supplement,* 17 December 1999). *Reproduced* with kind permission of *Times Education Supplement.*

Figure 6.4   Classical research

ACCORDING to 'High art: bald men with cellos' (*TES*, December 17) the National Foundation for Educational Research draws conclusions regarding high art and the attitudes of young people, based on questions to 20 teenagers.

While accepting that the opinions stated are those of the 20 young people, we would like to suggest that the sample is too small for the conclusions to be of value.

This letter is written jointly by nearly 200 young people of widely differing backgrounds who happen nonetheless to have an interest in classical music, popular music and many other art forms. Some of us are even cellists, some are male and none of us is bald!

We hope that, far from making 'depressing, if predictable, reading' for arts professionals and educationists alike, the Gulbenkian Foundation and Arts Council will take no notice whatsoever of this report until they have a much larger and much more representative set of views.

167 members of the Oxfordshire County Youth Orchestra and the Oxfordshire Schools Senior Orchestra Education Department, County Music Service, Oxford School, Glanville Road, Oxford (*Times Education Supplement*, 28 January 2000). Reproduced with kind permission of the *Times Education Supplement.*

The overall issue here, and raised by the 167 students form Oxfordshire County Youth Orchestra, would appear to be one of representativeness. The researchers do seem to have made their claims based upon interviews with just 20 students. The geographical areas are not representative of the whole of the UK – there is no representation of Wales where choir singing and brass band playing are important cultural heritages, which may be linked to attendance at concerts.

However, the report findings are prefaced with a comprehensive review of literature associated with the research in three areas:

- attendance at cultural venues;
- attitude and barriers to attendance;
- the role of schools, families and cultural organisations in encouraging young people's attendance.

Knowing this do you feel this in any way adds to the validity of the research? How representative is the reply given by 167 members of the Oxfordshire County Youth Orchestra it comes from? Is it any more valid than the actual research claims to be?

Having tried to offer some insight into sample size and its representativeness, how does one choose a sample? There are a number of ways, as shown in Table 6.1. Which of these methods you choose will of course, as always, depend on your actual research and access to students.

As a final word it is likely that for MEd work, especially if no *inferential* statistics is planned and so generalisability to a population is not required, the sample size will rely more on access to students and the time for, and purpose of, the research, than hard and fast rules to actual numbers. As an example, see Figure 6.5. In this case you could just take your teaching group as a sample. You have a representative sample (assuming mixed gender if this is important) and they are likely to be the easiest to access.

There are issues in this choice, though, about researcher *bias,* that is, being predisposed to a particular outcome and looking for this. In addition, being your students, they may also give less than truthful answers – especially if it puts you in a bad light. Taking all students would probably be too time

Table 6.1 Possible forms of sampling

Random	Select subjects at random from a list
Systematic	Every 20th person
Stratified	Subdivide into groups (male/female) and randomly select from subgroups
Cluster	Restrict one's selection to a particular subgroup (randomly selecting schools from one area)
Convenience	Choose nearest individuals and continue until you have the requisite number
Purposive	Subjects are hand picked by research on basis of his/her estimate of their typicality
Snowball	A small number of subjects is identified with the requisite characteristics and these identify others who are appropriate etc.

Sample size

Assume you were ascertaining student's views to the introduction of a new method of teaching and decide to do this first by using a questionnaire. The new teaching method was carried out with twelve mixed ability groups with 30 students in each. You and three others teach the groups, having three groups each, but you are not interested in any comparative analysis between each other. What sample do you take?

Figure 6.5 Sample size

consuming. If you have good relationships with the other colleagues teaching the groups you might select a group from each lecturer – but be sure to ensure anonymity for both the student and lecturer.

Pilot study

Undertaking a pilot study is an important part of designing a questionnaire but all too often this task is marginalised by a beginning researcher or sometimes worse, ignored.

> Questionnaires do not emerge fully-fledged; they have to be created or adapted, fashioned and developed to maturity – it has to be piloted. Piloting can help not only with the wording of questions but also with procedural matters such as the design of the letter of introduction, the ordering of question sequences and the reduction of non-response rates. (Oppenheim, 1992: 47)

So the kind of questions a pilot study can answer include:

- How long did it take to answer the questionnaire?
- Were the instructions clear?

- Were any of the questions unclear or ambiguous?
- If so, which and why?
- Did you object to answering any of these questions?
- Anything major omitted?
- Was the layout clear and attractive?
- Any other comments?

Any pilot also needs to be representative of the main sample or population to be studied:

> For it to work effectively the pilot sample must be representative of the variety of individuals which the main study is intended to cover. Pilot investigations do not need to represent, in the statistical sense, the correct proportions of different types of individuals in the population because the purpose is not to estimate the true proportions of such types but to cover the entire range of replies which might be given to any of the possible questions in the first draft of the questionnaire. (Sapsford and Jupp, 1996: 103)

A final note about undertaking a pilot study is that it is not wise to include the students used for it in the main research. Those undertaking the pilot will have become sensitised to the questions so that any answers they give in the main study will be influenced in a different way from those who have not.

Distribution and return

There are two formats here, self-administered questionnaires and postal questionnaires.

SELF-ADMINISTERED QUESTIONNAIRES

These cause little problem. They are generally easily distributed, explanation of purpose and identification and correction of any misunderstandings can be made, control over order of completion can be maintained and, almost inevitably, a high response rate is achievable.

POSTAL QUESTIONNAIRES

Basically these have all the advantages of a self-administered questionnaire as disadvantages. This being the case the issues of layout and piloting mentioned earlier are crucial. However, there are steps one can undertake to ensure as high a response rate as possible:

- Explain the purpose of the questionnaire and why the particular respondent was chosen and make the issue of confidentiality explicit.
- Send the questionnaire in a neatly, personally addressed envelope – stamped not franked (like most 'junk' mail).

Postal Questionnaire Issue

You have sent out a postal questionnaire to 100 people but you find your response rate is only 40–50%. Financial considerations mean you have the option of doubling your sample size, i.e. you send out another 100 questionnaires or you send a reminder to those who have not replied from the first round with an additional incentive for participation. What do you do?

Figure 6.6 Postal questionnaires

- Include a stamp addressed envelope for the return of the questionnaire.
- Be prepared to send reminders when the rate of response drops.

If you do undertake a postal questionnaire the latter point can become very important. Consider Figure 6.6 (adapted from Sapsford and Jupp, 1996: 50).

On the face of it, extending your sample size seems reasonable. As Sapsford and Jupp point out though, the key point is that the 'non-respondents are likely to differ in important ways from those who do respond' (1996: 54). In this sense increasing the sample size will not help. You would then be much better sending second or even third reminders and doing an analysis to see how these differ from those who responded first time around.

Types of questions

So far we have only considered practical issues associated with questionnaires, that is, their layout, sample size and administration. It is now time to turn our attention to the content of a questionnaire – the questions themselves. There are two general types of questions, closed questions and open questions.

CLOSED QUESTIONS

These are ones in which the respondents are offered a choice of alternative replies. They are easy to answer and the answers easy to quantify. In this sense they follow a positivistic approach. However, because they limit choice, respondents' views may not be catered for which may cause them frustration. These types of questions include those shown in Table 6.2.

OPEN QUESTIONS

These questions allow free response and no preconceived replies (unless the question is worded badly) are imposed by the researcher. In these cases one

Table 6.2   Types of closed questions

Yes/No	Do you hold a current driving licence?
Category	Please indicate your age group by ticking the appropriate box ☐ 16–19 ☐ 20–29 ☐ 30–39 ☐ 40–49 **Here the selection can only be from one category**
List	Please tick the box for any of these acronyms, all associated with education in the UK, that you are familiar with? ☐ DfES ☐ GNVQ ☐ OfSTED ☐ NGfL ☐ BECTa **Here any, or all of the options, can be selected**
Ranking	Please place these motivational factors in order of importance to you in your work as a teacher by indicating with a number from 1 (most important) to 5 (least important). A good teaching environment _____ Less paperwork _____ Supportive management _____ Appropriate remuneration _____ Professional development opportunities _____
Scale	If the present educational criteria for the diploma in nursing programme are lowered, more people will be encouraged to take up nursing as a course of study (Fan, 1997) VSD SD D A SA VSA **Here respondents were asked to ring their answers and VSD = Very Strongly Disagree, VSA = Very Strongly Agree. There are issues here about the number of scales used and interpretation (Cohen et al., 2000: 253–5). Respondents here had to make a decision as they could not opt for a middle ground, which would occur if there had been an odd number of scales. In addition one respondent's SA could be another's VSA or A providing inconsistency.**
Quantity	How many times over the last month have you been to the cinema to see a film _____?

obtains replies, which reflect the spontaneity of the respondent in their own language. The problem of course is that although such questions are easy to ask, they may be difficult to answer and even more difficult to analyse. There is also a tendency to resist writing answers to such questions, especially from students. This could be simply because of the time needed to do them, in that one needs to think more about composing answers or, in some cultural settings, a feeling of personal inadequacy in being able to answer in the language required. In this latter instance you would do well to consider another research procedure such as interviewing. Deciding which types of questions to answer is one thing but writing good questions even when you are clear of the type is quite another. This is discussed comprehensively elsewhere (Bell, 1999: 121–5) but we can cover the main issues through examples. Go through each of the questions in Figure 6.7 and write down what you think the problem with them is and a possible solution to them. They all highlight some difficulty of setting questions whether for interview purposes or questionnaires.

Your problems with the questions in Figure 6.7 may not reflect those noted here, but the fact that you perceive there may be a problem with any of these question is worthy of it being looked at and discussed and of course shows you why a pilot study is so important. Let's look at the issues and possible solutions, question by question.

1 Unless you give 'types' of schools as a list how can you ensure *conformity* in answering this question and so make analysis straightforward.

2 Could you answer this – even if you had only just left primary school? The issue here is one of *memory*. Memories are notoriously fallible and so this type of question is really of limited, if any, value.

3 Think about any course you have undertaken and ask yourself could I answer this question? It is an issue of *lack of knowledge*. Again try and avoid such questions.

4 This is a *double-barrelled* question. Break it up into two questions and then you analyse for learning both.

5 This is a *leading* question. It is difficult to answer no to it. Your way round it is to ask if they are consulted about initiatives and then from here if this concerns them. You might also think about exploring this issue through an interview rather than questionnaire.

6 This is *hypothetical* and so any respondent might take the view 'Why should I think about it?' The solution is to try and avoid such questions.

7 This is *restrictive* inasmuch as it does not allow you to take the opposite view, namely that older teachers are better than younger ones. Split it into a category question asking the respondent which type of teacher they think is best (you will probably need age ranges as well) and then an open question as to why they think this.

8 There is an issue of *quantification*. What is a great deal for one person may be just a certain amount for another. The solution is to quantify the time as with a category question selecting sensible time periods.

9 This is very *offensive* and should never be asked. If you really did want to look at links between age and taking up in-service courses you would ask these points separately and use your analysis to get an answer.

10 Did you understand the question? This is termed a *highbrow* question, which will cause the respondent to switch off. There is no easy answer to the problem although again it would be better to develop the answer through an interview rather than a questionnaire.

Questionnaires – Asking questions

1   What type of school does your child attend?

Problem_____

Possible solution _____

2   How were you taught spelling at your primary school?

Problem_____

Possible solution _____

3   What criteria were employed in allocating your personal tutor?

Problem_____

Possible solution _____

4   Do you think it is a good idea to learn Mandarin and English at School?

Problem_____

Possible solution _____

5   Do you agree that teachers should be consulted about any new initiatives, not just expected to implement them?

Problem_____

Possible solution _____

6   If you could start your career over again, what qualifications would you take?

Problem_____

Possible solution _____

7   Do you think younger teachers are better than older teachers?

Problem_____

Possible solution _____

8   How much time do you spend on studying this module?

A great deal   ☐   A certain amount   ☐   Not very much   ☐

Problem_____

Possible solution _____

9   If you are over 40, and have never attended an in-service course of any kind during your entire teaching career, put a tick in the box marked **NEVER** and a tick in the box marked **OLD**?

Problem_____

Possible solution _____

(Continued)

10 What particular aspects of the current positivist/interpretative debate would you like to see reflected in a course of developmental psychology aimed at teacher audiences?

Problem _____

Possible solution _____

11 Would you prefer a short, non-award bearing course (3, 4 or 5 sessions) with part day release (Wednesday afternoons) and one evening per week attendance with or a longer non-award bearing course (6, 7 or 8 sessions)?

Problem _____

Possible solution _____

12 Do you prefer abstract, academic-type courses, or down-to-earth, practical courses that have some pay-off in your day-to-day teaching?

Problem _____

Possible solution _____

Figure 6.7   Problems with questions

11 This is a *complexed* question almost certain to cause confusion resulting in either a no answer or, and probably worse, an erroneous one. Given the response is almost certainly going to be open ended you also have the problem of analysis. Again, if the individual components in it are important, split it into several questions and use your analysis to get what you require.

12 This is like the leading question above but regarded as a *loaded* question, that is, everything is driving you towards supporting the latter part of it. You might also argue that abstract and academic don't necessarily go together. Either split the question or change your procedure to an interview to ascertain answers.

Hopefully, with these few examples you are able to see that producing a questionnaire is not the straightforward procedure it might initially seem to be. The main issues concerned with designing a questionnaire have been addressed and their analysis will be dealt with in later chapters.

It has already bee noted that the major drawback with questionnaires is that they are not good for answering the question 'Why?' This is much better achieved through direct communication and as such we turn our attention to the next procedure – interviewing.

Interviews

Questionnaires, if well done, are useful in soliciting particular findings, for example, '45% of all students dislike lectures'. Although this is a fictitious finding used for the purposes of this book, the issue is that the questionnaire procedure is often not good at enabling us to explore such a finding in more detail, in short providing an answer to the 'Why?' behind it. Open-ended questions can be set to try and achieve such exploration but often fail to do so. This is primarily because many respondents are either not keen or don't feel confident in expressing their views, thoughts or feelings on paper, particularly if they are being required to write in what is not their first language. It is through the exploration of such findings as those above which gives any research its richness and value.

Purpose of an interview

Let us consider the fictitious finding again – '45% of students dislike lectures' – and assume little further detail about why this is the case has resulted from the questionnaire even though an open-ended question was asked to try and do this. Now also assume that one of the purposes to your research is to ascertain the most appropriate method of delivery of material for a new course you are implementing and lectures are one such method. On the face of it this finding is not particularly encouraging is it? However, all you know is that this percentage of students dislike lectures, not 'Why' they dislike them. The purpose of an interview is to try and obtain such information. For instance eliciting, from an interview, that the general reason for this finding is due to the inability to hear the lecturer or see his or her overhead transparencies, would result in a completely different solution from the reason that the majority of the 45% responded negatively because they had lectures scheduled at 8 am three times a week!

Interviews should encourage respondents to develop their own ideas, feelings, insights, expectations or attitudes and in so doing 'allowing the respondents to say what they think and to do so with greater richness and spontaneity' (Oppenheim, 1992: 81). Although the value of interviews has hopefully been made clear, the complexities of undertaking them has not and we shall explore these now.

Interpersonal skills

Undertaking an interview requires considerable interpersonal skills. As Oppenheim notes:

> The interviewer should be able to maintain control of the interview, to probe gently but incisively and to present a measure of authority and an assurance of confidentiality.
>
> Tone of voice, a pleasant and polite manner, deportment, choice of dress, the management of personal space, an acceptant and non-judgemental attitude and a willingness to listen should be among the interpersonal skills. (1992: 70)

Not everyone possesses, or indeed can develop these interpersonal skills and before you consider embarking upon interviewing you should give careful attention as to whether you feel you could act as an interviewer. This sounds very critical and to be fair most people can, albeit with practice, make an acceptable job of interviewing and the exercise given in Figure 6.8 will hopefully allow you to get a feel for the skills needed as an interviewer. You might like to note the other issues raised about this exercise before trying it out.

The exercise in Figure 6.8 is not one which just considers the process of actual interviewing, it also raises the issue of designing interview questions. We have already dealt with types of questions earlier in this chapter and the issues raised there are just as pertinent here.

Interview schedule

However, if as we have stated, the purpose of an interview is to encourage respondents to say what they think and to do so with greater richness and spontaneity, then questions need to be asked which will promote such a response. Take the last suggested topic in the exercise 'What makes for a good lecture?' As an interviewer you could simply expand upon findings from a questionnaire by asking the following interview question:

> From the questionnaire I undertook I found out that most students thought lectures were good if they were timetabled after 9 am, the lecturer was audible, gave good notes, showed clear overhead transparencies and captivated their audience. Do you agree?

Apart from this being an impossible question and so should not be asked if you were to ask it then you shouldn't be surprised if all you obtained was 'Yes' as an answer – and little else. Each of these separate findings could generate much more information though if asked in a way that encouraged their exploration and development. Look at the following:

• What do you feel is the most appropriate time for lectures to take place? [Prompt, if needed, with further questions of why. What might be the problem of having lectures before 9 am (a questionnaire finding) if not alluded to.]

Exploring the role of an Interviewer and Interviewee

The aim of this exercise is to enable you to get a feel for the process of interviewing and being interviewed. Although the exercise structure will remain the same the suggested topics presented here can of course be varied according to particular interests. The whole exercise can take no longer than 30–40 minutes but requires the ability to give and receive constructive criticism to be of most advantage.

1 Work in a group of 3. One person, A, will carry out the interview, B is the respondent and C will act as an observer. Each person will experience each role.
2 Have person A provide a topic for interview (of general significance) and allow them 5 minutes to jot down 3 or 4 questions they want to ask. Meanwhile person B can be considering their views of the topic given and person C on what they are going to concentrate their observation on.
3 Allow A to interview B with C observing for 5–10 minutes.
4 Then repeat the process so each person experiences the different roles.
5 Undertake a small group discussion for 5–10 minutes and jot down any questions you have about interviewing.

Suggested topics

- What will education look like in the twenty-first century?
- Can creative thinking be taught?
- What is the value of school league tables?
- Is streaming essential in a meritocratic society?
- What makes for a good lecture?

Figure 6.8   Exploring the role of an interviewer and interviewee

- What do you look for in the presentation by a lecturer, which would make you feel they had given a good lecture? [Prompt, if needed, with issues of audibility; handouts (what they look for in these and why); quality of visual presentation material; anything else.]
- My questionnaire indicated that a good lecture was one, which was captivating. Can you tell me what this means to you? [Listen carefully and develop anything, which sounds interesting.]

Now what we have done is encouraged open responses to each of the issues raised by the findings of the questionnaire. The above is often regarded as an interview schedule and is a critically important element in ensuring an interview goes well. It is quite structured and we will discuss this and other formats of interviews a little later. You could also present just the questions to the interviewee prior to the interview to enable them to have time to think about his or her answers. Although some would argue this damages the spontaneity of answers it can also help to develop the depth of an interview. There is no right or wrong approach so long as any interview is well prepared. If you have time, try a variant of the exercise in Figure 6.8, with A letting B see the questions for 5 minutes before answering them. You can then discuss this change in practice afterwards. It is also important to negotiate with C what they actually observe. It may be aspects of the interviewer, for example, how clearly they asked questions; did they give time for the interviewees to respond; did they 'listen' to answers and build upon them; did they 'lead' the interviewee in their answers; how were they sat with respect to the interviewee; did they make the interviewee feel comfortable, and so on; or the aspects of the interviewee, for example, did they appear at ease with the interviewer; did they appear to understand the questions. In this way C can focus on particular issues that A or B might have some concern over.

Contextual factors in undertaking interviews

The last section started to look at the contextual factors when undertaking an interview and these are worth considering here in a little more detail. Sapsford and Jupp (1996: 97) provide a useful overview to this area considering the following to be important:

- The legitimacy of the interviewer i.e. what right has, or is claimed by, the interviewer to ask the questions they wish to ask.
- The perception of the interviewer's visible characteristics as perceived by the respondent, e.g. accent, dress, ethnic origin, gender.
- The power relationships between interviewer and respondent, e.g. whether the interviewer is in a position to influence the respondent's life chances.

Each of these will have a bearing not only on the quality of the interview undertaken, but crucially the value of its findings. Assume you were going to interview students for whom you ultimately had some input into their exam results and you were interested in finding out their perceptions of your teaching style. How critical do you think your students would, or could, be to questions from you in this area? Of course this situation should never arise as it raises one of the main issues of research ethics discussed by Pat Sikes in Chapter 2 (p. 24). It is, of course, in this context, a wholly inappropriate research procedure and even if undertaken one would seriously question the validity of anything resulting from it.

Stages in preparing for and carrying out interviews

So far we have concentrated mainly on the process of undertaking an interview. This section looks at the preparation stages for an interview. Again there are no hard and fast rules but as with any research there is often a positive correlation between the quality of the preparation and the quality of its outcomes.

Preparing the interview schedule

We have touched upon elements of this earlier, but stages in its preparation should include:

- carefully and thoughtfully translating research questions into interview questions;
- deciding on the degree of structure in any questions;
- ordering of questions;
- deciding how responses will be collected (something we will discuss in more detail later).

Although, as we have noted on more than one occasion, the objective of a good interview is to encourage respondents to say what they think and to do so with greater richness and spontaneity, achieving this does not come easily. As with designing a questionnaire the best way of doing this is probably to move from more structured to less structured questions as the interviewee becomes more at ease with the interview.

PILOTING

There is considerable similarity here with the discussion of the value of piloting a questionnaire discussed earlier in this chapter. You should:

- carry out a pilot study in order to eliminate any ambiguous, confusing or insensitive questions;
- check the length of time of the interview and inform your interviewees how long you intend to take up their time for – and, unless the interviewee obliges, stick to this timing even if it means you don't finish the interview;
- check that confidentiality and anonymity are, where required, maintainable.

SELECTING THE RESPONDENTS

- consider carefully your choice of sample;
- ensure you negotiate access with individuals and their institution.

We have discussed the issue of sample selection but this is now a somewhat different set up. Let's assume you have distributed a questionnaire to say 100 students and, if self-administered, achieved a pretty high response rate.

Interviewing 100 students is not going to be feasible. There are no hard and fast rules but practicalities dictate that it is unlikely you will have, for an MEd, the time to undertake and most importantly analyse, the findings from more than 10 interviews. In many cases the numbers interviewed will be less.

There are no hard and fast rules. For example, of the 100 students above you may wish to undertake a group interview with 10 of them rather than undertake 10 individual interviews. This needs careful handling to ensure no dominance by any one strong character and that all participants get their say. It may be though that the findings need collaboration by other involved parties, such as teaching colleagues and/or management, and so you would just interview a section of them and none of the students.

As an example, an MEd student of mine distributed a questionnaire to approximately 40 of her ex-students to ascertain their views on the poly-technic course they had just completed. These students were all working in environments associated with their course and as it was a rapidly develop-ing area she was particularly interested in their views on the need for continuing professional development. She chose not to interview any of the students because of difficulty of access but did interview two senior colleagues in other educational establishments offering continuing professional develop-ment in this area to see if there was a link between student suggested develop-mental needs and existing provision.

THE INTERVIEW

For the interview:

- choose an appropriate venue which offers a degree of privacy and assured uninterruption;
- carefully consider seating arrangements;
- if you have not made the interviewee aware of questions to be asked then make sure you give a briefing and explanation of the interview, such as, its purpose, how the data it generates will be used;
- negotiate the method of recording well in advance, for example, whether just taking notes or using a tape-recorder, or video camera;
- conclude the interview with thanks, detail of future contact and how you will give feedback.

In today's world of mobile phones, assuring privacy is not always easy but you ought to try as any interruption to an interview has the potential for destroying it. You also must negotiate how you will record the interview. I well recollect a colleague, who although she was more than open to being interviewed, took strong exception to not being asked if a tape-recorder could be used in the interview she was giving. So much so she asked for it to be switched off which in her words 'threw the interviewer into a state of

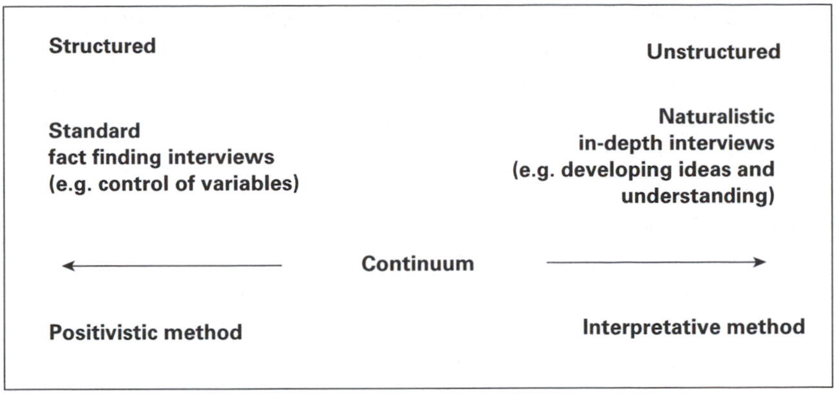

Figure 6.9 The level of structure of an interview and its link to research paradigms

turmoil such that he went to pieces and seemed to get little value out of the interview'. This may sound harsh but the lesson to be learnt is assume nothing – ask permission for the use of any electrical recording device and if it is not given then rethink how you will record the interview – or even whether you will do it.

Styles of interviewing

The term structured has been mentioned in the sense of setting up an interview schedule and it is worth looking at this term again in the sense of the overall interview. In Chapter 1 we looked at two research paradigms – positivistic and interpretative – and these can be mapped on to the structure of an interview, as shown in Figure 6.9. The decision as to where one puts an interview on the continuum shown leads to a variance in the style of interview and these are presented next.

STRUCTURED INTERVIEWS

A structured interview is similar to a questionnaire in both form and use. They impose a formality on a situation and any results are often used to try and make generalisations. Such interviews often use large samples and are often organised round a prearranged schedule of questions, which are short, direct and capable of immediate simple answers. Such responses lead to ease of data analysis and the style of questions leads to research free bias, as compared with semi- and unstructured interviews. Examples of this type of interview are the door-to-door market research interview or shopping centre survey.

Although a structured interview can be more flexible than a questionnaire, particularly if space or time is left for other categories or feelings to be explored, it generally will not reveal any complex or emergent features, which shape the social worlds of institutions. It is then difficult to see how this form of interviewing could meet the stated purpose of an interview as outlined in this chapter and details of it are given really as a means highlighting one end of the continuum shown in Figure 6.9.

SEMI-STRUCTURED INTERVIEWS

These are a more flexible version of the structured interview which will allow for a depth of feeling to be ascertained by providing opportunities to probe and expand the interviewee's responses. It also allows for deviation from a prearranged text and to change the wording of questions or the order in which they are asked.

Although provision for negotiation, discussion and expansion of the interviewee's responses is made, the semi-structured interview will also impose an overall shape to the interview and help prevent aimless rambling. Given the timescale normally attributed to an MEd thesis, both for collection of data and its analysis, it is a procedure often used by educational researchers.

Semi-structured interviews have to be carefully worded but yet provide more latitude of response than the structured interview. This being the case, a good technique is to ask an initial question which can be followed by probes, as in the example interview schedule shown earlier. Providing this flexibility brings other problems though.

There is now the possibility of researcher bias creeping in. The relationship between the questions asked and the conclusions drawn are no longer straightforward. One has to accept that no matter how well thought out you think a question might be, it may have a different meaning for, and so result in a different answer from, the interviewee than the one you intended. Minimising these problems is no easy task but to do so requires a realisation of how important it is to establish a rapport between the interviewer and the interviewee and to be aware that social meanings are complex.

UNSTRUCTURED INTERVIEWS

This type of interview presupposes nothing about the direction of the interview or what will be learned. In short it will follow the interviewee's flow of ideas. They centre round a topic or topics predetermined by the interviewer and often can provide large amounts of information for analysis, particularly if the interviewee's answers cannot be predicted or are generally unknown. In this sense such an interview format allows for what we have regarded as desirable – for respondents to develop their own ideas, feelings, insights, expectations or attitudes. Given what we have already said though, it doesn't take much extrapolation to see that the unstructured interview just intensifies the problems of focusing the mind of the respondent on the issues during the interview, researcher bias and time required for the analysis and interpretation

Summary of interview structures

Structured

- controlled by interviewer
- less flexible
- guided by researcher's predetermined agenda
- may provide easier framework for analysis

Semi-structured

- less control by interviewer than structured interviews
- more flexible
- not completely predetermined
- mixed framework for analysis

Unstructured

- control more evenly distributed between researcher and respondent
- very flexible
- direction unpredictable
- likely to be more difficult to analyse
- may throw up unexpected findings

Figure 6.10   A summary of types of interview structures

of data collected. For this reason novice interviewers or those undertaking research at MEd level are advised not to embark on this kind of interview.

If you do decide to carry out an unstructured interview then considerable thought needs to be given to the range of questions to be asked, and their possible sequence before the interview takes place. It would also be prudent to outline the content to the interviewee at the start of the conversation to help focus on its central points.

A short summary (see Figure 6.10) of each of these interview types will hopefully help you to clarify their advantages and disadvantages.

Collecting interview data

The method of collection will depend to some extent on the interview structure used. *Structured interviews* will normally just require simple answers, such as yes/no, or circling of a possible answer in a given Likert scale, and so the use of a predesigned grid for answers will suffice. Such grids are also likely to have codes allocated to them for analysis purposes. As it is unlikely this type of interview will be used to any great extent for educational research no more will be said about grids and codes and further information can be obtained elsewhere (Sapsford and Jupp, 1996: 165).

Semi-structured interviews may use grids and coding for any factual questions but in addition will almost certainly require some form of notetaking for any open-ended questions. It is always possible to code open-ended questions (Sapsford and Jupp, 1996: 166), but in doing so you could well miss certain categories and limit the richness of the response given by the interviewee. There is no easy answer and as we have indicated in numerous places in this book the decision will be based on your research questions and the time you have available to work on them.

The issue of how to take notes also raises questions. At the MEd level of working hand written notes are often sufficient and can usually be comfortably undertaken by the interviewer. There is of course the possibility of taping either sections, or all, of this type of interview but you need to ask yourself some important questions before you decide to do this. First, and this may sound obvious but is so easily forgotten, do you have suitable recording facilities? If you do, will the setting for the interview be conducive to tape-recording? I recall arranging to interview a student in Singapore about his MEd work and that we would conduct it in the privacy of his room. Unfortunately the noise of builders meant we had to move to a quiet cafeteria area. Although all seemed well I had forgotten how good the tape-recorder was, and the secretary transcribing my tape had some problems deciphering my interviewee's comments from those of distant patrons – especially as their conversations were in Chinese.

Will you have the time to transcribe or at least relisten to the interview tapes? Is the recording essential? If the answer to the latter question is no then don't do it. Is your interviewee happy to be tape-recorded? Remember to ensure permission to do this and if your interviewee changes their mind you must accede to this request.

The last part to this section highlights the advantages and disadvantages of tape-recording and notetaking and they are worth looking at as a preliminary to any decision you may take about recording any interview you are thinking of doing. There is also an exercise on categorising text obtained from interviews given later (see Chapter 7) when we consider issues of data analysis.

Unstructured interviews, because of their very nature, will require either considerable notetaking which, although it can be done manually, almost invariably necessitates the use of a tape-recorder. In some instances video recording is more appropriate but given the complexities and costs of setting this up it is unlikely to be the technique employed for MEd work although we will refer to it again in the last section of this chapter.

RECORDING INTERVIEWS

We have already noted issues about recording interviews and this last section just provides an overview of the advantages and disadvantages of notetaking and tape-recording (see Figure 6.11).

Tape-recording versus Note-taking

Tape-recording	Notetaking
ADVANTAGES	
Preserves natural language Objective record Interviewer's contribution also recorded Data can be re-analysed later	Central facts recorded Economical Off-record statements are not recorded
DISADVANTAGES	
Too much data Time-consuming to transcribe Presence of recorder off-putting Irrelevancies collected	Recorder bias Interview interference Status of data recorded is questionable

Figure 6.11   Advantages and disadvantages of notetaking and tape-recording interviews

Questionnaires and interviews are likely to be the mainstay of educational research at MEd level. However, these two should not be seen as the only procedures open to you. In fact a third one, observational research, has the potential for providing even greater insights into educational research associated with exploring issues to do with actual practice. In this way it allows the researcher to observe what is actually happening rather than relying on perceptions of what is happening which might result from, say, interviewing. By its very nature though it opens up practise for detailed scrutiny and so is not necessarily welcomed, particularly in some cultures, by those being researched.

Observational research

It might appear that employing this procedure should be quite straightforward, after all we spend our lives observing. However, nothing could be further from the truth and it is worth pausing for a short while and undertaking the exercise in Figure 6.12 in order to start to get a feel for the difference between observational research and the everyday observations we undertake.

Your answers to the exercise will undoubtedly vary but hopefully you will come to the general view that observation in everyday life helps us to gain information or knowledge to inform our actions, for example when, as a teacher, to intervene in a classroom discussion and allows us to continually test our common-sense theories about the social world. In short such observations are for personal consumption and add to our individual knowledge.

Defining Observational Research

Jot down your answers to the following questions and then, if possible, spend 10 minutes or so discussing your answers with other students undertaking some educational research.

1   What do we use observation for in everyday life?
2   What do you think the differences might be between your answer to the first question and observation in research?
3   Can you think of any advantages and/or limitations of observational research?

Figure 6.12   Defining observational research

In contrast, observational research is planned and conducted in a systematic way rather than occurring spontaneously and haphazardly as in everyday life. Its aim is also to produce *public* knowledge rather than just add to an individual's knowledge and to achieve this requires that such observations are systematically recorded, and carefully interpreted and analysed.

The last question in Figure 6.12 asked you to look at advantages and/or limitations of observational research. If you are inexperienced at educational research you may have found this difficult but the following presents some possible answers.

Advantages of observational research:

• Information about the physical environment and about human behaviour can be recorded directly by the researcher.
• The 'observer', unlike participants, can 'see the familiar as strange'.
• It can provide information on the environment and behaviour of those who cannot, or will not, speak for themselves.
• Data collected can be a useful check on, or supplement to that obtained by other means.

Limitations of observational research:

• People, consciously or unconsciously, may change the way they behave when being observed.
• Observations will inevitably be influenced by observer 'interpretation'.
• It can be very time consuming.

More or less structure

As with interviewing it is possible to vary the degree of structure associated with observational studies. Those less-structured are typically associated with long-term ethnographic studies and the impracticality of these for MEd work has already been noted in Chapter 5. It is worth noting that the term unstructured is used in some texts to reflect less structure, but neither case mean that data collection proceeds with no aims or idea of what to observe. It simply infers a flexible, open-minded approach to the observational research being undertaken and a preparedness to change its focus as required. As an MEd student time, and probably experience, will not permit you to pursue a less structured approach to observational research and so we will concentrate on one that is more structured. As Bell notes:

> it would be unwise to undertake unstructured observation unless you are already experienced and are very familiar with the techniques involved. In order to derive worthwhile information from the data, you will probably need to adopt a more structured approach and to devise some form of recording in order to identify aspects of behaviour which you have identified beforehand as being of likely relevance to the research. (1999: 158)

The reality is, of course, as with other research, that both more and less structured approaches may be employed within the same research (Sapsford and Jupp, 1996: 63) and whether either or both are used will be determined by what you are seeking to find out. If you are particularly interested in reading more about less-structured approaches to observational research and ethnography you are recommended to look at the following texts by Brewer (2000), Cohen, Manion and Morrison (2000) and Wragg (1999).

If we accept the need for a structured approach to observational research the key issue for the researcher is how to do this as objectively as possible. Although we have already discussed the advantages and disadvantages of using tape-recording (see Figure 6.11) and made a passing argument against the use of videoing due to the complexities of setting it up and its costs, it is worth rehearsing these again here in the context of observational research as well as looking at two other methods of recording observational data.

Tape-recording, videoing, photographs and field notes

With tape-recording the transcripts can be used to provide a check against bias or misinterpretation and although the classroom is often not the most conducive place for tape-recording it might have a role in a relatively closed situation, such as in small group work.

Video-recording helps make sense of non-verbal activity but brings with it technical problems, for example focusing and ensuring good sound quality, and for these reasons alone it may prove more troublesome and time consuming than it is worth.

Photographs can provide another valuable layer of description but the danger here is that the image presented can become quickly detached from the context in which it was taken and as such it loses its value.

Field notes can include records of conversations, discussions and interviews as well as the observed behaviour of the subjects. In this way an effort to reflect the holistic view of the setting is made. One advantage of field notes could be that as the research progresses, and theoretical ideas begin to develop, focus on particular aspects of behaviour or situations can be made. However, it is impossible to record everything and herein lies the disadvantage. As selection is inevitable and invariably necessary this in itself will influence the outcome of the research.

A major influence on the accuracy of field notes is when they are made. The later this is done the more inaccuracy and bias will creep in. Sometimes field notes can be made as the research is being undertaken, but in other cases where the social norms do not allow, for example in the social area of a staff room or where 'covert' research is being undertaken, and recall the ethical issues here, such notetaking practices are not an acceptable activity. Having noted possible means of recording observations there is clearly a need to systematically record observations and we shall now turn our attention to how this may be carried out.

Recording observations

You may recall from the first chapter that we qualified procedures for collecting data broadly into two groups – qualitative and quantitative. The former seeks to understand the social world and is based on the anti-positivist research paradigm where individuals' values and self-interpretation and representation of their experiences are of prime importance, while the latter is more concerned with the positivist tradition locked into outwardly measurable criteria which can be verified by observation. The advice offered has been to employ a more structured approach to observational research and so lends itself to the positivist research paradigm. Although by no means exclusively the case, classroom observations are usually quite structured and as such:

> The purposes of the observation, the categories of behaviour to be observed and the methods by which instances of behaviour are to be allocated to categories, are worked out, and clearly defined, before the data collection begins. So, in this sense, there is maximum prestructuring. A variety of different techniques is used to record behaviour, but all involve some sort of pre-set, standardised observation schedule on which a record (often ticks or numbers) of the type of behaviour can be made. (Sapsford and Jupp, 1966: 60)

What then are these pre-set, standardised observation schedules? In his book *An Introduction to Classroom Observation* Wragg (1999) provides a very informative discussion of quantitative methods applicable to observational research. It is not the intention to go into great detail about these methods here, so discussion will be limited to an overview of them along with an example of one of my MEd student's use of observational research.

Table 6.3 Examples of areas applicable to observational research

Personal traits	The traits of either the teacher or the pupils: for example, whether the teacher is warm or aloof, whether certain pupils appear to prefer collaboration or disruption
Verbal interaction	What teachers and pupils say to each other, who does the talking and about what, question and answer, choice of vocabulary and language register
Non-verbal	Movement, gesture, facial expression like smiles and frowns
Activity	The nature of pupils' tasks, what the teacher does
Management	How the teacher manages pupil behaviour, the use of resources, the organisation of group or individual work
Professional skills	Questioning, explaining, arousing interest and curiosity
Affective	Teachers' and pupils' feelings and emotions, interpersonal relationships
Cognitive	The nature and level of thinking in the classroom: for example, the level of reasoning necessary to answer a question, or the degree of understanding pupils appears to have of a topic or concept
Sociological	The roles people play, norms, codes, the effects of social background, status, power

Source: Wragg, 1999: 20

It is worth starting from the position of the purposes for which one might use observational research. What is provided here are some of the more common examples pertaining to classroom activity, arguably the environment where most observational research takes place (Table 6.3). Whether your area of research is applicable to quantitative observational research is likely to be a matter for discussion with your tutor but what is crucial is that you discuss and decide what is to be quantified with those being observed in advance of any observation taking place. Not to do so raises philosophical dilemmas as well as lead to a much less satisfactory piece of research. Clarifying with those being observed what is to be investigated and setting boundaries is also ethically sound. How then might we record our observations?

Wragg (1999) goes through a range of possibilities such as using rating scales and time lines. Rating scales have a similar drawback to Likert scales, namely, not really knowing if the rating given by one observer means the same as the same rating given by another observer. Time lines are simply lines whose length reflects the time spent on a particular activity being observed. Frequency counts can be employed where you are interested in how many times a particular behaviour occurs or you may be interested in behaviours which occur for a given interval of time, for example just how students set about beginning practical work or access resources. From a positivist position having a simple grid and simply ticking every time a particular occurrence happens would work. Although perhaps on the face of it limited in its value, it could form the basis of further, more qualitative work as indicated next.

I recall being at a lecture where the speaker was talking about gender issues and the time that her school went coeducational. It had always been a girls' school and was taking boys for the first time and the speaker wanted to be sure she gave equal attention to both genders. She asked a colleague to simply note every time she spoke to a girl or boy in a class she was teaching. This was done and then the tallies looked at and the numbers were 47 for boys and 24 for girls. She was adamant the observer had the headings round the wrong way as in her class of 24 students she only had 9 boys! In fact the headings were correct and although disturbing to her this simple observation led to further observational research analysing what she was actually saying to either gender, question types used, student–teacher interaction, and so on.

Probably the most valuable mechanism for recording observations is through the use of what is known as a category system and these are discussed from what is probably the most influential category system, the Flanders Interaction Analysis Categories or FIAC as it is more commonly known.

Recording using category systems

As Wragg points out the, FIAC system is described:

> not because it is the best system, indeed there have been many refinements and modifications of it, but rather because it is an example of a simple category system that has been widely used in its original or modified form in teacher training, lesson analysis and research. (1999: 38)

The FIAC categories are worth considering (Flanders, 1970; Sapsford and Jupp, 1996; Wragg, 1999) but rather than repeat them verbatim I will look at how they have been very slightly adapted in the research work of another of my MEd research students (Seethepalli, 2002).

Seethepalli undertook three case studies in a pre-school setting, observing the teacher's use of ICT and in particular sources from the internet. Data for the three case studies were gathered from questionnaires, teacher diaries, informal dialogues, field notes and through the use of a structured observation sheet using a slightly modified FIAC (see Figure 6.13). Her recordings were taken every 30 seconds (rather than 3 indicated by Flanders) and from these she derived a number of total tally figures as well as producing an interaction matrix and one example of both of these are shown here (see Figure 6.14). The latter is based on a two-dimensional display devised by Flanders which, while preserving the sequence of events, also shows where the action is. Basically a string of categories (using Seethepalli's coding) such as might occur in a classroom, teacher information (5) – teacher question (D) – pupil answer (8) – teacher praise (B), are recorded in the matrix as pairs 5-D and 8-B. The example shown not only indicates the number of tallies corresponding to teacher talk and student talk but the grid shows where in the main this occurred – in teacher giving facts and contents (5-E) totalling (18) occurrences. Seethepalli qualifies this particular outcome by noting that the latter five minutes of her field notes showed

FIAC observation sheet

(Adapted from Flanders Interaction Analysis Categories 1970)

Teacher: _____   Class:_____

Subject/Learning area:_____   Date: _____

Organisation of students in IT lesson: whole, individual, pair: _____

Recording time: 10 minutes (coded at 3 second intervals per minute)

Category (teacher)	Code Number
Accepts feeling	1
Praises	2
Uses ideas of student	3
Asks questions	4
Gives facts, content	5
Gives directions	6
Category (students)	**Code Number**
Pupils response to teacher	8
Pupil talk – self-initiation	9
Silence/confusion	10

Figure 6.13 Adaptation of FIAC categories (Seethepalli, 2002)

the teacher was explaining the necessary skills required for the individual activity that was to follow the introductory lesson. Directions for setting up of student pairs, rules for the computer activity and other formal classroom instructions were also part of this teacher – talk recorded as (5-F = 3). (2002: x)

It needs to be noted at this point that one does need to exercise care in interpretating such matrices and realise there are no, as Wragg puts it, 'good or bad patterns' (1999: 44).

An interesting point to note with Seethepalli's work is that, with mutual researcher–teacher consent, there was an agreement to omit the FIAC category 7 (Criticism) from all observations. It is not appropriate to discuss the reasons for this in this text, although you might ponder upon them, but it does highlight the importance of negotiating what will be observed in any research with those being researched.

One final thing before leaving this section is that one needs to be aware of the weaknesses of the FIAC. For example with Category 2, cursory praise such as 'Good', and 'Fine' are not distinguished from more substantial praise such as 'That's a very good answer. Well done.' Similarly Category 5 does not distinguish between information which is factually correct or incorrect. Further details on these, and other weaknesses of the FIAC and how they might be addressed can be found in Wragg (1999: 39).

	A	B	C	D	E	F	G	H	I	Total
1		1		1	4	3		1	3	13
2				2	2		1			5
3	1									1
4	1	1		1	1		3	1		8
5	3	1	1	2	18	3	1	8	4	40
6					2			1	1	4
8	1	1			2	1		3	1	9
9	8			1	5		2	3		19
10		1			5				6	12

Figure 6.14 Interaction matrix for observational research undertaken in one class

Participatory and non-participatory roles

So far we have looked at the advantages and limitations of observational research and methods of recording observations. A third and concluding issue to be considered with regard to observational research is the role the observer takes. The two main roles are as a participant or non-participant.

As the term suggests, a non-participant role is where the researcher has no interaction with the subjects during data collection and as such this role is most often used in structured observation. This role has the advantage that it can eliminate the 'reactivity' of the presence of the researcher. However, the observer has to accept that they cannot ask the subjects being observed questions and therefore may fail to appreciate the perspectives of the subjects and to understand the social meanings which underpin the interaction. It also limits the behaviour and settings that can be observed. For example it is very difficult to maintain this role in settings you have some familiarity with, such as in your own school, which is where a lot of MEd work is carried out. In such settings it is more likely that some form of unstructured observation involving a participant role where the observer interacts, to varying degrees, with subjects will occur.

A participant role can take one of three broad forms, with each influencing the balance between the objectivity and subjectivity of the research:

- *Observer as participant* Where the observer interacts with the subjects but does not take on an established role in the group. For example, the observer could be listening to student conversation and categorising its form and perhaps prompting answers to issues but not actually engaging with those answers. In this way the researcher maintains a large degree of objectivity.

- *Participant as observer*   The researcher takes a more participant role, for example, as a part-time teacher, for the bulk of the research. Here the observer may not only note conversation but engage with it. Here the researcher will inevitably lose some objectivity and probably influence the outcome of the research.
- *Complete participant*   Here the researcher is fully immersed in the participant role but uses their position to conduct research. The main issue here is the researcher has greater possibility of influencing the people he or she is with and if it involves 'covert' activity this could be considered ethically unacceptable.

Summary

This chapter has presented three research procedures which are deemed the most relevant to MEd work questionnaires, interviews and observational research. Questionnaire design layout, types of questions asked, ordering of questions and sampling have been discussed as well as the issues behind undertaking postal questionnaires. This is seen as more of a 'positivistic' procedures as although allowing for open-ended answers it does not usually result in more 'interpretative' data collection and seeking answers to the question 'Why'?

Interviewing has much greater potential for encouraging respondents to develop and relate their own ideas, feelings, insights, expectations or attitudes to an issue. Interviews are not a straightforward procedure to use and the various interpersonal skills required to ensure they are effective have been discussed. Similarly the style of interview whether structured, semi-structured or unstructured will result in more 'positivistic' or 'interpretivist' data being collected, which in turn will impinge upon the kind of analysis possible.

Finally observational research provides the third procedure generally suited to MEd work. This also lends itself to taking on either a 'positivistic' or 'interpretivist' stance and the implications for this have been presented. In particular the role of the observer in respect of the level of objectivity attainable in this kind of research is crucial.

The next three chapters now move on to looking at the analysis of qualitative and quantitative data. Ann-Marie Bathmaker (Chapter 8) and Mike Pomerantz (Chapter 9) look at analysing qualitative data using the computer software NUD·IST and ATLAS.ti, but before that Clive Opie (Chapter 7) considers the analysis of quantitative data using the computer software EXCEL and SphinxSurvey.

7 Presenting Data

Clive Opie

Let us assume you have given careful consideration to your methodology (as you should always do and detail in your thesis); have decided on your research methods and procedures; have devised any data collection tools; and have given due consideration to any ethical considerations. You might now think you are ready to go and undertake the research. Unfortunately, too often this is exactly what does happen, but your actual research should not commence at this point. You have at least one more vital question to consider, and one so many new to research forget, namely: 'How are you going to analyse any data you actually collect?' This may sound strange. Your research procedure, for example a questionnaire, may yield quantitative data but is this to be used for descriptive or inferential statistics and with the latter are you interested in parametric or non-parametric tests (see also Chapter 10)? This can all begin to sound somewhat unwieldy and problematic, but recall the opening chapter, which indicated that in most cases with MEd work descriptive statistics would suffice and that these are a simple summary of findings. However, if you do want to undertake inferential statistics, and you know what you are doing and have suitable support there is no reason why you should not. You will though, need to know what type of data is appropriate for any analysis you want to perform which in turn will dictate the questions you ask.

What if you are seeking to explore values, feelings, attitudes and so on, that means undertaking more interpretative research? This will almost certainly employ the use of interviews, so you now need to be able to handle more descriptive – qualitative – data. The chapters that follow by Ann-Marie Bathmaker (Chapter 8) and Mike Pomerantz (Chapter 9) focus on exploring the analysis of qualitative data in more detail. Whether you are intending to collect quantitative or qualitative data, the important point to keep firmly in mind is that shoddy, ill-conceived or inappropriate data analysis can render an otherwise sound research project worthless. The essence of this chapter is to begin to highlight various points you need to be aware of when collecting and analysing data.

This text cannot provide the kind of in-depth discussion needed to be conversant with all quantitative and qualitative data analysis techniques. What it does do is aim to provide an introduction into data analysis. To try and achieve this the first part of this chapter discusses different types of quantitative data, what you can do with it and some advice on its presentation. It also starts to explore the analysis of this type of data with the help of computer programs, in particular SphinxSurvey (Scolari, 2002) and Excel (Microsoft, 2002). Some may argue that this chapter does not go far enough, but for the purposes of clarity its contents are restricted and a more detailed summary of terms and techniques used in quantitative analysis, particularly statistical analysis, is given in Chapter 10.

The second part of this chapter gives an introduction into the analysis of qualitative data using Word (Microsoft, 2002) and the textual analysis features of SphinxSurvey. This is then complemented, as already noted, by Chapters 8 and 9 which look specifically at the analysis of qualitative data through the use of two computer software packages – NUD•IST and ATLAS.ti – from Scolari (2002).

PART 1: QUANTITATIVE DATA

Types of quantitative data

Our starting point has to be an understanding of types of quantitative data and what you can do with it. Although a number of texts refer to four types of quantitative data – nominal, ordinal, interval and ratio (Sapsford and Jupp, 1996) – it is easier to reduce this to three where interval and ratio data are considered together. The fine distinction between interval and ratio data is discussed elsewhere (Moore, 1997) and for our purposes linking them will not be problematic. These types of data and a brief explanation of their differences are shown in Table 7.1.

It is not always easy to reconcile what type of data you have but it is crucial you know this, as this in turn will determine what you can do with it. For example nominal data only provides non-parametric statistics, which can measure mode frequencies and the use of the statistic analysis Chi square (χ^2). Ordinal data offers other non-parametric statistical analysis such as Spearman Rank Order and Kruskal-Wallis tests. It is only with interval and ratio data that you can undertake parametric statistics such as ANOVA and t-tests. You may be getting worried at the terms in this paragraph but they are all explained in the Glossary (see Chapter 10), and keep in mind that for MEd work in many instances you may well not need to undertake anything more complicated than frequency counts, which are an aspect of descriptive statistics.

Table 7.1   Types of quantitative data

Type of data	Function
Nominal	This simply puts data into categories – nothing more and nothing less. For example different types of ethnic groups.
Ordinal	This indicates that the order of numbers is meaningful but they have no arithmetical significance, i.e. the intervals have no constant difference between them. For example, grading students by exam marks. The order is meaningful but you cannot say that someone scoring 80% is twice as good as someone who scores 40% or that the difference between 45% and 55% is the same as that between 60% and 70%.
Interval/Ratio	This refers to numbers, which have regular intervals between them and so can have meaningful multiplication carried out on them. A student getting 10 correct answers would have got twice as many correct as a student who got five correct. Note this is not the same as saying the first student is twice as good as the second.

It is helpful, even if you don't intend to use any of them, to get some insight into types of data. Try the exercise in Figure 7.1, and although answers are given in Table 7.2, try it for yourself first.

Apart from learning a little more about data types the exercise will hopefully help you to realise (particularly from Question 6) that there are occasions where actual data items can be regarded as different data types. You do not need to worry unduly about this unless of course in your research you are aiming to undertake various statistical analyses. My advice then, as it has been in several places within this text, is to talk with your tutor to ensure you are collecting the data items you will need and you know which are the appropriate statistical tests to use on them.

There are examples detailed later for both parametric and non-parametric tests (see Chapter 10) and you are advised to look at these and other texts to clarify which data types are relevant to each. Those detailed in this text should aptly cover the needs of any MEd thesis and in addition Cohen et al. (2000: 80) provide a useful overview of the statistical tests appropriate to each data type noted above. What follows is a short introduction into the kind of statistical data analysis arguably more appropriate to MEd work that you can undertake using SphinxSurvey and Excel, but before leaving this section the answers to the exercise in Figure 7.1 are now given (see Table 7.2).

Statistical analysis of quantitative data

We have already noted that at MEd level it is very likely you will be undertaking little more than descriptive statistics. Put this way this may sound like a lesser form of statistics – it is not. Admittedly it will not allow you to: 'draw

Data Analysis – Issues of scales

Identify the scale of each of the following variables as nominal, ordinal, or interval/ratio:

1   The concentration of Calcium in a sample of milk, in milligrams per litre.

Type _____

Why? _____

2   The species of insect in a sample plot of ground.

Type _____

Why? _____

3   The responses to the question: It is natural for people of one race to want to live away from people of other races.

Strongly agree   Agree   Undecided   Disagree   Strongly disagree

Type _____

Why? _____

4   The pressure in kilogrammes per sq metre required to crack a specimen of copper tubing.

Type _____

Why? _____

5   The position of schools in a league table.

Type _____

Why? _____

6   The scores in an examination.

Type _____

Why? _____

Figure 7.1   Issues of data scales

conclusions about a wider population from your sample data and to examine differences, similarities and relationships between different variables' (Sapsford and Jupp, 1996: 230), as inferential statistics will do. As we have noted, though, educational research undertaken at MEd level is often time limited and, quite acceptably, only concerned with one's own practice. In these circumstances descriptive statistics, which do nothing more than describe the data you have, are not only sufficient but perfectly appropriate.

Table 7.2 Answers to questions in Figure 7.1

Question	Type of data	Why
1	Interval/ratio	You can calculate other meaningful values from this data.
2	Nominal	This provides no more than a list of species, nothing is inferable from this list.
3	Ordinal	The categories provide a list of answers but they are not operable on mathematically.
4	Interval/ratio	From these results extrapolation can take place to find other values.
5	Ordinal	You cannot say that out of 50 schools the 1st is twenty-five times better then the 25th.
6	Ordinal or Interval/ratio	If you measured the scores as grades, say A, B, C or D then although you know B is higher than C you do not know by how much so measured this way it would be ordinal data. If you used percentages then you could say 70% was twice as much as 35% and view it as interval/ratio data. Note this is not saying the student who got 70% is twice as good as the one who got 35%. What this example shows is that 'the scale of a measurement depends mainly on the measuring process, not on the property measured' (Moore, 1997: 179).

Table 7.3 An example of descriptive statistics

19	20	21	Group Total	22	23	24	25	26	27
50	73	55	178	26	10	5	4	2	1
22.0%	32.2%	24.2%	78.4%	10.5%	4.8%	2.2%	1.8%	0.9%	0.4%

Descriptive statistics

As an example of descriptive statistics look at the information in Table 7.3, taken from Bell and Opie (2002), based on the description of the ages of the students that were involved in the survey carried out by Fan (1997) for his MEd work. One could argue that Fan might have improved his description by considering the groupings as shown in Table 7.4, but nevertheless what he did was appropriate and relevant.

Fan could have gone on to calculate other descriptive statistics from his data such as the mean, median and standard deviation of the ages (see Chapter 10), and the fact that he did not, highlights a crucial question when undertaking any data analysis, namely, 'What purpose does any analysis serve?' Too often, and here perhaps advances in technology must take some of the blame, researchers provide what I would call superfluous data for no better reason than it is easy for them to do so. Tables of mean values or standard deviations, or correlation coefficients are often given which, if I was to be highly critical, serve little purpose other than in helping to fill up a page.

Table 7.4 A variation on Table 7.3

Age range	Group total	Cumulative percentage (%)
19–21	178	78.4
22–24	42	96.9
25–27	7	100

Take the data presented in Table 7.3. The mean of this data is simply the sum of all the ages, divided by the total number of ages, which in this case would be 4666/266 or 20.65. The median is the middle value of a set of values, which would be 20. Neither are difficult to compute but the question is why would you want to know them? What purpose or value do they add – arguably in this case, none.

By way of another example (and this was from a PhD thesis) I recall looking at pages of correlation coefficients. If appropriate, these are fine, but what intrigued me was the number, which had the value +1. This simply means a perfect positive relationship between the variables being looked at. Those of you who are not perhaps conversant with correlation coefficients might see nothing strange so you will have to accept that finding a correlation of this value is almost certainly unlikely to occur in educational research. In short what the student had done was measure two variables, which he knew to have a predictable and positive straight line relationship and simply reported these along with his other measurements. He had not thought about what he was doing and had just let his computer slavishly print out results.

Further discussion of descriptive statistics can be found elsewhere (Cohen and Holliday, 1996; Hopkins et al., 1996) but measures of mean, mode, median, standard deviation and frequency counts are defined with examples in the Glossary (Chapter 10). An aspect of descriptive statistics, which needs to be given careful consideration, is that of sample size and this is also discussed later (see p. 220). Sample size is even more important for inferential statistics and it is to this type of statistics we now turn.

Inferential statistics

Here the term again explains what these statistics do – they allow you to infer something from the data you have. These statistics involve two types of tests non-parametric and parametric (see Chapter 10) and it is important that you use the appropriate test for the data you have collected.

NON-PARAMETRIC

Non-parametric tests are associated with nominal or ordinal data obtained from populations where no assumptions are made about the distribution

Table 7.5 Table of observed and expected results

	Yes	No
Observed answers (O)	84	20
Expected answers (E)	60	60

Table 7.6 SphinxSurvey calculation of Chi square (χ^2)

Classtype	N°. ans.	Percent
Yes	84	70.0%
No	36	30.0%
TOTAL OBS.	120	100%

Note: Dependence is highly significant (Chi2 = 19.20, df = 1, $1-p$ = >99.99%). Chi2 is calculated with equal expected frequencies for each value label.

within these populations. In other words the findings cannot be extrapolated to other populations. As an example take the descriptive statistic that 70% of school-aged girls in a mixed school said 'yes' when asked if they preferred to be taught in single-sex classes. Let us assume this result was obtained from a questionnaire to 120 girls in one 10–16 school. We can use a non-parametric test – Chi square (χ^2) – to determine the level of significance (see Chapter 10 for a description of this term) of this result. Had there been no preference we would have expected (E) there to be a 50:50 split. However, what we observed (O) was a 70:30 split which is shown as student numbers in Table 7.5.

We can calculate whether this is statistically significant (see Chapter 10). This is quite easy to calculate by hand but if we had collected the answers in SphinxSurvey we could get this computer package to calculate Chi square (χ^2) for us. In this case this would show Table 7.6.

SphinxSurvey is a relatively straightforward program to use and is, in short, as its manual introduction notes, 'an integrated package for the design, administration and analysis of questionnaire based surveys' (Scolari, 2002). It provides the facility to design a questionnaire; then allows its use for direct entry mode; subsequent immediate analysis of any data collected; a broad selection of powerful yet easy-to-use statistical functions; and then assists in the final generation of any report. It will also allow for data to be transferred from other spreadsheets and databases and as we shall discuss in the second part of this chapter, it also has a Lexica edition, which enables various analyses of qualitative data.

Excel allows you to perform the function CHITEST, which returns the probability for the number of degrees of freedom (see Chapter 10) for the χ^2 result. Putting the results in an Excel worksheet and selecting CHITEST would give you the result p of 1.17713E-05, which you might like to confirm

Table 7.7   Excel calculation of Chi square (χ^2)

Observed values	Expected values
84	60
36	60
Chi-square =	19.2
CHITEST =	1.17713E-05

matches $1-p$ = > 99.99. For completeness, Table 7.7 shows the calculation of χ^2 using the formulae shown (see Chapter 10, p. 204) but it is not needed to ascertain the significance of the result.

Either way of calculating χ^2 shows that the result is statistically significant. It is, though, only significant for this group of 120 girls. We don't know the social background of these girls, details of the school they are in, how old they are and how they are presently taught, and so we cannot extrapolate to other compulsory school aged girls. This, however, is not important as we are stating the result of a non-parametric test. We are not intending to extrapolate from this result to say, all girls in 10–16 schools. Again my experience tells me that often research students feel they need to be able to undertake such extrapolations otherwise their work is somehow inferior. This could not be further from the truth, and particularly as many are involved in education, non-parametric tests are invaluable as:

> They have the advantage of being tailored to particular institutional, departmental and individual circumstances. They offer teachers a valuable opportunity for quick, relevant and focused feedback on student performance. (Cohen et al., 2000: 318)

You will find other worked examples of non-parametric tests, such as the *Kruskal-Wallis test* for finding out if three or more independent groups belong to a single population (see Chapter 10, p. 210) and *Spearman's Rank Order* which allows one to find out if there is a significant relationship between two sets of ordinal data (see Chapter 10, p. 221), and it is likely these will be more than enough for Masters work.

PARAMETRIC TESTS

Parametric tests on the other hand are designed to allow for extrapolation from sample populations to whole populations and use statistics applicable to interval and ratio data. They are often considered as more powerful but this comes at a price. Their use requires careful attention to the characteristics of the population and to issues such as their reliability and validity. This is not to say that reliability and validity are not important in non-parametric tests, as noted in Chapter 3, but with parametric tests they have to take on

Table 7.8 Pearson moment correlation calculation from Excel

Predicted A level result (X)	Actual A level result (Y)	Pearson product moment correlation value (PEARSON)
30	34	
38	36	0.908915195
60	42	
65	60	
43	42	
50	48	
58	52	
72	66	
64	48	
80	72	

statistical significance. This text is not intended to provide an overview of such issues and should you wish to explore them you are advised to consult other texts such as Cohen and Holliday (1996), Hopkins, Hopkins and Glass (1996) and Wright (1997), with the latter looking in more detail at the application of the computer program SPSS (Statistical Package for the Social Sciences). Chapter 10 does provide details and examples of the parametric tests considered to be of most value to Masters work: *ANOVA* (p. 199) for testing if the difference between the mean of more than two samples is statistically significant, *Pearson's Product Moment Correlation (r)* (p. 218) for ascertaining the strength of relationship between two interval scales variables, and the *t-test* (p. 224) for testing the level of significance between the means of two samples.

However, rather than repeat unnecessary detail, only the value of using the computer programs Excel and SphinxSurvey for calculating *Pearson's Product Moment Correlation (r)* is shown here. Putting the two sets of interval scale variables into EXCEL then selecting another cell and **I**nserting the **F**unction PEARSON should, after following the request for the data, result in Table 7.8. The same data can be inserted into SphinxSurvey and the results shown in Figure 7.2 are obtained. On the face of it there appears to be considerably more information supplied with SphinxSurvey but much of this is unnecessary, although that is not to say it may not be useful or of value. The key thing is, as we would expect, that the value for $r = 0.909$ is the same no matter what program we have used to calculate it.

As already noted there is not space in this text to go into the range of features that are useful when undertaking quantitative analysis using either Excel or SphinxSurvey, and indeed many of them are well beyond the needs for MEd work. Should you wish to explore the potential of these computer packages for quantitative analysis then given the ubiquitous position of Excel in the marketplace, a look at its help guide is a good starting point and for SphinxSurvey the following website should provide a comprehensive introduction: lesphinx-developpement (2002).

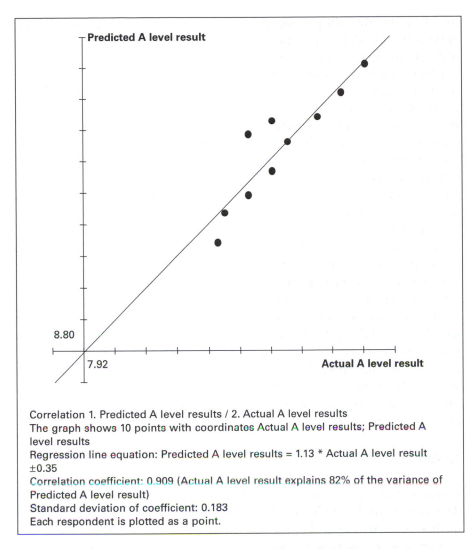

Predicted A level result

8.80

7.92

Actual A level result

Correlation 1. Predicted A level results / 2. Actual A level results
The graph shows 10 points with coordinates Actual A level results; Predicted A
level results
Regression line equation: Predicted A level results = 1.13 * Actual A level result
±0.35
Correlation coefficient: 0.909 (Actual A level result explains 82% of the variance of
Predicted A level result)
Standard deviation of coefficient: 0.183
Each respondent is plotted as a point.

Figure 7.2   Pearson moment correlation calculation from SphinxSurvey

Having looked at the types of data one can work with and their analysis,
we need to consider the presentation of the data and it is to this aspect we
now turn.

Presentation of data

Getting this aspect of your work correct is probably one of the most important considerations when producing your thesis – and yet so often it is the
least considered and most badly done. To some extent technology must take

the blame for this. By putting data into a spreadsheet and pressing a few buttons it is possible to produce what looks like the most wondrous variety of charts and graphs. For example with Excel column, bar, line, pie, X-Y scattergrams, doughnut, radar, surface and others are all possible and unfortunately are all too often used just because they look good. The application of colour often doesn't help either, as the capability of modern printers usually serves no more than to provide a cacophony of variety and hues. On more than one occasion I have had students present me with bar charts containing a minimum of 15 bars, all of different colours and displayed in 3D, with legends that stretch two to three times the size of the chart. Such presentation results in little more than a mess hiding any potential value the data might have to offer. This may sound very negative, and to be fair put to appropriate use technology is useful and colour advantageous. Too often, though, what is ignored is the question 'What is the best format to represent my data so that it reflects accurately yet straightforwardly what I am trying to show?' If students took some time in answering this question it would save them a lot of editing work at a later date.

It is not possible, within this text, to go into a wide range of presentation techniques or (given it is in black and white) to highlight the problems of misuse of colour. What we will do though is look at the basic presentation techniques most suited to MEd work, namely tables and charts, and try to highlight some of the problems of using these. Other texts provide a much more comprehensive discussion of organising and displaying data and one which covers more than sufficient material for MEd work is that by Moore (1997).

Tables

Tables provide one of the commonest ways of organising a large amount of data and correctly produced offer a very convenient and straightforward method of displaying it. They are also, though, probably the format most open to poor representation as the following exercise aims to show (Figure 7.3).

You probably have a number of criticisms with the example Table 3.3, and I must admit to removing various bits and pieces to make it worse than when it was originally presented. The basic problems with it are:

- there is no title or indication of what the numbers mean;
- how have the literacy and numeracy levels been measured?;
- what is the source of the data?

I have rectified these points on the other example of Table 3.3 (see Figure. 7.4), however, there are still issues, which one needs to raise about the data in it.

One, which should be immediately obvious, is that actual totals are not given. As this is a longitudinal study, it is likely that some people who were included in the sample at birth are not now included for a whole range of

Data Analysis - Tables

Data Analysis – Tables

Take a look at the following table and the notes written with it. Ask yourself does the table seem to reflect the data? Does the table present the data in the best possible way?

Table 3.3

Age on leaving full-time education	Low literacy	High literacy	Low numeracy	High numeracy
Under 16	22	78	67	33
16	25	75	59	41
17–18	10	90	36	64
19–20	6	94	25	75
2l and over	0	100	12	88
All 37 year olds	18	82	47	53

In 1995 the National Child Development Study collected information on the basic skills levels of 37 year olds. This is a longitudinal study of 10 per cent of all people born in Great Britain in a single week in 1958, with data collected at birth, 7, 11, 16, 23, 33 and 37 years. It showed that in general, the earlier someone had left full-time education, the more likely they were to have problems with basic skills (Table 3.3). For example, over 60 per cent of those who left full-time education by the age of 16 had low numeracy scores compared with only 12 per cent of those who left at the age of 21 and over. Women tended to have lower numeracy levels than men, but there was not much difference between the genders of literacy. Overall, far fewer had low literacy scores than low numeracy scores.

Figure 7.3   Example of data and the table produced from it

reasons. I wondered also whether there had been any change over time, with for example, people returning to learning. We are also told in the accompanying notes that there are gender differences, though this is not indicated in the table, although as the source is given this means that this information could be tracked down if it was necessary to do so. Producing a table is not necessarily that straightforward even with what looks like uncomplicated data. It is likely that any table produced for an MEd thesis will be a lot simpler than the example shown here, but this should not negate the need to follow some simple guidelines. The things to remember are:

- Simplicity – keep your table as simple and uncluttered as possible. Make sure it highlights the main issues you want to get over.
- Labels – ensure these are clear, comprehensive and explanatory. For example, always have a title, give units of measurement, make sure columns are headed and that the year of collection is indicated.

Table 3.3 Social Trends 1997

Literacy and numeracy standards of 37 year olds: by age on leaving full-time education, 1995

Great Britain
Percentages

Age on leaving full-time education	Low literacy[1]	High literacy[2]	Low numeracy[1]	High numeracy[2]
Under 16	22	78	67	33
16	25	75	59	41
17–18	10	90	36	64
19–20	6	94	25	75
2l and over	0	100	12	88
All 37 year olds	18	82	47	53

1 People generally not able to demonstrate skills above The Basic Skills Agency's foundation standard.
2 People generally able to demonstrate skills above The Basic Skills Agency's foundation standard.

Source: **City University from the National Child Development Study**

Figure 7.4 Improvement on the example Table 3.3

- Totals – these should be presented, especially where percentages are given, as otherwise there is no indication of what these represent, for example, whether 10% represents 50 or 5 items.

Charts and graphs

These can be very valuable methods of presentation of data because people can find it easier to see spatial relationships than numerical relationships. However, their production is not without problems. The lure of technology and misuse of colour have already been mentioned, so here we will look at other aspects of producing charts and graphs which one needs to take care with.

BAR AND PIE CHARTS

Bar charts are used to represent frequency data, that is, the number of occurrences in a particular category. Moore (1997: 205) suggests bar charts are more useful, but my own view is to use whatever most appropriately presents your data. To present some insight into this we will look at some examples.

Figure 7.5 is an example of a simple bar chart, using some fictitious data, produced using the graphing features in Excel. I have in fact changed the colours of the bar chart to black and white for ease of viewing. In this case with only two colours the presentation should be quite straightforward but

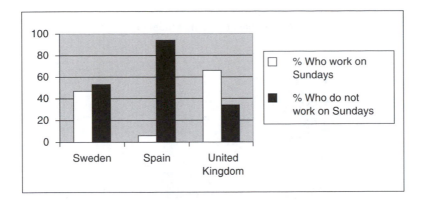

Figure 7.5   Examples of a simple bar chart

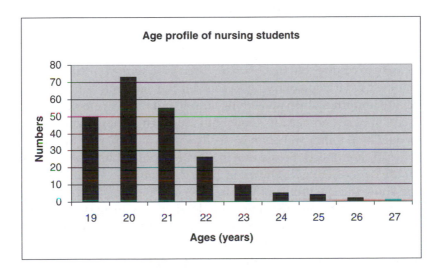

Figure 7.6   Table 7.3 represented as a bar chart

when you have more data items things can get quite difficult to interpret. So here is a piece of advice: to ensure ease of interpretation limit the number of bars in any graph. I know it is simplicity itself to take all your data, insert it into something like Excel and with the press of a few keys produce a bar chart. Take, for example, the data shown earlier in Table 7.3 which has nine pieces of data; inserted into Excel and produced as a bar chart gives Figure 7.6.

Is this bar chart easier to read than the table of results? Should it be provided in place of or in addition to the table? The answers to these questions

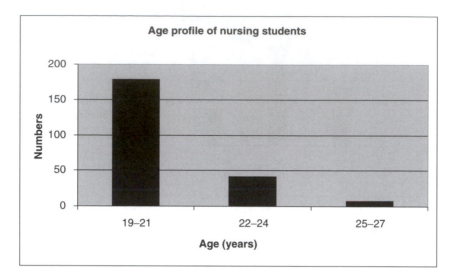

Figure 7.7   Table 7.4 represented as a bar chart

are not easy to resolve, but this is where discussion with your tutor will help. Ask yourself what you are trying to show. If the age profile of the students is crucially important, then go with the graph, but if not the table would suffice. I certainly see no need to show both although I know many a student who would and, if they were honest, really for no more reason than to fill up the pages of their thesis. Before moving on ask yourself whether the groupings of the data of Table 7.3 shown in Table 7.4 would be any better as a bar chart to show the age profile of the students (see Figure 7.7)? I would probably argue yes, as it seems to show more clearly the main age groupings and, with only three bars, the profile as well – but it isn't easy to decide, is it? As I have noted, though, showing say fifteen bars, even if it looks pretty in all its colour glory, is almost certainly going to be difficult to read.

Returning to Figure 7.5, how else might we improve this bar chart? We might want to include some axes labels (as with Figure 7.6 and 7.7) for clarity, or vary the background colour and/or show grid lines. How does the variation (shown in Figure 7.8), of the earlier bar chart (Figure 7.5) appear to you? I would suggest this looks clearer but you may wish to differ. The point is that the technology will allow you to produce an infinite variety of formats. Here is a second piece of advice: whatever you produce, ensure it is clear and simple to understand. You can still pick faults with this chart (Figure 7.8). As we noted when talking about tables, what numbers do these percentages refer to? When was this data collected? Is the data representative of the whole populations of these countries? There is no suggestion all this detail needs to be placed on the graph. In fact this would almost certainly result in a messy result but it needs to be somewhere, and close by. A possible solution is given (Figure 7.9) but this

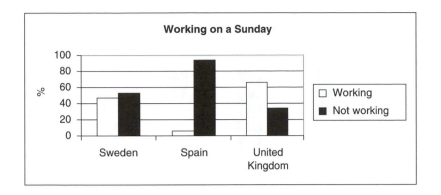

Figure 7.8   Variation of the bar chart from Figure 7.5

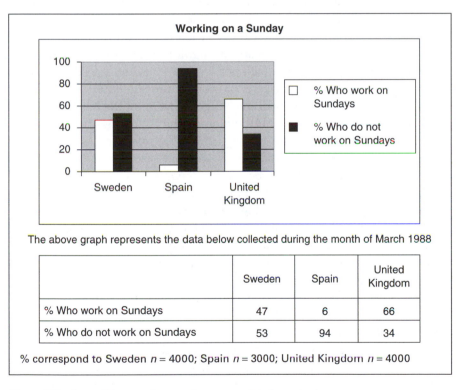

The above graph represents the data below collected during the month of March 1988

	Sweden	Spain	United Kingdom
% Who work on Sundays	47	6	66
% Who do not work on Sundays	53	94	34

% correspond to Sweden $n = 4000$; Spain $n = 3000$; United Kingdom $n = 4000$

Figure 7.9   A possible way of presenting source data for a chart

is by no means a definitive solution – and remember all the figures are fictitious. One could probably go on and you would need to stop somewhere but this is where communication with your tutor is again important.

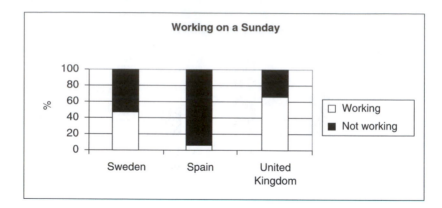

Figure 7.10   Stacked bar chart

It is also possible to produce a bar chart in various formats. So, with the same data as in Figure 7.9, you could produce Figure 7.10. This is a stacked bar chart, which compares the percentage each value contributes to the total across the categories. Is it any clearer in highlighting the percentage differences between those who do or do not work on a Sunday in the countries detailed? Might there be any clearer or more appropriate display?

To conclude this section, we can change the style of the bar chart. Using other data (see Moore, 1997: 214), which of the following do you prefer? Figure 7.11 shows a 3D image, and Figure 7.12 is produced as a horizontal bar chart with values on it. There is, however, a strong argument that the dependent variable (%) should be on the Y-axis so, as the second of these fails on this account, the first should be used. Perhaps a combination of the two formats would be better (see Figure 7.13) with a label to the X-axis given.

Not easy is it? And, given that the three Figures 7.11–7.13 were produced within a few minutes of each other by just formatting the basic graph produced by Excel, hopefully you can see how presentation of data may not be as straightforward as you might first have thought.

Let us return to our first set of bar chart data showing those working and not working on a Sunday in Sweden, Spain and the United Kingdom. The same data of course would not be suitable, in its entirety, for treatment as a pie chart. Pie charts show the percentages related to a whole. So, a pie chart of any of the above countries on its own would be fine, or producing resultant percentages of those who did work, as shown in Figure 7.14, would also be fine – wouldn't it?

Words of caution: look carefully at the percentages shown here compared with the percentages in Figure 7.9. If you look closely, the percentages it displays do not match those in the table we showed for the bar chart. The pie chart percentages in Figure 7.14 are a recalculation based on the actual numbers in the original table and so do not correspond to the percentages

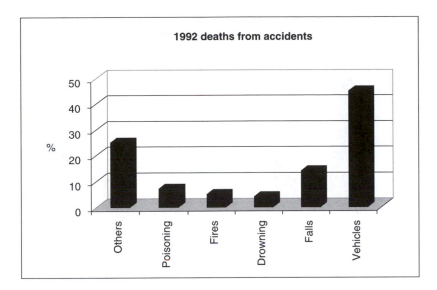

Figure 7.11   3D bar chart

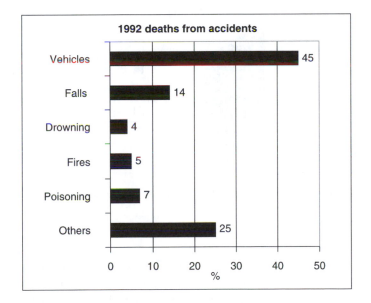

Figure 7.12   Horizontal bar chart

per country and this could easily lead to misinterpretation. This is always the case and as long as you explain this, all is well, but it may be advisable to keep pie charts for those cases where true percentages of an overall total are to be shown. If this is followed then all that needs to be considered is the actual form of presentation.

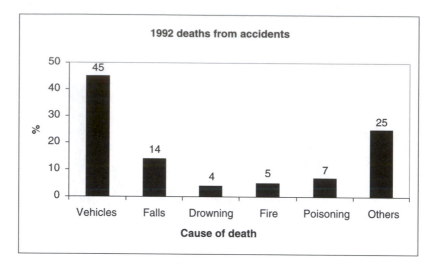

Figure 7.13 A combination of figures 7.11 and 7.12

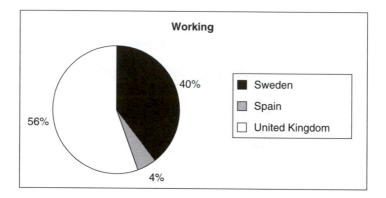

Figure 7.14 Pie chart of percentages of the population who work on a Sunday

Look at the two pie charts in Figures. 7.15 and 7.16, shown in bar chart form earlier (Figure 7.11). Both reflect the same data and all I have done is change the format of presentation. Again which do you prefer? Again the answer is not easy. I have also used different 'fill effects' to identify each area. It all goes back, I would argue, to the same basic issue, of using the format which shows the data you have in the simplest and easiest way for it to be understood.

GRAPHS

We have no real need to dwell on too many issues here, as most of them have been covered in our discussion on bar charts and pie charts. However, It is

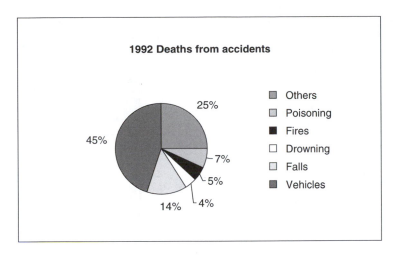

Figure 7.15   Pie chart example 1

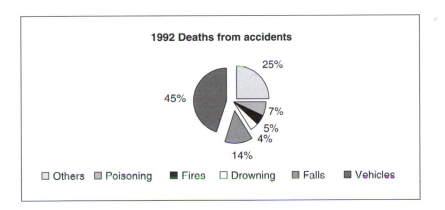

Figure 7.16   Pie chart example 2

worth reiterating these here and look at one other feature with respect to graphs – namely, distortion as a result of poor use of scales. The following principles should be considered when producing a graph:

- Labels: as before, ensure these are clear, comprehensive and explanatory, for example always include a title, and both the variable and unit of measurement are given.
- Variables: always place your independent variable (e.g. time) on the horizontal (x) axis and your dependent variable (e.g. number of pupils) on the vertical (y) axis.
- Vertical axis: this should always start at zero and the variable evenly spaced. Where there is a large jump this should be indicated by a break in the axis indicated by a ~.

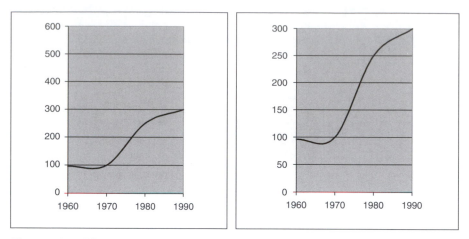

Figure 7.17   Effects of scale

- Impression: be sure the graph is not inaccurate or distorted by the incorrect use of scales.

The first three of these principles have been covered already and so we will turn to the last one. Look at the two graphs in Figure 7.17, which, for presentation purposes only, we will say show the number of households who have pets per thousand households. I have made the graphs smaller and not included labels so they can be seen side by side.

At a first glance these graphs look different and so give different impressions. The first would appear to indicate a moderate rise in the number of homes having pets while the second is a very steep rise. The truth is that the graphs show exactly the same thing. They are both accurate and it is only the fact that the scales are different which provides the first impressions. As Moore notes: 'Because there is no one "right" scale for a line graph, correct graphs can give different impressions by their choices of scales. Watch those scales!' (1997: 210). And to highlight Moore's comments, assuming the figures indicate supportive home environments for pets (and of course they do not necessarily do so), which two graphs would you use if you wished to show your country was becoming an increasingly pet supportive society? You may think the above comments just reflect the obvious but it is very easy to fall into the trap of making your graph misleading (Moore, 1997: Part II).

This section has attempted to provide you with a basic insight into types of quantitative data, its analysis and its presentation. We have noted though that such quantitative data although of value, especially given the time constraints of a typical MEd thesis, is limited in its capability for allowing us to explore the values and views of those being researched. To attempt to do this requires the use of more qualitative research methods, such as interviews, and it is to the analysis of this type of data we now turn.

PART 2: QUALITATIVE DATA

A momentary consideration might suggest there is an initial advantage to this area of data analysis in that, for most purposes and certainly I would suggest at MEd level, we do not have to consider the type of data as it will all be in the form of text. This text may have been collected from different sources, such as open questions in a questionnaire, interview transcripts or descriptions from observational research but it is technically all the same type. The source and the style of how it was obtained will undoubtedly affect the depth, quality and structure of the text collected, but it will not change its type. Unfortunately, the fact that all the data is of one type does not mean it is going to be easier to analyse. In fact the contrary is true as anyone who has undertaken the analysis of even the simplest open question or transcription of a few short interviews will quickly and often fervently confirm. The problem lies in creating some sort of meaning out of what can often be a vast quantity of data and to do so in such a way that any meaning attributed stands up to analytic rigour. This is no easy task as Fisher notes:

> If volume is one problem, complexity is another. Attempts to organise qualitative data typically run into difficulties on the question of what organising scheme to adopt. If the data may be organised in a logically infinite number of ways, each having its own unique validity, how can one organising method be chosen? Every decision implies an organising framework, from the simple use of chronological order for field notes, to 'case' methods (people, institutions, social situations etc.) to topical filing systems. The temptation is to put off decisions on the basis that to take any might restrict options to pursue other frameworks, and thus risk losing the essence of what the data contain. (1999: 113)

Just to remind us, with quantitative data analysis the type of data collected determines how it can be analysed and the tables and figures that result from any analysis appear to provide objectivity and an acceptable degree of reliability and validity to it. Note I say 'appear' in the last sentence, as by now I hope you have some understanding of the significance of the reliability and validity of data and these cannot just be assumed. We have also seen that the collection and analysis of quantitative data can be relatively straightforward and quick. Qualitative data analysis on the other hand has no such comfortable framework. The analysis of textual data is much more open to the subjectivity of the researcher and as such its reliability and validity are often seen as more suspect. Then, even without analysis, collection and transcription of qualitative data in itself is often time consuming.

Analysis of qualitative data is, as Fisher notes:

> a highly technical process … time-consuming clerical tasks, going through the data to locate every time a particular issue is discussed, and trying to see connections to other issues and to other factors, such as the type of social situation under investigation … interplay between clerical rigour and intellectual creativity,

a process so intense that few of us can maintain it at high levels for very long periods. (1999: 116–17)

This all sounds quite demoralising and begs the question why anyone should even think of undertaking qualitative research, especially with the time constraints associated with an MEd thesis?

If you have read the earlier chapters of this book then hopefully the answer to this last question is clear. It is only through qualitative data analysis that one can begin to get a feel for the social reality, which underlies any research findings. As we noted at the beginning of Chapter 5, the limitation of quantitative data analysis is that it cannot begin to provide any insight into why the findings are as they are. Only qualitative data analysis, even with all of its potential pitfalls, can offer this. To help us, as with quantitative data analysis, what would be of value is 'an analytic process (approach) which incorporates intuition and insight, but which is built on clerical thoroughness' (Fisher, 1999: 116).

We have already touched upon an approach to qualitative research, namely grounded theory, and noted the significance of one of its procedures which is the organisation of data into a set of themes or codes (see Chapter 5, pp. 93–4). The purpose of reminding ourselves of this here is that this grounded theory procedure can be considered to have influenced the development of computer aided methods for qualitative data analysis (CAQDAS). The next two chapters each provide details of two different CAQDAS programs – NUD•IST (Chapter 8) and ATLAS.ti (Chapter 9) – which the authors used to help them organise what, in each case, was the accumulation of a considerable amount of personal qualitative research data. It is arguable that the time needed to get to grips with the complexities of either of these two programs would make them improbable candidates for use at MEd level. Certainly the volume of qualitative data collected by each author is well outside the norms at MEd level but both chapters provide an overview of the programs and a critical analysis of their worth and as such are valuable contributions to this book. There are though other 'computer aided' analysis tools, which are available to help with qualitative analysis but require minimal effort to master and the rest of this chapter considers one of these, the lexical analysis element of the program SphinxSurvey which we introduced in our discussion of quantitative analysis.

Lexical analysis of SphinxSurvey

Again it will not be possible within the constraints of this book to consider all the features of the lexical analysis environment of SphinxSurvey (Scolari, 2002) but hopefully through the use of some exemplar material you will get some feel for its potential value for qualitative analysis. As I have already noted in this chapter, learning to use SphinxSurvey is, I feel, relatively straightforward.

I personally spent about a week coming to terms with many of its features and although not claiming to be an expert, feel I can adequately use the program to help me analyse both quantitative and qualitative data, making it a potential viable tool for use in MEd work. However, its use has to be predicated on the condition that it offers facilities which support the task of the analysis, not the other way round. In this way SphinxSurvey can be regarded as a tool and 'to focus attention in the responsibility of the students (researcher) to use the services of the program, rather than allow the programs to employ the services of the student (researcher)' (Fisher, 1999: 119).

I will, though, throw in one more caveat before moving on. Do not feel you have to use any CAQDAS program for any qualitative data analysis you undertake at MEd level, or that the use of any such program will either improve the reliability or validity of your data or somehow pull the wool over your tutor's eyes as to the quality of your work – it won't. I say this in all sincerity. Half a dozen half-hour interviews could be analysed perfectly acceptably without any recourse to a CAQDAS program, particularly if you have used a structured or semi-structured format. As a quick example have a go at the exercise provided in Figure 7.18.

I hope this exercise shows that you can categorise text without recourse to CAQDAS. It would be strange if you did not come up with similar categories to those expressed next in (Figure 7.19).

At this point you may be thinking why bother with the extra workload of learning how to use a CAQDAS program? The following chapters will help to answer this issue but returning to the exercise here, ask yourself how were the statements (Figure 7.18) arrived at? You need to realise that for the purposes of the exercise I have made things easy for you inasmuch as they were all embedded in quite a large number of interviews with both students and staff. Even with a structured interview format it would not be straightforward extracting them. This is where spending time looking at the facilities of programs such as SphinxSurvey might help, and may well provide you with insights to qualitative data analysis useful to any further studies you undertake – the PhD waiting in the wings, for example.

What I will aim to show is that the use of CAQDAS programs such as the lexical analysis aspect of SphinxSurvey can help in extracting and categorising qualitative data – always assuming this is what you want to do, and for MEd work I would hasten to suggest it is.

Figure 7.20 is an extract of three questions from a total of twelve, and of the responses from two interviews from a total of ten with recently qualified teachers. The original data have been altered slightly in terms of labels used for teaching groups and various people to try and ensure anonymity, but otherwise is verbatim. I have also pulled the answers to each question together for the convenience of presentation but this is easy to do with the cut and paste facilities of a word-processor – assuming your interviews are at least semi-structured.

Data Analysis – Categorising Text

The aim of this exercise is to enable you to get a feel for the categorising of data you get from the process of interviewing. There are no 'right' answers although it will be surprising if you do not come up with some similar categories to those offered. Take no more than 30 minutes.

These selected statements are from interviews of a sample of staff and students on a one-year initial teacher training PGCE course, examining staff and students' attitudes to the way in which knowledge was acquired on such courses. The findings were eventually published as *Acquiring Knowledge in Initial Teacher Education; Reading, Writing, Practice and the PGCE Course*, G. Squirrell, P. Gilroy, D. Jones and J. Rudduck (British Library Research Report 79, 1990).

Your task is simply to categorise the data.

1   I wanted them to get into the library.
2   We give you assignments because we need to assess you.
3   I went into school and told the teacher that I was doing these lesson plans and he said, 'Hey, see mine!' And in fact his was three words – 'Teach physiology, afternoon'. So they're not really that useful.
4   We give you work because we think it will do you some good.
5   My journal's awful. I pity who's got to read it. I just wrote down what happened at school.
6   Quite frankly, I don't think we've been given that much time for reading at all. I think that's a real problem.
7   Using the library is a bit like a Harrod's Sale – there's a rush and I arrive after all the bargains have gone.
8   I was suffering from complete exhaustion after my teaching practice. And then I had to write!!
9   They've given us so many of these tasks to do. You just end up feeling swamped.
10   What I'm going to tell you about my course and the tutors is confidential.
11   The only reason I read the *TES* is for the jobs. I don't think I've ever read an article in it.
12   I'd certainly want to go on reading when I've left the course, because there's so many ways you can go on improving.
13   The whole process of writing a journal has made me think.
14   They get a reading list beforehand and they get some guidance during the course.
15   Teaching practice was the most valuable bit of the course.
16   Just doing the teaching is the best preparation for the job, not reading.
17   Are you from the government?
18   To be quite honest, by the time I've got to the library there aren't any books left, so I've found it all a bit of a waste of time.
19   I don't want an external to read something so private and personal.
20   Oh, well, you learn to be very careful about saying anything you hear in lectures in the staffroom because it doesn't go down too well.
21   I can't imagine reading educational literature for pleasure, although it may happen with time.

22	I think if you don't watch out you end up being like a teacher – they've got all the ideas they could possibly want and that's it, full stop.
23	The course should be whether you're teaching or not and you're still getting the impression that the way to pass it well is to do quite a lot of written material.
24	I started off thinking who's going to read this – am I offending anyone, especially the person marking it?

Figure 7.18   An exercise in categorising text

My own categorisation is here to show you what constructions I came to. I broke it first into staff and students, which gave me:

STAFF   – 1, 2, 4, 14
STUDENTS   – 3, 5, 6, 7, 8, 9, 10, 11, 12, 13, 15, 16, 17, 18, 19, 20, 21, 23, 24
NOT SURE   – 22 (and I couldn't in fact fit it in)

Then putting STAFF and STUDENTS into various categories gave me

Categories	Staff	Students
Assessment	2, 4, 14	9, 23
Teaching practice (journals)	-	3, 5, 13, 19, 24
Teaching practice (work)	-	8, 15, 16
Reading (library)	1	6, 7, 18
Reading (general)	-	11, 12, 21
Confidentiality	-	10, 17, 20

Figure 7.19   Possible categorisation of sample statements

Given the example material in Figure 7.20 it would be perfectly feasible to just analyse it by reading it and pulling out various issues. This is in fact exactly what the interviewer did and quite successfully with all ten of the interview transcripts. It did, however, take five to six weeks to do this and even when completed the interviewer was unsure as to whether any links had been 'missed'. To help avoid this the interviewer could have searched for particular words using nothing more than a word-processor such as Microsoft Word, using its Edit–Find facility and then marking those found with its in-built highlighting tool for future reference. This would have ensured that no occurrences of any particular words were missed, which in turn would have enabled the kind of statements noted earlier (Figure 7.18)

Interviewer: In teaching the unit of 'energy' in Y7, which topic do you perceive the lowest confidence? Why? How do you cope with it?

A: 'Energy inter-conversions and energy converters' are abstract in nature, making these topics very difficult for students to really understand. Through my studying in my PGCE course, I gained insights for teaching abstract science concepts, for instance, by stating observable and concrete examples or analogies. For this topic, I would start with a simple demonstration. Then, students would be asked to identify the initial and final forms of energy in some processes of energy changes. Besides this, the principle of conservation of energy in nature would be introduced too.

B: The form of potential energy is comparatively difficult for students. Most students are not capable of distinguishing between potential energy and chemical energy. It has to emphasize that potential energy is related to changes in shape or position such as those examples of coiled springs and raised weights. Then, I'll ask students to give further examples.

Interviewer: How do you perceive your confidence in teaching physics topics at Y8? How do you handle the problems encountered in your teaching?

A: I have the lowest confidence in teaching the topic of 'forces and movement'. Fortunately, it is the last chapter in the Y8 curriculum and I usually don't have enough time to go over the whole topic. I just introduce the effects, the measurement and the unit of forces. Besides, I also teach students how to do simple calculations on forces and ask them to remember the method.

B: I have full confidence in teaching Y8 physics especially for the topic on 'electricity' because I have taken an 'electrical technician' course. Analogy would be used in teaching the concept of simple circuitry'. The analogy of electric current I used is a group of students, each holding a football, passing the balls to adjacent students. This may lead students to build up the idea of free electrons and atoms. Besides, I prefer letting students do many experiments when teaching physics. I want to comment that the equipment in the integrated science laboratory is not sufficient and needs to be improved. It is also true that there are too many topics in Y8 and we do not have enough time to teach the last unit on 'Forces and movement'.

Interviewer: How do you perceive your confidence in teaching 'electricity' in Y9 physics?

A: It is most difficult. I actually do not have much confidence. This is the first year I am teaching Y9 level. I have to call for help from the Head of Department to brief me on the content and theories and the laboratory technician especially to set up the demonstrations, which use EHT (Electric High Tension) power supply. I just don't know how to handle the electric circuits of this kind, which are very dangerous. If possible, I'll avoid using the dangerous apparatus, such as EHT, or complicated circuits.

B: Through my 'electrical technician' course, I had equipped myself with solid knowledge on electricity and electronics and I am quite sure that I can manage these topics in Y9. The 'electrical technician' course did not have direct relation to teaching junior secondary science and it did not contain much relevant material appropriate for my teaching. The course just strengthened my knowledge in this field. With this knowledge, I can find many other suitable materials from the library or bookstores for my teaching. As a teacher, you can't just wait for others to feed you. For the topics on 'domestic electricity' and 'electronics', I like to set a project for students. Although the project will not be easy for everyone, students will benefit from conducting the project and gain an understanding of what science and technology are all about. Besides, it would enhance the acquisition of proficiency and integration of science 'process skills especially those high-level skills which are difficult to develop. In this unit, there are also many, experiments some of which are demonstrations. I would modify the experiments in a more interesting way in order to hold students' attention as well as to aid them to understand the principles. For example, to demonstrate how to use the sparks produced by the Vande der Graaff generator to light up a Bunsen Burner, a light bulb or a series of fluorescent tubes.

Figure 7.20 An extract of interview data

to be extracted. Undertaking this task with a word-processor would have been quite time consuming, perhaps even more so than just reading the text, but still arguably doable. It could also quickly become very messy, as Ann-Marie Bathmaker notes in Chapter 8 (p. 166). What then might be useful is a tool that will maintain the integrity of the text while helping with its analysis, for example grouping similar comments together. This is where the lexical analysis of SphinxSurvey, or indeed any similar CAQDAS program, could help.

The data for CAQDAS often has to be in a particular format, and although SphinxSurvey offers you facilities for text preparation, typically all that are needed are either single sentences or lines of text. Other formats are possible, for example paragraphs, but analysis is more cumbersome with these larger chunks of text. It is quite easy to convert text into suitable formats. In WORD for example you could either insert a paragraph marker at appropriate points and save the resulting file as 'Text Only (*.txt)', or even simpler use the save function 'Text only with line breaks (*.txt)', which although it may not break the text exactly where you want is very quick to do. The above text in Figure 7.20 was saved with a paragraph marker at the end of each sentence (with the interview questions held as one sentence) and then as a 'Text Only (*.txt)' file.

There is no intention here to go through all the operations of the lexical analysis of SphinxSurvey, but loading the text file above and analysing the contents produces the opening screen shown in Figure 7.21. This shows the frequency table of the lexicon words and the first piece of text – the text corresponding to the first interview questions.

This initial presentation is in itself useful. The frequency list can begin to give you a feel for the contents and the type of key words, which may be useful for further analysis. Let's stay with this frequency table for the moment. As it stands it actually contains 294 words, far too bulky to make any real sense of and many of them are what are called 'tool words', for example, 'the', 'to', 'I', 'and' and 'in', which as the SphinxSurvey reference manual notes 'are needed for constructing language but convey little information on their own'. Removing these tool words is simple with the Reduce option. Doing this and transferring the outcome results in a reduced lexicon of 217 words, shown in Table 7.9. Although I have done a few minutes' work formatting the table for presentation here, the need for this is questionable. Reduction of the number of words or their presentation as here is not the issue. What is important, and has been noted already, is being able to rapidly get a frequency list of those in the text in order to get some idea of keywords for further analysis. Let's look at this now.

Marking various words in the lexicon automatically highlights them in colour in the text and changing View: (Figure 7.21) to Corpus allows you to scroll down the whole text viewing them. This is extremely useful in that it can help you get more of a feel of issues within the text. The text is kept as a

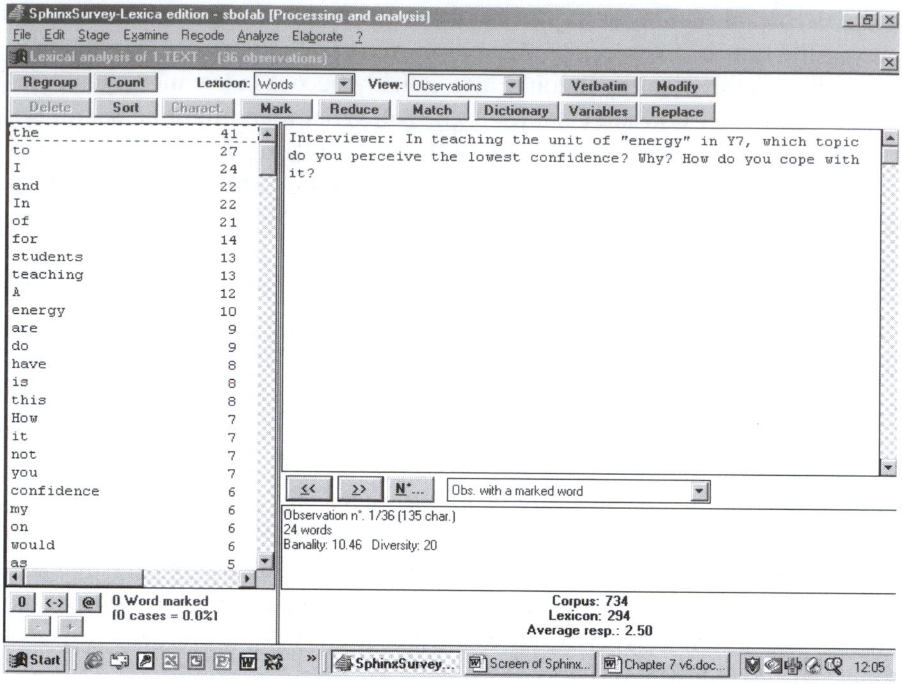

Figure 7.21 Initial analysis screen display of SphinxSurvey

whole and although it does not replace needing to read all the text in its entirety to get an overall feel for its contents, it does permit the picking out of possible links using intuition and insight, while ensuring clerical thoroughness.

Of perhaps more value is that particular words can be grouped for convenient analysis and this analysis transferred to file for further scrutiny. As an example I marked the words 'lowest', 'confidence' and 'teaching' and grouped these using Regroup (see Figure 7.21) as 'Teaching ability'. This term then appeared in my lexicon linking all three words. I could then use this 'grouping' within the Verbatim option (see Figure 7.21) to just look at the marked sentences resulting in extraction of these from the whole text with the marked words being conveniently converted to capitals as shown in Figure 7.22.

Rapid grouping of words with similar stems is also possible offering a further valuable tool. For example #teach* would link teaching, teach and teacher together while #electr* would link electricity, electrical, electric, electrons and electronic. In a similar vein it is possible to use Dictionary (see Figure 7.21) to either load up a predefined dictionary linked to a particular theme (see Figure 7.23), or to design your own dictionary specific to your needs and use these for analysis. It is not difficult to see within the example I have used that developing a dictionary for say Physics which had in it the

Table 7.9   SphinxSurvey Lexicon 217 list (with the number of cases for each word)

students	13	teaching	13	energy	10	confidence	6
science	5	topic	5	topics	5	Besides	4
difficult	4	electricity	4	forces	4	physics	4
technician	4	unit	4	Y8	4	electric	3
electrical	3	especially	3	examples	3	experiments	3
Interviewer	3	knowledge	3	perceive	3	potential	3
project	3	simple	3	Y9	3	abstract	2
Analogy	2	ask	2	changes	2	circuits	2
dangerous	2	demonstrations	2	EHT	2	electronics	2
enough	2	handle	2	High	2	laboratory	2
last	2	level	2	light	2	lowest	2
movement	2	nature	2	set	2	skills	2
teach	2	time	2	understand	2	used	2
acquisition	1	actually	1	adjacent	1	aid	1
Although	1	analogies	1	apparatus	1	appropriate	1
asked	1	atoms	1	attention	1	avoid	1
balls	1	benefit	1	between	1	bookstores	1
brief	1	build	1	bulb	1	Bunsen	1
Burner	1	calculations	1	call	1	capable	1
chapter	1	chemical	1	circuitry	1	coiled	1
comment	1	comparatively	1	complicated	1	concept	1
concepts	1	concrete	1	conducting	1	conservation	1
contain	1	content	1	conversions	1	converters	1
cope	1	current	1	curriculum	1	demonstrate	1
demonstration	1	Department	1	der	1	develop	1
direct	1	distinguishing	1	domestic	1	easy	1
effects	1	electrons	1	emphasize	1	encountered	1
enhance	1	equipment	1	equipped	1	everyone	1
example	1	feed	1	field	1	final	1
find	1	first	1	fluorescent	1	football	1
form	1	forms	1	Fortunately	1	free	1
full	1	further	1	gain	1	gained	1
generator	1	give	1	Graaff	1	group	1
Head	1	help	1	hold	1	holding	1
idea	1	identify	1	improved	1	initial	1
insights	1	instance	1	integrated	1	integration	1
inter	1	interesting	1	introduce	1	introduced	1
junior	1	kind	1	lead	1	letting	1
library	1	making	1	manage	1	material	1
materials	1	measurement	1	method	1	modify	1
more	1	needs	1	observable	1	order	1
others	1	passing	1	PGCE	1	position	1
possible	1	power	1	prefer	1	principle	1
principles	1	problems	1	process	1	processes	1
produced	1	proficiency	1	quite	1	raised	1
related	1	relation	1	relevant	1	remember	1
secondary	1	series	1	shape	1	solid	1
sparks	1	springs	1	start	1	stating	1
strengthened	1	studying	1	sufficient	1	suitable	1
supply	1	sure	1	taken	1	teacher	1
technology	1	Tension	1	theories	1	true	1
tubes	1	understanding	1	using	1	usually	1
Vande	1	wait	1	want	1	way	1
weights	1	whole	1	Why	1	Y7	1
year	1						

'1.TEXT' : Response extracts Teaching_Ability (the responses are reduced to sentences containing one marked word)

n° 1 : In TEACHING the unit of "energy" in Y7, which topic do you perceive the LOWEST CONFIDENCE /

n° 3 : Through my studying in my PGCE course, I gained insights for TEACHING abstract science concepts, for instance, by stating observable and concrete examples or analogies /

n° 11 : How do you perceive your CONFIDENCE in TEACHING physics topics at Y8 / How do you handle the problems encountered in your TEACHING /

n° 12 : I have the LOWEST CONFIDENCE in TEACHING the topic of 'forces and movement' /

n° 16 : I have full CONFIDENCE in TEACHING Y8 physics especially for the topic on 'electricity' because I have taken an 'electrical technician' course /

n° 17 : Analogy would be used in TEACHING the concept of simple circuitry /

n° 20 : Besides, I prefer letting students do many experiments when TEACHING physics /

n° 22 : How do you perceive your CONFIDENCE in TEACHING 'electricity' in Y9 physics /

n° 23 : I actually do not have much CONFIDENCE /

n° 24 : This is the first year I am TEACHING Y9 level /

n° 28 : The 'electrical technician' course did not have direct relation to TEACHING junior secondary science and it did not contain much relevant material appropriate for my TEACHING /

n° 30 : With this knowledge, I can find many other suitable materials from the library or bookstores for my TEACHING /

12 quoted responses

Figure 7.22 SphinxSurvey analysis of text on grouped word 'Teaching ability'

VERB_REGROUPMENT_DICTIONARY

#accept=accept=accepted=accepting=accepts
#accuse=accuse=accused=accusing=acuses
#act=act=acted=acting=acts
#admit=admit=admitted=admitting=admits
#agree=agree=agreed=agreeing=agrees
#ask=ask=asked=asking=asks
#be=be=been=was=am=are=were=is=being=m=re=will=ll
#beat=beat=beaten=beating=beats
#become=become=became=becoming=becomes
#begin=begin=began=begun=beginning=begins
#believe=believe=believed=believing=believes

Figure 7.23 Part of the Verb Regroupment Dictionary within SphinxSurvey

group electrics linked to terms such as #electrics=electricity=electronics=EHT=electric=circuitry=current=electrons=atoms, might be of use.

In conclusion SphinxSurvey offers other lexical analysis features, such as various statistical analysis of expressions, which may prove of value but space does not permit their description here. Hopefully, this whole section has provided you with some insight into the potential at MEd level for the use of the CAQDAS programs, and in particular SphinxSurvey Lexical Analysis, for qualitative data analysis. The use of such programs may also help to redress the resistance to qualitative research often apparent in MEd work and so help rebalance the usual quantitative focus in MEd thesis.

Summary

This chapter has provided an overview of the analysis and presentation of the data obtained from quantitative or qualitative research. With quantitative research the type of data obtained dictates how it can be analysed and what statistics, descriptive or interpretative, can be applied to it. Knowing the type of quantitative data your research will result in and what you can do with it is clearly a crucial aspect of your research design and one which requires careful attention before you embark upon any data collection.

Once analysed the presentation of quantitative data is also something that requires careful consideration although too often, as this chapter tries to show, it does not receive the due care and attention it deserves. The presentation of tables, charts and graphs are all considered and the common pitfalls in their production highlighted.

The final section looks at the analysis of qualitative data with the help of the CAQDAS program SphinxSurvey Lexical Analysis. Its purpose is to show that even at MEd level, where the amount of interview data is likely to be quite limited, the use of such a package can offer considerable support for qualitative analysis. Indeed the relative ease of use of this package offers the potential for the increase in qualitative research at MEd level. Whether what you get with such computer aided qualitative analysis is what you intended is another question and one, which is addressed in the following two chapters.

8

Using NUD·IST

Ann-Marie Bathmaker

This chapter outlines the use of a software package for analysing qualitative data called NUD·IST (Non-Numerical, Unstructured Data Indexing, Searching and Theorising). In the study referred to in the chapter, NUD·IST was used to analyse a set of semi-structured interviews with staff and students in a further education college, which formed the basis for a case study of teaching and learning in further education. The chapter provides only a brief outline of the research study, as the main purpose of the chapter is not to report on the findings from the research, but to consider the practicalities of using NUD·IST, and to examine some of the critiques of the software in the light of experience. The chapter concludes with recommendations for new users.

About the research

The research on which this chapter is based was a study of the changing system of 16–19 education in England in the 1990s. In 1993, a new vocational qualification was introduced for young people studying in schools and further education colleges, called the General National Vocational Qualification (GNVQ). GNVQs are intended to provide a broad, work-related qualification for students in post-compulsory education. They are available at three levels, Foundation, Intermediate and Advanced, representing levels 1, 2 and 3 of the National Qualifications Framework in England (Qualifications and Curriculum Authority, 2001). The qualifications are mainly taken by young people aged 16–19 who are studying full-time in schools or colleges. In 2000 GNVQs at Advanced level were replaced by Advanced Vocational Certificates in Education (AVCEs), and in 2001, vocational General Certificates in Education (GCSEs) were introduced, which are intended to replace some Foundation and Intermediate GNVQs.

A considerable amount of quantitative information is available about GNVQs. A nationwide survey of GNVQs from 1993 to 1997 was undertaken by the Institute of Education in London directed by Alison Wolf (Further Education Development Agency et al., 1997). The Awarding Bodies Edexel, City and Guilds and OCR (Oxford, Cambridge and Royal Society of Arts Exam Board), provide data about entries and completion rates; the Department for Education and Skills (DfES) provides tables showing completion rates of GNVQ by institution. The Further Education Funding Council (FEFC) collected statistical data about uptake and completion of GNVQ programmes in colleges (data now held by the Learning and Skills Council).

The goal of my research was to move beyond the statistical information available, and also to get behind the rhetoric of success offered in official announcements by the Awarding Bodies and by the National Council for Vocational Qualifications (NCVQ) (now the Qualifications and Curriculum Authority (QCA)). I wanted to examine the perceptions of teaching and learning in post-compulsory education expressed by staff and students involved in GNVQ. The intention was to use this to develop ideas about teacher and learner identity, linked to notions of learner autonomy and self-esteem. I also wanted to consider what insights the research offered about the development of 16–19 education for the future, particularly in the light of demands for a unified system and the increasing importance attached to lifelong learning.

The research took the form of a case study of one college of further education, using semi-structured interviews with staff and students in the college as the main research instrument. I aimed to get an overall picture of GNVQ at all three levels and across a range of different vocational areas. I selected three areas: Business, Information Technology and Science. The choices included one of the most popular GNVQs (Business), a GNVQ related to a traditional academic subject (Science) and a 'new technology' GNVQ (Information Technology). To cover the three different levels of GNVQ – Foundation, Intermediate and Advanced – I also interviewed staff and students in Foundation Studies, because the college organised the teaching of Foundation level separately. In addition, two senior managers in the college were interviewed. Three external verifiers, who are employed by Awarding Bodies to check the quality of assessment procedures, were interviewed; two were connected with the college, working as the college Edexel external verifiers for Business and Science. In addition, an external verifier for OCR was interviewed to gain a view from another Awarding Body.

Forty-Seven interviews were conducted in total. All the interviews were carried out by one interviewer (myself) over a period of one year. Interview schedules with a list of areas to cover in the form of questions were used as the basis for the interviews (see Figures 8.1 and 8.2). However, the schedules were not followed rigidly; interviewees were encouraged to talk about their

---

INTERVIEW SCHEDULE FOR STUDENTS

1 Choosing GNVQ
 Why did you choose GNVQ?
 How did you choose GNVQ?
 Views about doing GNVQ
 Academic achievement at school
 Views of: parents, school, peers

2 Why did you choose this college?

3 What's it like doing GNVQ?
 What do you enjoy?
 What don't you like?

4 What does doing GNVQ involve?
 Give an example of what you have to do for a unit or an assignment.
 What do you do in timetabled sessions?
 What do you do for/What do you think about:
 Grading themes   action planning
                    information seeking and information handling
                    evaluating
 Key skills   communication
                    application of number
                    IT
 Do you work in groups/individually? Which do you prefer?
 When and where do you do GNVQ work?

5 What makes a good GNVQ student?
 What makes a good GNVQ teacher?

6 What are you getting out of doing GNVQ? (emphasis on vocational

 knowledge or key skills or something else?)

7 Would you encourage friends or people in your family to do GNVQ?

8 Do you have a paid job as well as doing GNVQ?

9 The future
 What do you want to do next?
 What is your goal in approximately 3 years' time.
 Why?
 When/how did you decide?
 Who has helped you decide what to do?
 Has GNVQ affected your decision?

10 Conclusion of interview
 One thing you would change about you and what you have done so far?
 One thing you would change about GNVQ?

Figure 8.1   Interview schedule for students

experience, and questions were asked which followed the flow of the discussion, rather than following the order of the questions as listed. The schedules
were used to ensure that all areas were covered in each interview.

INTERVIEW SCHEDULE FOR GNVQ LECTURERS

1   Tell me a bit about what your job involves.

2   What is it like teaching GNVQ? What does it involve? Is it different to
    teaching on other qualifications?
    What's good about GNVQ?
    What's bad about GNVQ?

3   What do you think of
    Key skills
    Grading themes?

4   Who are your GNVQ students and what are they like?

5   What sort of skills do you need/what sort of person do you need to be to
    teach on GNVQ programmes? What makes the ideal GNVQ teacher?

6   What do you see GNVQ as for?
    Vocational qualification?
    Broad-based transferable skills?
    Route into employment?
    Route into education?

7   Would you encourage your own children to do a GNVQ?

8   How do you see the future and the place of GNVQ?

9   How did you come to be teaching in FE?

10 Do you see FE as having a particular role in the education system?

11 How do you see the future for you?

Figure 8.2   Interview schedule for GNVQ lecturers

By the time I had completed the interviews, I had a box full of tapes,
which translated into hundreds of pages of transcription. One interview was
anything from 7 to 26 pages of transcription, with longer being the norm. I
was faced with an enormous pile of interview transcriptions each of which
covered the issues in my interview schedule, but in no particular order; fur-
thermore the questions in my schedule did not necessarily appear in the
transcription, because an interviewee might talk about an issue without
prompting.

While I was the sole interviewer, two people completed the preliminary
transcription of the interviews from the tapes. I then checked the transcriptions by listening to the tapes and making corrections. Both processes are
very time consuming. It took experienced audiotypists using a transcriber (a
special tape-recorder with a foot pedal) approximately seven hours to transcribe one hour of tape. I spent a further three hours checking each hour of
tape.

Once transcribed I found that I rarely returned to the tapes. Pauses, hesita-
tions, coughing, and laughter were indicated in the original transcriptions,

though these were not used in the final presentation of findings. Tone of voice was often important but difficult to capture, and if it was not recorded as part of the transcription it was soon lost. I aimed to be as accurate as possible; however, every time I listened to a tape it sounded different. It was easy to become obsessed with trying to record accurately everything that was on the tape. For a small-scale study such as a Masters dissertation it is worth thinking carefully about whether it is necessary to complete full transcriptions of taped material. Tape-recordings may be used to assist with detailed notetaking for example, and transcription could be reserved for sections, which are particularly relevant to the study. However, I should warn that it may not be easy to determine what is relevant at an early stage; what turned out to be important in my study came from studying the transcripts at length.

At all stages of collecting the data, while interviewing, listening to the tapes, and reading the transcriptions, I was starting to develop ideas and make connections between what different interviewees were saying. When listening to the tapes I was able to think through what had been said and consider what was going on. Reading the transcriptions later presented the information in another way, and what Denzin (1998: 314) refers to as 'tales of the field' began to develop.

Organising and analysing the data

Qualitative researchers handle their data in different ways, but all face the need to organise the data collected for a study, and to analyse it in a way that offers a credible and meaningful account of the data in relation to the research questions they have identified. The User Guide for the NUD•IST software suggests that 'most qualitative researchers are assisted by developing a system of categories for thinking about their data, and by organizing it to some extent as their understanding develops' (Qualitative Solutions and Research, 1997: 74).

A number of options faced me as I began the process of organising and analysing, and settled into quiet panic as the quantity of data grew. First, I could approach the task manually, the method typically used by qualitative researchers. I was wary however of my ability to create chaos by chopping up bits of text and lose sight of where they had come from, based on the experience of cut-and-paste when writing papers. Second, I could use the advanced features of a word-processing package such as Microsoft Word. But at a seminar where the possibilities of this software were demonstrated, I got so confused about what I was doing to my text, which seemed to be either hidden (so I did not know what was there) or visible, but containing squiggles and highlighted text everywhere, that I abandoned this approach as a complicated and confusing activity. Third, I could use a dedicated computer-assisted qualitative data analysis software (CAQDAS) package such as NUD·IST. I did not undertake a detailed evaluation of different software.

I selected NUD·IST because the two programs readily available to me were Ethnograph and NUD·IST, and I preferred the flexibility of NUD·IST (it allows the user to make changes rapidly and easily). A further advantage was that a colleague had recently used NUD·IST, so I had ready access to advice from someone with experience of using the software. It is clear from the above comments that the decision to use NUD·IST was pragmatic and not based on thorough research of all the alternatives. Although the latter may be recommended, other potential users may well opt for similarly pragmatic solutions.

However, the study on which I was working was a more extensive piece of work than would be expected for a Masters dissertation, and the scale of any intended study needs to be taken into consideration when deciding whether to use qualitative data analysis software. I had 47 long transcripts; with smaller datasets it is worth thinking through the intended approach to analysis and considering the time involved in learning and using the program, which may detract from rather than support the process of working with the data.

Using NUD·IST

Overview of what NUD·IST does

Using NUD·IST is very straightforward. The software includes an introductory tutorial, which takes about five hours to complete. At the end of the five hours I was confident in using NUD·IST and understood how to seek further help from the printed manual and the help feature in the software, both of which are very clear and indexed in detail. At its simplest level, NUD·IST operates as a 'code and retrieve' program. The program has more complex features, which can be learned or ignored as the user develops familiarity with the software.

Textual data are imported into NUD·IST as separate documents. These data can then be 'coded', using categories defined by the researcher – the themes or headings, which are being used for analysing and making sense of the data. Codes are allocated to portions of data in each document by the user. All the data appearing under one category or code can then be called up or 'retrieved', turned into a separate document, and viewed or printed off. The headings or codes, which are called 'nodes' in NUD·IST, can be free-standing, but the user is encouraged to develop an index tree which gives a hierarchical structure to the coding system (see Figure 8.4, p. 170). Nodes can be moved, deleted and merged with other nodes at any time, so there is plenty of opportunity to change and adapt the index tree.

Memos can be written and attached to nodes and to the documents created through the coding process, so that ideas and thoughts about the data can be noted as the user is working with the data. The coding system can be modified, and links can be made between nodes so that Boolean searches can be carried out (linking codes by using AND, OR or NOT). NUD·IST is also designed to allow system closure, which means that any search done on the dataset and any memo can become an additional part of the data and can be searched in its own right. Probably the best and quickest way to learn how to use the software, and to get a hands-on idea of what NUD·IST can do, is to complete the introductory tutorial.

Preparing text for coding

Data are imported into NUD·IST in text files which remain as source files within a NUD·IST project throughout. Naming the files is an important consideration. I soon realised that for easy identification it was easier to work with files, which had a name (the name of the interviewee) rather than a number, a view shared by Buston (1997). I had to rename all my files, as I had originally saved them using numbers. Where names are going to be changed in the original data to preserve anonymity, it is worth doing it at this point. I found that if I changed names at a later stage, I ended up with some data using original names, and some using pseudonyms.

Within NUD·IST text is coded in units. This means that the user has to determine what a 'unit' is, usually either a line or a paragraph of text. It is not possible to highlight and code text starting and finishing in the middle of a line. This needs to be considered at an early stage in preparing data. Word-processing packages allow documents to be resaved as text with line breaks (see Figure 8.3), but if paragraphs are to be used as the unit of analysis, it is necessary to ensure in advance that the paragraph breaks are meaningful as separate units for coding. The paragraph breaks in the transcription of my interviews, for example, equate with the change from interviewer to interviewee. An interviewee might cover a number of issues in one response (paragraph), which would lead to irrelevant text appearing under a particular code. I imagine that many users, like myself, therefore use each line as a text unit.

Coding data

Once text has been prepared, the files containing the text are imported into a NUD·IST project and can then be coded. The user is required to name 'nodes' which can then be used to code the text. The approach to coding in NUD·IST encourages the user to work top-down. The first node or code in a tree denotes higher level, general, overarching relationships, followed by

AMB: Are the teachers different in college?
SUSANNE: Yeah, the teachers are much different. They're more like normal people.
            Teachers at school are just like, they don't even seem like people. You
            couldn't imagine them having a lifestyle. The teachers at college they
            just seem nice, like people you can just talk to, and they tell you the
            work to do and just help you through it.

Figure 8.3 Excerpt from an interview with a student, formatted as text with line
breaks

increasingly specific nodes. It is possible to start with free nodes, which stand on their own and are not related to other nodes, but the system encourages the user to create a tree, which I did. It means that the first coding of text, which takes place is attached to nodes which appear at various levels in the hierarchy of the index tree.

Weitzman and Miles suggest that 'This is quite different conceptually than the normal situation in which all your codes are at the same level, with varying levels of abstraction above them' (1995: 252). They believe that normally a researcher would start by coding or categorising the material at one level, then start to see relationships which bring things together and only then link these together at a higher-order level. This is in fact what I eventually did, but I did so by abandoning NUD·IST and working with a combination of printouts from the nodes and the full transcripts of the interview data. Initially, though, I drew up a list of themes to look for and created an index system with these themes. I then read through each interview on screen and coded the text. As I worked through the interviews, I added new nodes or codes to the index system resulting in a long index tree (see Figure 8.4).

Richards and Richards (1995) describe two approaches to coding: a bottom-up, data-driven method, where the researcher builds up hierarchical categories by starting to code with specific categories then thinking about more general categories which link specific categories together. The other approach is a top-down theory-driven approach, where general categories are determined in advance, and the purpose of the research is to test out a hypothesis, and to show whether the categories apply and are elucidated in the data.

They offer a number of principles of tree construction, including these important points:

- The relationship between higher level nodes and those which branch off below them should be general to specific: kind to instances, thing to parts, concept to examples.
- The description of a category should apply to all categories in the sub-tree, for example canines/types; behaviour/types. Canines should not be used as a category for both types and behaviour.

```
(1)         /identity
(1 1)       /identity/staff
(1 1 1)     /identity/staff/biography
(1 1 2)     /identity/staff/future
(1 1 3)     /identity/staff/work on GNVQ
(1 2)       /identity/students
(1 2 1)     /identity/students/biography
(1 2 2)     /identity/students/destinations
(2)         /GNVQ
(2 2)       /GNVQ/compare other quals
(2 3)       /GNVQ/perceptions
(2 3 1)     /GNVQ/perceptions/future
(2 3 2)     /GNVQ/perceptions/your children
(2 4)       /GNVQ/purpose
(2 5)       /GNVQ/students
(2 7)       /GNVQ/R staff students
(3)         /T&L GNVQ
(3 1)       /T&L GNVQ/teaching GNVQ
(3 2)       /T&L GNVQ/learning GNVQ
(3 3)       /T&L GNVQ/assessment GNVQ
(3 3 1)     /T&L GNVQ/assessment GNVQ/exams
(3 3 2)     /T&L GNVQ/assessment GNVQ/assignments
(3 4)       /T&L GNVQ/paperwork GNVQ
(3 5)       /T&L GNVQ/tracking
(3 6)       /T&L GNVQ/monitoring progress
(3 7)       /T&L GNVQ/progression
(3 8)       /T&L GNVQ/GNVQ programme
(4)         /key skills
(4 1)       /key skills/staff
(4 2)       /key skills/students
(4 3)       /key skills/communication
(4 4)       /key skills/application of number
(4 5)       /key skills/IT
(5)         /grading themes
(5 1)       /grading themes/action planning
(5 2)       /grading themes/information
(5 3)       /grading themes/evaluation
(6)         /FE general
(6 1)       /FE general/perceptions of FE
(6 2)       /FE general/teaching in FE
(6 3)       /FE general/changes
(6 4)       /FE general/T&L not GNVQ
```

Figure 8.4   NUD·IST index tree for GNVQ project

- A rule of 'one place only' should be applied, meaning that one topic or idea should occur only in one place in the index system.

I read this advice retrospectively, and the index tree in Figure 8.4 did not always adhere to these principles.

   In the middle of coding the interviews I went on holiday. On my return, the index tree seemed to have developed a life of its own. What did each node mean? I had given definitions to some but not others. There seemed to be unidentifiable but very fine nuances between different nodes. A combination of the break, and reading the printouts, led me to reorganise coding and to recode quite a lot of text. I think this was partly because I allowed myself to be seduced into using a hierarchical tree structure when I should have coded on one level only, a problem raised by Stanley and Temple (1995).

I found there was a difference between the way I originally organised the data, and the categories, which developed as the analysis progressed. I started out using categories which reflected the questions in the interview schedule, such as students' and teachers' biographies, perceptions of doing key skills and grading themes, views about assessment, and plans for the future. My eventual categories for analysis cut across these organising themes, and focused on a range of factors affecting perceptions of teaching and learning, including individuals' previous learning career, the relationships between teachers and students, and imagined futures.

Nevertheless, patterns were beginning to emerge which were important to my overall interpretation of the data. For example, the relationship between staff and students was coming up again and again, and my most pertinent question turned out to be 'Would you encourage your own children to do GNVQ?' (to staff) or 'Would you encourage your friends or family to do GNVQ?' (to students). There was more information about people's perceptions of GNVQ, its status, and its future from this question than from any other.

Working with the coded data

Once data has been coded, a report can be made for each node in the index tree, bringing together all material gathered under a particular coding, which can then be printed off and Figure 8.5 shows what such a report looks like. The report ensures that the user knows where the printout is from, and what it refers to, by showing the number allocated to the node which has been printed off in the top left-hand corner (2 3 2) and the name which has been given to that node next to it (GNVNQ/perceptions/your children). The report also shows the definition which the user has given to the node (Definition: Would you encourage your children to do GNVQ?). The report then contains chunks of text from different documents, which have been allocated to that node. In the example, text from two original transcript documents are shown, first from Mike's transcript, and second from Louise's. For each of these, the origin of the text is shown (for example, online document: Mike), and what percentage of the whole of the original document this represents (for Mike, 20 units out of 1756, = 1.1%). The printout also shows which text units from the whole document the excerpt represents (for Mike, text units 1309–1328). Thus each report allows the user to locate the origin of any text quickly and easily.

(2 3 2)   /GNVQ/perceptions/your children
*** Definition:
Would you encourage your children to do GNVQ?
+++
+++ ON-LINE DOCUMENT: MIKE
+++ Retrieval for this document: 20 units out of 1756, = 1.1%
++Text units 1309–1328:

AMB: Yes, yeah. So I don't know if you've got children, but would you encourage
your children to do a GNVQ?

MIKE: I have got twins, a boy and a girl and I would think it would be very suitable for
my daughter, because she's a sort of average performer academically and it
would be, she's quite interested in certain types of jobs. She's 14 at the moment
so I could see her doing something like a Health and Social Care or a, if not that
then an NNEB type thing perhaps as a prelude to going to college to train as a
teacher or something or maybe, I suppose the GNVQ would be the better one,
really. Whether I'd say that about my son I don't know 'cause he goes to a
grammar school and he's got a reasonable chance of doing OK in his GCSEs
and A-Levels. So, but if wished, if he came at 16 and said I really don't want to
carry on doing this I want to do Theatre Studies GNVQ or Media Studies
I'd say well, if that's what you want to do.

AMB: Yeah

MIKE: Do it, it's your life. I think there is a certain snobbishness about would you let
your children come to this college. There is an issue, I think there definitely.
+++
+++ ON-LINE DOCUMENT: LOUISE
+++ Retrieval for this document: 4 units out of 442, = 0.90%
++Text units 351–354:

LOUISE: I wouldn't encourage my own children to come to the college. There is not enough
control now, so a young student can drift. That's to do with the contact time and the lack of
whole group teaching. I think the GNVQ is OK, it's the college environment that I'm less
happy about.
++

Figure 8.5   NUD·IST printout for one node

Once I had coded the data, by allocating all data to 'nodes', I printed off
reports for each node, and worked from the printouts. This was very important to me; although I write straight onto the computer a great deal, I find
reading on screen very different from reading printed text. I feel that I understand

things differently and better through printed text. Reading the reports for each node told me whether I had bracketed the extracts sufficiently so that what I had coded included enough information either side of a comment to make sense and give enough context. It also told me whether I was applying my categories in the same way across the data, or whether when I worked on one interview I put things under one node, and when I worked on another, I coded differently. In addition, I went back to my recollections of the interviews and considered whether what I was reading fitted in with how it had seemed then.

This contextual locating is important for interpreting qualitative data. Fielding and Lee comment that 'how one interprets a particular utterance in an interview, say, depends on the context within which that utterance is made' (1998: 57). It is therefore important to be able to retain the original context in the analytic process and switch back and forth between analytic material and the original data. They believe that the process of returning to the data time and again transforms the analysis 'as one's familiarity with the data increases, one's analytic understanding of it is transformed' (1998: 57). They argue that the process is made easier with computer software, because data can be located more quickly. However, this apparent benefit is seen as a disadvantage by critics of CAQDAS, who believe that the software may distance researchers from their original data. Just as a researcher may never listen to the tapes again once they have been transcribed, this may equally apply to the transcriptions once they have been coded in NUD·IST, and the researcher may never look at the transcription as a whole again, concentrating instead on chunks of text and the index system.

Reflections on using the software

The index system

The index system is central to software such as NUD·IST. Weitzman and Miles (1994: 241) describe it as 'the real heart of the program'. It is this feature of NUD·IST which indicates the real intentions of the software. The software developers Richards and Richards (1995), express two very clear views about categorisation; first, that categories emerge from the data, and second that more important than the categories themselves is the link which is made between categories.

> Coding bits of data as particular categories supports the process of theory emergence and theory construction only if the categories and their links to each other are structured and explored. (1995: 80–1)

They encourage the user to create a hierarchical index tree system and then to study the relationships of codes and believe that:

> unstructured categories do not present us with an organizational structure, making systematic surveying, orderly analysis and retrieval, and the presentation of one's concepts as an ordered system with meaning and coherence, impossible. (1995: 91)

This orderly, accountable approach is supported by Buston who describes the role of NUD•IST as allowing the creation of a comprehensive and systematic indexing system, 'facilitating the development of theory in a highly organised and systematic way' (1997: para. 10.5).

For Stanley and Temple (1995) these issues are problematic. They disagree with the view that categories and meaning are in the data waiting to be found. Instead, they argue that researchers develop their own interpretations and need to try to make this explicit. They also question the use of variable analysis, because it places an emphasis on causal links between variables:

> Built into variable analysis is a related assumption, that if variables can be correlated, then this means that the link between them is causal, with one variable (the independent variable) causally affecting the other (the dependent variable). (Stanley and Temple, 1995: 177)

Similarly, Weitzman and Miles are not convinced of the benefit of hierarchical structures:

> Working with a hierarchically structured tree of codes (or nodes) forces you to think about the relationship among your codes and strongly encourages you to do it in hierarchical terms. This may or may not be a good thing. (1995: 252)

Although I did not develop any form of variable analysis, I found that as I worked with NUD•IST, I became immersed in the index system rather than the data itself. Weitzman and Miles warn:

> The one real drawback here is that NUD•IST tends to distance you from your data. You develop a very intimate feel for your index system, and can retrieve from it easily, but you don't see your hits in context. The only time you work from a view of your text is when you code, though you can keep text windows and document report windows open on the screen and go back and forth to explore things. (1995: 255)

Indeed, that is exactly what LeCompte and Preissle (1993), proponents of NUD•IST's approach, would encourage. They state that:

> Theory-building programs consequently allow the researcher to move away from the raw data, to concentrate on the conceptual notions they contained, and to ponder and visualize these concepts. The classificatory system, used as an organizing tool in descriptive-interpretive studies, is refined and elaborated. Patterns are discovered and complex new categories created from simple ones by establishing relationships, until the system becomes the result of the study. (LeCompte and Preissle, 1993: 304)

Does all this matter if the software is only being used to cut and paste? As Stanley and Temple, who are critical of such software, suggest:

> The Ethnograph and NUD·IST are particularly good at retrieving and placing in a separate file a range of pieces of text which have been coded or indexed in a particular way, complete with the line-numbers of this text. (1995: 189–190)

However, what this meant in practice was that I used NUD·IST to cut and paste, and then abandoned the software and worked from the node print-outs and my original transcriptions to continue with the analysis. Although I found the coding of material useful, the findings developed away from NUD·IST, as I immersed myself in the data in more traditional ways, by reading notes, transcriptions and printouts, and comparing my data with other literature in the field. The findings I eventually reported were derived in part from the original analysis I did using NUD·IST, but they were also based on a considerable amount of further work, which did not involve developing a complex index tree, but immersing myself in the data.

Concerns about the use of CAQDAS

There is considerable debate about the strengths and limitations of using computer software programs for qualitative research, and the effect they can have on the research project. While LeCompte and Preissle unquestioningly recommend the use of qualitative data analysis programs and claim of computers that 'in themselves, they have no influence on the research process' (1993: 279), other researchers, including the designers of NUD·IST (see Richards and Richards, 1998) are more cautious, and discuss the possible effects of CAQDAS in some detail.

There is some concern about the emphasis given to code and retrieve methods, which may encourage researchers to see this method as the only way to deal with qualitative data. The designers themselves (Richards and Richards, 1998) point out that many researchers do not use code and retrieve, and many more would not if the software did not support it.

> Before computers, many researchers did not code segments of text. Rather, they felt through, explored, read and reread … . This required a simpler and more complex form of data management, as researchers compared and systematically built upon data records, keeping growing memo records about the accruing evidence and their exploration of its narrative and convincing body. Theory was arrived at and tested not through the retrieval of text chunks but through complex processes of evidence analysis, including consideration of knowledge about the site or story that is not in the text. (Richards and Richards, 1998: 214)

The concern with an orderly, organised system links with claims made by programs such as NUD·IST to achieve enhanced validity, reliability and generalisability. These claims appear to be based very much on understandings from quantitative research. Fielding and Lee (1998), for example, suggest that the software makes replication of a study much more feasible. The facility to keep a log or trail of analytic procedures, which many CAQDAS programs offer, appears to allow for easy replication. It may also make larger-scale research easier, both in terms of numbers of researchers involved and the size of the study. Fielding and Lee thus believe that CAQDAS can give legitimacy and credibility to qualitative research, suggesting that:

> There is sometimes a suspicion that the analyst has done little more than string together a series of 'juicy' quotes extracted from transcripts. By contrast, the computer encourages users to be clear about what they are doing. (1998: 58)

And Richards and Richards claim that CAQDAS is an important means of validating qualitative research:

> critical examination and reporting of the indexing process is central to validation. By reflection on and documentation of the process of category construction, the researcher accounts for and argues for interpretations. Categories need to be documented by an 'audit' trail recording not only the relationship of categories to each other, but also the origins and histories of categories. (1995: 81)

However, Coffey, Holbrook and Atkinson are very critical of the above views and warn that:

> It is important to avoid the misapprehension that coding and computing lend a scientific gloss to qualitative research. The growing 'respectability' of qualitative methods, together with an adherence to canons of rigour associated primarily with other research traditions, can lead to the imposition of spurious standards. (1996: para. 7.6)

In their response to Coffey, Holbrook and Atkinson (1996), Lee and Fielding (1996) argue that: 'Far from propagating an orthodoxy, developers, popularizers and commentators have often stressed the need for epistemological awareness and debate in relation to software use' (1996: para. 2.2). They believe that computer-based methods allow for the multi-tooling of qualitative researchers, 'making available to them more or less at will a wide range of different analytic strategies'. However, even if one agrees with Lee and Fielding, the caveat should remain: 'did you *want* to do that?' (Richards and Richards, 1998: 212), or in the words of Stanley and Temple:

> researchers need to commence any piece of research by asking some fundamental and linked questions about just what kind of analysis they want to carry out and what kinds of analytic outcomes they want the research to produce. (1995: 178)

Conclusion: Do you want to do that?

NUD·IST allowed me to bring together relevant text from 47 interviews a great deal more easily than if I had attempted to manually cut and paste the material. However, the interpretation of the data, and telling the story, came from detailed reading of the interviews, talking about them to others, as well as reading the excerpts placed under each theme, and I did not exploit the theorising capabilities of the software. I would suggest to others considering using such programs to try out the software using the tutorials provided. While doing this, it is important not to be seduced by what the software can do, but to ask: 'did you *want* to do that?' (Richards and Richards, 1998: 212). As Buston suggests: 'What is important is for the researcher to be aware of why he/she is doing things, and to ensure that these things are not just being done because the package can do them, quickly and easily' (1997: para. 13.5).

I conclude with three common commitments for qualitative researchers, identified by Denzin (1998: 339):

- First – 'the world of human experience must be studied from the point of view of the historically and culturally situated individual'.
- Second – 'qualitative researchers will persist in working outward from their own biographies to the worlds of experience that surround them'.
- Third – 'scholars will continue to value and seek to produce works that speak clearly and powerfully about these worlds'.

I would not wish the power of CAQDAS to allow the authority of the carefully constructed index tree to replace these underlying commitments of qualitative research.

Summary

This chapter offers a helpful insight into the potential value and possible pitfalls in the use of CAQDAS programs, such as NUD·IST, for qualitative data analysis. Working from personal experience the chapter starts with an overview of how NUD·IST was used to help with the analysis of 47 interviews obtained during a research project designed to examine the perceptions of teaching and learning in post-compulsory education expressed by staff and students involved in General National Vocational Qualification (GNVQ). This in itself is of value and amongst other things highlights the importance of getting to know someone who has used any particular CAQDAS you have available for your own use in order to advise you.

It does not stop at this pragmatic level though as it then addresses the more important procedural question of how might the application of CAQDAS affect one's analysis of the data? It presents an answer to this question, through the viewpoint of various authors, concerned with the debate about the strengths and limitations about the use of CAQDAS. Many of these authors are not directly quoted but can be found within the web pages quoted in the references.

Overall then this chapter provides a constructive and informative discussion which will undoubtedly be of value for Masters students coming to the area of CAQDAS, possibly for the first time.

9

Using ATLAS.ti

Michael Pomerantz

What is ATLAS.ti?

ATLAS.ti is an innovative and imaginative computer software application that allows the user to study and analyse text (such as interview transcripts) and add additional coding so that it is easy to categorise or code short or long text segments for comparisons and easy retrieval at a later time.

I have been asked to write this chapter with the needs of those relatively new to research in mind. There are all sorts of technical instructions, messages and warnings to convey to beginners but readers can find this elsewhere. In particular the Atlas.ti website http://atlasti.de/index.html, provides a wide variety of sources of information and available support for example a bibliography http://www.atlasti.de/bibliography.shtml and online tutorials provided by Thomas Muhr who devised ATLAS.ti http://www.atlasti.de/demo.shtml. Given my intended audience it seems more appropriate, before going into detail about this application, that I provide a story as to why and how I use it.

My background is in educational psychology and my original training was in America with a quantitative bias to conducting educational research looking at reading and motivation. For years I used SPSS (the Statistical Package for the Social Sciences) in its various versions and still do quite happily when I need to analyse numerical data. I was trained to conduct psychological research with experimental and control groups who were subject to different teaching methods. We then used statistical procedures like analysis of variance to measure the effects.

Then I came to work in England 26 years ago, employed as an educational psychologist. Beginning in 1983 I was appointed as an associate tutor to the postgraduate programme training educational psychologists at the University of Sheffield. This has afforded me ample opportunity to work with students learning the basics of conducting research primarily in educational settings. The procedures used by our students have included mostly questionnaire surveys, interviews and observations.

Several years ago I was involved in designing and launching a new doctoral training programme for practising educational psychologists in England. The target student audience and the staff seemed to demonstrate a preference from the start for qualitative research methods rather than activities that resulted in the production of large batteries of numbers. Our researchers were more interested in making good qualitative descriptions about what they saw or heard rather than proving a hypothesis that had been previously stated. They were seeking a better understanding of fundamental educational processes. They were attracted to a grounded theory approach and were reading texts on this area by Strauss and Corbin (1998) and Miles and Huberman (1994).

Imagine yourself at the conception or early development phase in a research project and trying to discover the 'best' way to gather and then interpret information. Researchers often begin to ask questions of people in one of two ways, either by drafting a written questionnaire or by interviewing subjects with a set of questions. As we have seen (Chapter 6) there is considerable latitude as to just how highly structured these questions are.

It is here where some basic decisions will be taken that will move you down a route that is predominantly quantitative or qualitative although the dividing line between these two extreme methodology positions is not always that clear. The questions could be structured in a variety of ways. If it calls for the respondent to make forced choices like we see in the Likert type rating scale (see Chapter 10, p. 212) it would produce basically quantitative information. If a sample of respondents answered these questions orally or in written form we could build up a statistical summary showing us the average or most frequent responses. Different groups or samples could be compared in the way they responded.

Alternatively the questions could be devised with less structure and with just a few probing questions and the request that the respondent respond orally or write a paragraph as the response and the result would be much more qualitative. The result would not lend itself to rigorous number crunching data analysis.

If you are learning the art and science of conducting research it would be preferable for you to explore and use a range of methodologies (see Chapters 1 and 2) along the quantitative–qualitative continuum. You will probably discover some hybrid methods where the technique employs both ends of the spectrum.

My colleagues and students were more prone to want to interview people and engage in real live dialogue (with all its attendant problems like subjective bias) than remain with the more structured questionnaire format that results in such a paucity of information even if you ask a lot of questions.

I had been reading the output of many such investigations at the Masters and doctoral level where researchers were interviewing people with a tape-recorder and then having the interview session tapes transcribed either by a secretary or by themselves prior to embarking on a textual analysis of what was being said. The grounded theory approach suggests that the researcher first read the transcriptions to get a feel for what is being communicated and to generate a range of themes or ideas that appear in the discussions. From this the researcher starts to place codes in the text perhaps through underlining or making notes in the margins. If the volume of transcribed data is manageable the reader might analyse the transcripts several times looking to be thorough and to capture the essence of what is being stated through the use of codes. However, when there are a lot of long interviews this can become a huge task and there is a limit to how much coloured ink one can add to a transcribed text before it becomes difficult to read.

ATLAS.ti attempts to make the coding and all the subsequent analysis easier for the researcher. Like many other tools it will take some time to learn how to use it but the dividends are potentially enormous. My preferred introduction would be in a gentle tutorial with a guide who is familiar with the use and practice of ATLAS.ti. But you are probably not there yet. You probably need some convincing before you think of accessing the product and teaching yourself how to use it for your unique research problems.

To assist I would like to share with you the experience that I had and why I made the decision to use ATLAS.ti and in this way hopefully help you decide whether or not to look further at information technology tools to facilitate qualitative research.

For a start I was around all these colleagues and students who were committed to interviewing people and then painstakingly studying the resultant word-processed transcripts. Those with information technology inclinations started to look at the wide range of products on the market that addresses this research need. One colleague seemed interested in ATLAS.ti amongst others and that is where it started for me. He had attended a number of taught courses at another university each addressing a different software application.

Later we obtained a site license for ATLAS.ti and that is where the story begins. I did not ever attend a taught course but I did repeatedly run through the numerous brief online recorded tutorials that Thomas Muhr has made available for beginners. I read the manual and I practised a lot. It was helpful to share experiences with the colleague who had also completed some training and who was using ATLAS.ti for his own research.

In 2000 I took a study leave from my university position with the expressed intention of conducting a research project looking at the needs of able underachieving pupils. I intended to interview them and use ATLAS.ti to assist with the coding, analysis and interpretation of the data. The project then would result in both doing the research and getting 'hands-on' experience with ATLAS.ti.

Project methodology overview

This introduction is intended to show the reader some of the preliminary concerns and outcomes of the project thus far. The original plan was to investigate the behaviour and the views of pupils in secondary education described as being able but tending to underachieve. The key research questions from the start were:

1   What causes able pupils to underachieve in school?
2   What interventions could be implemented to reduce underachievement?

Context

This particular survey project is nested within a larger programme that has wider intentions and applications. I was planning to write a longer paper addressing issues like change within schools, separating pupils into sets based on ability, preferences and needs, the new summer schools for gifted pupils, best practice innovations coming from the literature and comments made by staff during the survey. I was privileged to be able to work closely with a Local Education Authority (LEA) Adviser in researching policy statements about More Able Pupils (MAPs), to teach in three summer schools for MAPs, to train Newly Qualified Teachers (NQTs) about the needs of MAPs and to work to create a network to support teachers interested in MAPs.

The wider project was also intended to provide a focus for me to test out the computer software ATLAS.ti that allows researchers to scrutinise interview transcripts with greater depth, precision and thoroughness than has applied with more traditional qualitative research methods employing a grounded theory foundation.

Selection

A decision was taken to interview randomly selected Year 9 able underachievers (AUs) using a set of 36 questions in a semi-structured format, which was tape-recorded. All interviews were done with the same interviewer for continuity. The interviews took place during the summer term of 2000.

The work took place within one large predominantly rural LEA where a cross-section of 11 comprehensive schools was selected randomly. Subsequent analyses comparing these schools with the remainder of the LEA secondary schools on the basis of GCSE results and school size showed that the randomisation procedure had been effective and that the selected schools were not statistically different from the other schools in those areas where comparative measures were used.

Next, headteachers (HTs) were approached both by telephone call and later by letter with the recommended protocol for randomly selecting a small number of AUs to interview (see Figure 9.1). The letter to them appears below and is reproduced here just to give you yet another example of a way of seeking the involvement of participants in your research. You may find this letter a little too informal but ask yourself does it grab my interest more than a formal request for involvement might? Could I use this semi-informality in my own setting and culture? What advantages or limitations might its use have? Note that for brevity I have removed the normal courtesy introduction about the project and the final part of thanking the receiver for their antici-pated support. The actual letter was also in a larger font.

HTs responded to this invitation with enthusiasm although there were some problems with the CAT score criteria that were included as a safe-guard. Basically we wanted to use multiple selection criteria to avoid inter-viewing candidates who might not be that able but just appeared so to the teachers. Unfortunately some HTs either did not have the CAT data (as with a pupil transferring into the LEA from a school that did not use CAT tests) or felt inclined to offer candidates slightly below the 115 standardised score. In a few cases the figure might have dropped to 112. Rather than discard the candidate he or she was included as planned.

When 26 AUs were identified and we had both individual student and parental permission to interview, the selection process stopped. In the end 26 pupils were interviewed from 11 comprehensive schools. There were five girls and 21 boys in the cohort. None of those interviewed were from an eth-nic minority group.

Interview procedure

The subjects were interviewed individually in a small quiet room in their school at a mutually agreed time. Sessions lasted from 20 to 30 minutes on average. After a brief introduction with reassurances about the research pro-ject and confidentiality the planned 36 questions were administered with follow-up questioning as and where appropriate. The intent was to elicit as much information as possible from the candidate in their individual responses. All sessions were tape-recorded and subsequently transcribed by a word-processor operator who was unaware of the scope of the research project.

Interview schedule content

Prior to writing and editing the 36 questions for the semi-structured inter-views, the literature on able, talented and gifted pupils was addressed to produce a range of constructs that might have some bearing on the processes

Dear ....

By way of introduction I am writing to seek your assistance with a research project that focuses on underachievement amongst more able Yr. 9 pupils in secondary education. I hope to interview about 24 pupils during June and am asking if you can help with the careful and unbiased selection of this student cohort that I wish to interview. I trust that by the time you have this letter in your possession we would have discussed the proposal and my specific request over the phone. What follows is designed to add to what we have already discussed.

You will be aware that underachievement is a cause of serious concern that has implications both for schools and for students. The size and the scope of this have never been accurately measured and the current research project is not intended to do this. Rather it is an exploratory study designed to listen to pupil perspectives on the causes of underachievement and suggestions to reduce underachievement.

Here is a bit of an analogy to whet your appetite. You might want to compare the functioning of a newly commissioned ship with an older vessel. The new one is fast and the old one is slow when moving through the water. The new one has a sleek hull and it cuts through the water like a knife. If the latter boat is placed in a dry-dock it becomes immediately apparent that its hull is encrusted with thick deposits of barnacles and seaweed which introduces tremendous drag when cruising through the ocean. Underachievers have the potential to slow substantially the attainments of schools by introducing drag and a wasteful deployment of scarce resources.

The analogy gets worse when one studies the toxic effects of chemical treatments designed to stop the damaging adherence of barnacles on hulls. Special paint might have seemed like an elegant preventative measure initially but the steps taken to solve the problem have actually introduced new and serious poisonous side effects that now need to be addressed. Prior to making systemic suggestions about how to reduce underachievement this local research activity is designed to ask more able young people who are underachieving to give us their views on causation and intervention.

I have randomly selected a few local secondary schools of which yours is one. If you are willing I would ask that you consult colleagues and produce a list of pupils whom you would describe as more able underachievers. To meet the criteria they would need to satisfy the following conditions:

- In Yr. 7 the pupil scored 115 or better on the non-verbal CAT sub-test
- The staff would describe the pupil as a more able underachiever
- The parents would agree that the pupil is a more able underachiever
- The pupil himself or herself agrees that they are underachieving

If you were to look at the top 20% of your Yr. 9 student population (based on CAT scores) this might amount to about 36 pupils in a school with 180 in a year group. Amongst these 36 pupils I would ask you to identify up to 12 whom the staff feel are talented but not working up to their potential. This cautiously amounts to one third of the group. The selection ought to include both boys and girls and pupils from ethnic minority groups if present. In smaller secondary schools we would obviously be expecting less candidates.

If you could supply me with a list of names then I would like to randomly select about three or four so as to minimise any bias that might creep into the selection procedure. I really do want to avoid any subsequent criticism that schools pre-selected subjects who were deemed to be co-operative or particularly willing. We would then need to secure the permission of both the parents and the pupils in allowing me to conduct these student interviews that should only last for about 30 minutes each. If we fail to secure permission for a given student we would randomly choose a replacement.

Yours sincerely,

Michael Pomerantz, PhD

Senior Educational Psychologist

Figure 9.1   Example letter to headteachers seeking research involvement

underlying underachievement. The initial list of bipolar constructs is reproduced in Table 9.1. Using this list as a starting point questions were drafted and then subjected to two separate pilot exercises to assess their suitability and usefulness. Questions that appeared ambiguous, confusing or redundant were revised or omitted. We did not want interviews to run over 30 minutes. In the end the final list of questions that was used is reproduced in Figure 9.2.

Analysis of the audio transcripts with ATLAS.ti

All the tape-recordings were transcribed and stored as MS Word files. A cross-section was checked for transcription accuracy and were found to be very good reproductions of what was said in the interviews. There were very few instances when the word-processor operator was unable to transcribe what was said and this inevitably was caused by background noise for example when bells were ringing in schools and the volume of noisy conversation outside the interview room increased. When it was really interfering the interviews were temporarily interrupted. If ever considering the use of tape-recording interviews in noisy environments then consideration should be given to the problems of background noise that could make subsequent transcribing very difficult indeed if not impossible (see also Chapter 6, p. 120).

Subsequently the 26 Word transcripts were converted into narrower width text files (about 10 cm across) with line breaks. This is easily done within the 'save' options found in MS Word. This was done to facilitate importing the text into the ATLAS.ti hermeneutic unit which is where all the text and the codes are stored. Think of a hermeneutic unit as a container.

By importing the 26 narrow width transcripts with line breaks into the ATLAS.ti software application with each containing dialogue associated with the 36 key items with follow-up questions, the user is able to analyse the resulting matrix of text or prose. In summary the entire set of transcripts contain over 65,000 words. Each word belongs to one of 936 cells formed by the cross-section of 26 subjects by 36 questions. This would very roughly average about 70 words in each cell. This is considerably more data than, for example, might be obtained using a quantitative approach such as a written questionnaire with 36 Likert type (forced choice) responses being requested and the researcher getting 36 responses times 26 subjects with a grand total of 936 bits of data. This would be only one or two percent of the data that the qualitative method obtained from the respondents.

This is no small difference when it comes to assessing what the research has to address. While the qualitative method gets us much more data to study we are subsequently challenged to find a rigorous method to analyse that same data. This is where ATLAS.ti comes to the rescue if one takes the

Table 9.1   Bipolar constructs influencing achievement and underachievement

Positive pole = facilitating	Negative pole = debilitating
1 Anxiety (positive)	Anxiety (negative)
2 Aspirations (high)	Aspirations (low)
3 Attribution (internal)	Attribution (external)
4 Boredom (low)	Boredom (high)
5 Challenge appropriate	Challenge inappropriate
6 Competition helps	Competition hinders
7 Concentration good	Concentration weak
8 Confidence strong	Confidence weak
9 Conformity fosters achievement	Conformity hinders achievement
10 Curriculum appropriate	Curriculum inappropriate
11 Culture: Success is comfortable	Culture: Success is not comfortable
12 Dependency (low)	Dependency (high)
13 External reinforcement	External punishment
14 Fears are constructive	Fears are not constructive
15 Fear of failure (low)	Fear of failure (high)
16 Identity established	Identity not established
17 Learning model (adult)	Learning model (child)
18 Mentor available	Mentor not available
19 Mistakes promote learning	Mistakes interfere with learning
20 Motivation (high)	Motivation (low)
21 Needs met	Needs unmet
22 Opportunities are present	Opportunities are absent
23 Parent attitudes (positive)	Parent attitudes (negative)
24 Parent behaviour (positive)	Parent behaviour (negative)
25 Parent expectations (positive)	Parent expectations (negative)
26 Parent pressure (positive)	Parent pressure (negative)
27 Peer attitudes (positive)	Peer attitudes (negative)
28 Peer behaviour (positive)	Peer behaviour (negative)
29 Peer expectations (positive)	Peer expectations (negative)
30 Peer pressure (positive)	Peer pressure (negative)
31 Persistence (high)	Persistence (low)
32 Pupil culture and social world (positive)	Pupil culture and social world (negative)
33 Repetition infrequent	Repetition excessive
34 Research skills developed	Research skills under-developed
35 Responsibility (high)	Responsibility (low)
36 Risk taking (positive)	Risk taking (negative)
37 Role models (positive)	Role models (negative)
38 Self-discipline established	Self-discipline missing
39 Self-esteem (high)	Self-esteem (low)
40 Self-assessment (high)	Self-assessment (low)
41 Setting high standards	Setting low standards
42 Sibling attitudes (positive)	Sibling attitudes (negative)
43 Sibling behaviour (positive)	Sibling behaviour (negative)
44 Sibling expectations (positive)	Sibling expectations (negative)
45 Sibling pressure (positive)	Sibling pressure (negative)
46 Teacher attitudes (positive)	Teacher attitudes (negative)
47 Teacher behaviour (positive)	Teacher behaviour (negative)
48 Teacher expectations (positive)	Teacher expectations (negative)
49 Teacher pressure (positive)	Teacher pressure (negative)
50 Teamwork (positive)	Teamwork (negative)
51 Time management (positive)	Time management (negative)

Able Underachiever Interview Schedule (Revised)
20 May 2000

Number:
Pupil:
School:
Date:

Curriculum:

1   What gives you a buzz or excitement in and out of school?
2   What turns you off or bores you in or out of school?
3   When do you find the work really demanding in school? (Elaborate)
4   Have you ever had the opportunity to join an interesting activity or group either in or outside of school? (Elaborate)
5   If something really interested or excited you in school how would you develop this?

Attributes:

6   Tell me what your favourite teachers are like.
7   What do some teachers do that cause you to dislike them?

Influences:

8   What do your teachers do to encourage or discourage your progress in school? (Probe if necessary)

Who do you live with at home?

9   What do your *parent(s) [or carer(s)]* do to encourage or discourage your progress in school? (Probe if necessary)
10 Tell me about the other pupils that you like to spend time with. What are they like?
11 What do other pupils do to encourage or discourage your progress in school? (Probe if necessary)
12 Would your friends say the same thing?
13 Do your brothers or sisters exert any influence on your work and if so how?
14 In this school what do your friends think about clever pupils? (If the response is negative probe for reasons and interventions to change attitudes.)
15 How often do you feel there is a conflict of interest between advice from your teachers and your friends?

Self:

16 What do like about yourself?
17 What do you dislike about yourself?
18 Do you think that worrying interferes with your learning in school? (Probe for examples)
19 What characteristics do you feel you possess that are not valued by your teachers, friends, or parents?
20 Do you believe that you are not really working up to your ability? (If 'Yes,') how do you know this?
21 What do you do differently to other students in school who achieve at a higher level than you do?
22 Do you think in general that you are good at learning?
23 How do you know that?

Interventions:

24 How do you learn best?
25 Have you developed your own study skills? ... What are they?

(Continued)

26   What do you do when you are bored or not engaged that helps to get you back to serious work?
27   Does this tend to work?
28   What would make you work harder?
29   If you were to design a new school course and ways of teaching it that would inspire you, what would it be like?
30   Imagine your teachers want you to do A. Your friends want you to do B instead. Think of an example. What do you usually tend to do?
31   If you were studying underachievement what question would you ask students ... I'd like you to answer your own question?
32   Are the standards set for you high enough?
33   Who would you be inclined to blame for your underachievement?
34   On average how much do you spend on homework each night?
35   Do you have any plans to attend college or university later in life?
36   If I were to come back and see you in a year would the situation have changed? Would you be working harder?

Figure 9.2   Interview schedule

time to explore its potential. If readers want more information about ATLAS.ti software they can visit the ATLAS.ti website at http://atlasti.de/index.html and download a trial version of the software for demonstration purposes. This will allow the reader to see sample screen shots that may facilitate interpretation of what follows. For demonstration purposes the screenshot shown here is of my project (Figure 9.3).

Coding quotations

With the text in the left-hand panel on the screen the user can create visible codes in the right-hand panel alongside the associated text. This is usually done by selecting or highlighting the text that one wants to code. There are many coding techniques but for now let us take a simple example. On the left of the screen is the dialogue that is both the question Number 9 and the 17th interviewee's responses to this. This text can be selected in its entirety and given the code of 9. In future if the user ever needs to get back to this particular quotation it can be easily found. I would recommend that the researcher use an Intelligent Mouse with a scroll knob in the centre as this makes coding ever so much easier.

All 26 transcripts were carefully read and coded by the same interviewer. Eventually over 130 codes were generated for this textual archive. By employing the codes then the user can systematically retrieve the highlighted quotation associated with any individual codes or a combination of codes. Effectively all 65,000 words were surveyed and codes were applied to those words or phrases or sentences or paragraphs that were selected where the user might want to get back to them at a later date.

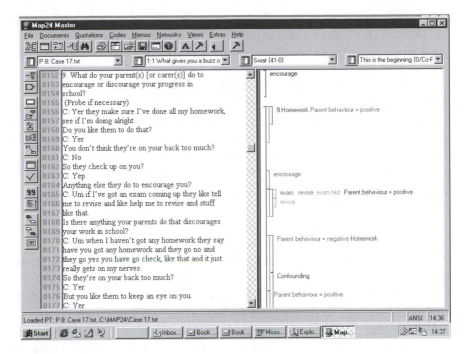

Figure 9.3   ATLAS.ti screenshot example from the project

Initial use of coding

The first analyses performed focused on having ATLAS.ti produce a summary of all the highlighted quotations stored against each of the codes 1–36 that were used to identify the semi-structured questions. For example, it was an easy task to get ATLAS.ti to generate paper output of all the text transcribed that was associated with Question 9. These operations were performed for all 36 questions that facilitated the textual analysis in the results section.

This would be one of the most basic tasks that ATLAS.ti could assist in performing. If the researcher wanted to look at all the responses (in their entirety) to a given item like question 9 then ATLAS.ti would be asked to print out just those lines and the researcher could then study the output and draw conclusions as appropriate.

More interesting is the subtle use of coding where an idea or a notion emerges as the reader scans the text. A word might recur with some regularity such as 'praise' which occurred 11 times within the text surveyed. Perhaps having seen this word appear a few times I might have coded it 'in vivo' which means that the code used to identify the word 'praise' was 'praise' itself. Once the code has been stored within ATLAS.ti it is easy to auto-code the 26 transcripts asking that wherever the word 'praise' appears in the text it would be so identified with the matching code 'praise' which will appear in the right-hand margin associated with the text. All such incidences of the code could then be pulled out of the data at any time for subsequent analysis.

Another example of coding would be to use an open code where the reader wants to tag an element (word, phrase, sentence, paragraph, etc.) with a new code that originates in the imagination of the reader. For example, in reading some of the interview dialogue the reader might feel that a segment might represent an example of what we call 'teacher behaviour = negative'. This particular label or code could be used widely wherever the reader feels that the pupil is talking about some aspect of a teacher's behaviour that the student feels is negative, such as teasing or humiliating someone.

In my coding I generated the list of codes given in Table 9.2, by the process of reading each transcript and adding codes where it seemed appropriate. What you see is an assortment of what we might call first-generation codes. They came from a variety of sources. Some were in my mind as a result of the literature search that I did that produced the original list of 51 bipolar constructs that I brought to the project building on the work of others.

To deny that these constructs were in my consciousness would be quite dishonest. They helped to generate the questions that I asked the students who were interviewed. Many other codes however emerged from the uninhibited voices of the pupils. Some were memorable such as the suggestions that some teachers need to laugh, loosen up and get a life outside of teaching. If grounded theory is in operation here it was essential that something 'value added' emerge rather than that we just recycle truths or beliefs stemming from the literature on able underachievers most of which is written by adult professionals who undoubtedly hold different views from the pupils themselves.

What follows the coding?

It took a long time to conceptualise this project, review the literature, design the questions, find the appropriate able underachieving Year 9 pupils, interview them, transcribe the interviews, learn to use the ATLAS.ti software and then code the 26 interview scripts. I had had the great benefit of working with a wide range of colleagues and students who favoured the application of qualitative methods which result in harvesting a rich collection of bold statements, hidden beliefs, positive and negative attitudes, fine grain snapshot opinions, harsh judgements, over-the-top criticisms, humorous material, sad stories, plausible suggestions, recommendations we ignore at our peril, and more.

It is all so much more valuable to place respondents' replies in a discourse context where it is readily possible and advisable to ask follow-up

Table 9.2 List of preliminary codes used to analyse the data

Activity = disliked	Laid back & loose = valued	Strength
Activity = preferred	Laugh	Stress
Ambition	Lea Green	Stressed
Anger	Learning = difficult	Strict
Assertive	Leisure activities are valued	Strictness
Award	Locus of control is self	Success not embarrassing
Biased	Loner	Swat
Blame	Look down or patronise less able	Target
Blame self for underachieving	Lost opportunity	Teacher assessment = negative
Boredom	Missing mentor	Teacher attributes = negative
Boredom strategy	Missing role model	Teacher attributes = positive
Cadet	Moan	Teacher behaviour = negative
Camp	Mood	Teacher behaviour = positive
Causation	Music	Teacher doesn't recognise ability
Challenging activity or demanding	Music week	Teacher influence = nil
Clever pupils	Nagging	Teacher recognises ability
College or university	Newspaper	Teacher relations
Compromise	Next year	Teacher relations = negative
Conflict of interest	Onset	Teacher relations = positive, teachers pet
	Parent attitude = positive	
Confounding	Parent behaviour = negative	Teachers under pressure
Contradictory response	Parent behaviour = positive	Tease
Copy or writing	Parent controlling	Teasing or tormenting
Costs	Peer achievements	Test
Curiosity	Peer attributes	Top dogs
Curriculum	Peer attributes = positive	Unappreciated personal attributes
Deadline	Peer influence = negative	Underachievement
Decision	Peer influence = neutral	Unhappy
Detention	Peer influence = positive	University
Develop an interest	Peers = average ability	Weakness
Geeks	Rewards	
Goal	School = positive	
Groups	Scouts	
Guitar	Self assessment = negative	
Happy with friends	Self assessment = positive	
	Self assessment = underachievement	
	Self blame	
	Setting	
	Sexist	
	Shout	
Homework	Sibling influence	
Humour or laughter or joke	Sibling influence = negative	
Illness	Sibling influence = nil	
Incentive	Sibling influence = positive	
Interesting activity	Small classes	
Intervention: Compromise	Spoff	
Intervention: school improvement	Square	
Intervention: set higher Standards	Standards?	
Intervention: Study Skills	Strategies	
Jealousy	Streaming	

questions in the light of what one hears. This would never really be possible when studying the findings of a quantitative questionnaire survey.

Just getting to hear and then read what the respondents had to tell us was a privilege. It was consistent in what we have learned of late from studies on inclusion. If we listen to a broader audience we find new problems and better yet new answers to the questions we keep asking of our professional colleagues and ourselves. Predictably it was not simply a rehashing of what one could read in the published literature. It showed us some fresh insights and new paths for exploration.

The initial coding was a learning experience in that it opened up the study to further tasks of reducing the commentary and the codes into clusters or summaries or second generation codes which attempted to occupy a superordinate status incorporating what the initial codes said in batches or groups or categories. The new derived secondary codes are built on top of the primary codes. They should be economical and capable of holding a group of ideas together as a wider concept.

Findings from the data analysis

Having done all the above it was time to start writing up the project and this meant looking to be economical in reporting the essence of what these 26 Able Underachievers had to say about the causes and remedies of their school underachievement. By moving from individual captured and coded responses I began to see the emergence of trends or themes that seemed to reveal material that we could use elsewhere such as in training exercises with teachers and talks with both pupils and parents. MAPs generally have advocates and much has already been written about their met and unmet needs within education generally. Able Underachievers are (I suggest) perhaps less well advocated. So it was beneficial to gather up the thoughts presented and convey them as a list, which hopefully does justice to what a range of AUs are telling us. What follows is a brief summary of what the AUs revealed:

- AUs have no great love of learning in traditional academic subjects with preference for social life and recreation, performance, hands-on practice and creative activity.
- AUs are bored by excessive copying, sitting passively, lack of variety, lack of relevance, dull lecturing, uninteresting topics, silence, waiting and poorly planned lessons. There is a power imbalance and AUs do not feel they own the problem.
- AUs do not see demands and challenges with associated rewards in school as exciting and welcoming.
- AUs have little experience in school with bands, teams, clubs, group work but value adult oriented work in the cadets. This is a lost opportunity

as AUs do not seem interested in affiliation or organisation which is self-initiated.

- AUs do not seem interested or motivated to initiate extra-curricular activities to make school life more exciting. AUs identify obstacles and this is another lost opportunity.

ATTRIBUTES

- AUs value good relations with friendly, attentive, available, respectful, humorous, socially skilful teachers with whom they can communicate in a more adult fashion thus avoiding the 'cat and mouse' roles that prevent real dialogue. Sadly this is rare.
- AUs dislike unfair, boring, shouting, stressed, overly critical, disorganised and unassertive teachers. They are pessimistic about improvements and feel no sense of problem ownership. They are not in dialogue with anyone to repair the situation.

INFLUENCES

- AUs feel that teachers are influential in that they can stimulate or kill interest and enthusiasm. With the latter AUs do not use their talents, inventiveness or leadership to improve or rescue the situation in failing lessons.
- AUs mostly use parents in a limited homework surveillance role that gets mixed results. This is another lost opportunity for a much wider range of facilitative and stimulating communication that sadly only a minority seem to access. AUs seem arrested in a child like pattern.
- AUs really value friendships but seem to have little contact with or understanding of Able Achievers (AAs) and reject the social costs of being called a 'square', 'swot', 'nerd', 'spoff' or 'geek'. The peer group culture exerts considerable pressure on AUs. They fear that hard work and self-discipline might disadvantage their social life and make them boring.
- AUs do not appear to access much regular peer support and encouragement for academic work as they might do if they played for a team. The peer culture does little to encourage achievement.
- AUs believe their friends think more or less as they do about these issues.
- AUs can get valued help from siblings but the scope of this seems limited and underdeveloped.
- AUs have clear and worrying views about the social costs of becoming an AA but lack much opportunity to get to know AAs well and delve beneath the stereotypes. This is another lost opportunity.
- AUs perceive some conflict between meeting competing needs from teachers' and friends' expectations but tend to try to strike a compromise. They did not seem to fully grasp the nature of the conflict but tended to address it as a simple problem that requires a simple compromise solution.

SELF

- AUs could achieve a much higher level of self-esteem if they accessed and used a fraction of the underdeveloped talent that they possess in academic schoolwork.
- AUs are skilled at talking about themselves in a self-critical way but this does not appear to lead to successful interventions that might boost attainments.
- AUs do not overwhelmingly feel that worrying is a major problem in their lives although a fear of failure or being compared with others is worth exploring.
- AUs acknowledge that they possess talents, abilities, inventiveness and performance skills that are not particularly acknowledged or celebrated in school. They have mixed views about publicity and the peer culture's views on excellence need to be better understood. National Curriculum emphasis on citizenship and leadership could offer opportunity here.
- AUs acknowledge that they underachieve in school. They can be identified and singled out for intervention such as mentoring and target setting but I suspect they would value some recognition that they are not fully to blame for the problems. Without this they will be expected to adopt an internal locus of control and assume all responsibility for interventions and improvements.
- AUs know what they do differently from AAs but do not feel totally responsible for the discrepancies. They think the teachers own the problem. Unless teachers change their attitudes and behaviour AUs are unlikely to do much in terms of raising standards. We are stuck here with the status quo.
- AUs acknowledge their intelligence but often do not find school challenging. This is a lost opportunity again. AUs can back up claims to be good at learning with evidence. They are not being overly challenged at school. Their low attainments must follow decisions about not making more commitment. Perhaps they do not see the payoff. Who owns this problem?
- AUs know they are good at learning and can summon evidence to prove this. They acknowledge a lack of commitment to achieve better grades.
- AUs value diversity (like multi-media) in teaching and group work and prefer practical hands-on approaches involving performance other than exclusively in writing and they welcome research practice. They want to break out of the restricting binds of closely controlled classrooms where they can use more freedom and space as might apply to students in higher education.

INTERVENTIONS

- AUs seem to have developed a limited repertoire of study skills that does not match their creativity, spontaneity or imagination. This area could be developed.

- AUs have some strategies to address boredom and poor concentration but this area could be developed more using AUs' talents. Strategies seem short sighted and not systematic or dynamic. AUs accept boredom as part of school life with some detachment.
- While AUs claim the above strategies are partially successful AUs need to open a dialogue with teachers and peers about problem ownership, causation and preventative interventions. Lost opportunity here.
- AUs might work harder if teachers were less boring and generally improved the classroom. AUs seem to take little responsibility for this. Perhaps they do not feel teachers are interested in their suggestions.
- AUs could help staff design more stimulating and productive schools provided they thought teachers would listen to them.
- AUs do possess skills in the diagnosis of a conflict situation and they have some ideas about causation and resolution.
- AUs have strong hypotheses and unique personal experiences to account for underachieving but are curious to know more about causation and to a lesser extent intervention planning. They admire self-assessment.
- AUs might well work harder if expectations and standards were raised. Screening and subsequent mentoring with adults or peers might be helpful.
- On balance, towards the end of the interviews AUs want to accept responsibility for underachieving before blaming others. This suggests an internal locus of control.
- AUs see homework more as a burden than an opportunity. Some work gets done but it falls far short of what might be possible if the AUs were motivated and saw a better purpose to this work.
- AUs do have ambitions but a poor grasp of higher education and careers neither of which seem to exert much pulling power in terms of commitment and motivation. Homework often fails the relevance test.
- AUs categorically seem discouraged and pessimistic about teachers and schools becoming more interesting and stimulating. Nevertheless they plan to change their ways and work harder in Year 10 mostly because of GCSEs rather than a new attraction to the curriculum.

Higher order coding

In the course of writing up the above summary comments I found myself to be doing what grounded theory expects: namely to be generating second or even third generation codes which hopefully operate at a higher level of abstraction and are more economical in the use of language to describe a concept. At the present time my list of these advanced codes is reproduced below:

- Lost opportunities to use talents, imagination and leadership
- Missing communication with teachers, friends and family

- Lack of perception of problem ownership and responsibility
- Apathy and powerlessness
- Lack of a more adult or age appropriate culture as applies in higher education
- Over-reliance on restricting traditional teaching methods
- AUs' perceptions about causation and intervention not exploited by staff
- Where is the commitment to change?

Reflections on this project and conclusions

If I were to be asked (and this has actually happened) where was the point where 'the penny dropped' and something emerged that was unexpected and not previously found explicated in the literature or with the 51 bipolar codes at the start, it would have to be hearing the unspoken message of 'lost opportunity' that kept recurring. It was all about the conversations that the AUs *were not having* with their teachers but were with me in such an eloquent manner.

Within ATLAS.ti there is ample opportunity to 'play around with' what you discover in clusters and hierarchies of codes visually in what is called a network. For more sophisticated users this can be the environment where all the hard work starts to pay dividends. I actually made less use of this feature as the inspiration and the creativity seemed to arrive spontaneously. I felt cheated somehow that with other demands on my time I did not use this major feature as much as I could have done. It certainly would have generated some brilliant OHTs or PowerPoint presentations that would have conveyed more of what I want to express about the overall project. As I write this I am making a memo to remind myself to go back and work more on this feature of ATLAS.ti.

When students ask me about the attendant advantages of ATLAS.ti I'm inclined to argue that it allows the user to go back to the drawing board and start all over again in trying to make sense of the coding procedure. Preliminary or first-generation codes can be added, deleted, renamed or clustered into new codes. Codes can be divided up or merged as necessary. Codes can be parked in families of codes. Superordinate or subordinate relations can be created.

If a grounded theory qualitative researcher had decided to do all this by hand traditionally in order to get the 'feel' of the data, the result might be a floor space or a large wall covered with cards or papers in a spatial arrangement that makes conceptual sense at the time top of its physical construction. It helps to safeguard this precious workspace so that the research activity is protected from adventurous animals, inquisitive children, partners with a different need for the same space and vandals.

My interpretation of the use of ATLAS.ti is that it would allow the user to either stay with a given visual display structure that is working or file it away and start with a whole new structure in order to make sense of the codes and the patterns they create. This restructuring could be done at any time that the user feels the pattern of coding is not working. Those committed to a pattern that is up on a wall or occupying floor space might be more than hesitant about throwing the whole arrangement up in the air and starting again in case something might be lost. The ATLAS.ti user has no such fear as any earlier work, no matter how embryonic, temporary, cautious, tentative or crazy, can be easily stored away for later use. This is especially helpful when a friend, a critic, a student or a tutor comes along with the suggestion of another approach.

On reflection I feel the time invested was worthwhile and I would certainly do it again and recommend it to other researchers. Like any IT application it would require an investment and it would be easier for those who have already learned to use other computer applications. I would have been happier with hindsight to take a taught introductory course and to work within a team where others were using it and sharing skills with one another.

I joined two really interesting internet discussion groups, one of which focused on qualitative methodology and the other on ATLAS.ti, but in retrospect I did not devote the time needed to benefit from this and all the technical advice and tips that other users share with each other. For further information the reader might like to look at the website http://caqdas.soc.surrey.ac.uk/ for a wealth of suggestions for new users and those who are contemplating the use of software to assist with qualitative analysis.

What is written above is designed to assist the researcher who is looking for a method and the tools to examine the output that results when one asks language based rather than numerical rating questions of subjects in a study and is left with lots of text. What I have not yet revealed is that my co-researcher is my wife Kathryn and she elected to examine the exact same transcripts herself without the benefit of ATLAS.ti to assist. At this time we are finishing off the first phase of the project by writing a book together (Pomerantz and Pomerantz, 2002). We have the benefit of two sets of eyes looking at the same material but with a slightly different perspective. On balance I feel that we gained by really grappling with the text and the findings. Kathryn used notes in the margins and different coloured highlighters.

In the end we found congruence and could build on insights gained from how we approached the data. ATLAS.ti was always available to us if we ever needed to go searching for something elusive in the final stages of the project. I feel that I was able to handle the application at an intermediate level and could teach others to use it. It is now part of my kit and I am looking to use it in other contexts and have done so.

Summary

This chapter looks specifically at the analysis of qualitative research data (interview transcripts) with the use of specialised computer software ATLAS.ti. The data was obtained from a research project actually undertaken by the author who, although familiar with qualitative educational research procedures, was a first time user of this software. As such the detail in this chapter should resonate with the needs of those thinking of undertaking qualitative research.

There is a concern held by some that the use of 'computer analysis' can in itself either hide a particular analysis or divert the user into a particular line of thought (see Chapter 8). This concern is raised here inasmuch as the same data was analysed without the use of computer software. Perhaps it is comforting to see that the outcome of this was that both analysis methods led to congruence but ATLAS.ti was always available if there was ever the interest to go searching for something elusive.

10

Quantitative Analysis: A Glossary of Terms

Clive Opie

Analysis of Variance (ANOVA)

If a researcher wanted to show that the difference between the **mean** of two samples were statistically significant then they would most probably apply the **t-test** and this is described elsewhere in this glossary. If however, they had more than two samples the statistical test they would use is called analysis of **variance**, abbreviated to ANOVA. ANOVA is another **parametric test** using **interval scale** or **ratio scale** data, although as its name implies the calculation uses measures of **variance** and not **mean**.

Although ANOVA tests vary considerably depending on the experimental design being employed, and their calculation can appear to get quite complicated (Black, 1999: 441–84) they all conform to the basic principle of measuring the difference between what is called *systematic variance* and *random variance* which together make up the total variance of any set of results.

$$\text{Total variance} = \text{Systematic Variance} + \text{Random Variance}$$

Systematic variances are ones that are caused as a result of the variable being looked at while *random variances* are ones that would occur anyway just by chance. *Random variances* are always going to be present and deciding whether a **null hypothesis** should be rejected or not is based upon whether we observe any *systematic variances* above these *random variances* and, of course, whether these *systematic variances* are significant. To get an idea of how ANOVA works we will work through an example (based on Hinton, 1996: 122).

Assume we have three similar age range, completely mixed ability classes and all have been taught a particular topic, by the same teacher and for the same period of time but using different teaching resources. One class used only standard textbooks, another used only the internet, and a third used a combination of both these resources. When they undertook a test associated with the topic the results obtained suggested to the teacher that the classes might have achieved significantly different results. The teacher would like to test the *null hypothesis* that there is no difference in the results of the classes and to do so for a *level of significance* of $p = 0.05$.

This research is based on one *independent variable* (the teaching resource) with our *dependent variable* being the test scores. As this example uses only one *independent variable* the test is known generally as 'one-way (or one factor) ANOVA' and as we have **different** classes it is further described as an, 'independent measures one-way ANOVA'. In the table of results given later (Table 10.1) each column shows the results for a particular condition (a different teaching resource being used). Any variance **between** these columns is called a *between conditions variance*. This will be made up of *systematic variance* and *random variance*. If we consider **each column on its own**, the variance in each is called the *within conditions variance* but will only be made up of *error variance* because the subjects (pupils in the class) in each column have all been treated the same.

These terms are important as the ANOVA test is actually a measure of the ratio (F) of the *between conditions variance* and the *within conditions variance*:

$$F = \frac{\text{between conditions variance}}{\text{within conditions variance}}$$

The basis of the calculation of *variance* is

$$\frac{\sum (X - M)^2}{N - 1}$$

where X is each value, N is the total number of values and M is the *mean* of all the X values. The term $\sum (X - M)^2$ is known as the sum of squares and $N - 1$ is the number of *degrees of freedom (df)*.

Let's assume the table of results for our example are as shown (Table 10.1) where X_n are the set of values for each class. To calculate F we split the variances into their component parts. Abbreviating sum of squares to SS:

$$SS_{total} = \sum X^2 - (\sum X)^2 / N = 96880 - 2755600 / 30 = 5026.67$$

$$SS_{between} = \sum B^2 / n - (\sum X)^2 / N = 923600 / 10 - 2755600 / 30 = 506.67$$

note that the term $\sum X^2 - (\sum X)^2/N$ is the same as $\sum (X - M)^2$ but easier to calculate. So from our original formulae for total variance:

Table 10.1   Table of results for ANOVA calculation

	Class A (Books only)		Class B (WWW only)		Class C (Books and WWW)	
	X_1	$(X_1)^2$	X_2	$(X_2)^2$	X_3	$(X_3)^2$
	34	1156	34	1156	46	2116
	38	1444	46	2116	48	2304
	41	1681	47	2209	49	2401
	42	1764	53	2809	49	2401
	45	2025	54	2916	51	2601
	48	2304	58	3364	55	3025
	53	2809	60	3600	68	4624
	64	4096	62	3844	72	5184
	65	4225	71	5041	78	6084
	70	4900	75	5625	84	7056
$\sum X_n / n$	50		56		60	
$\sum X_n^2$		26404		32680		37796
$\sum X_n$	500		560		600	
$(\sum X_n)^2$	250000		313600		360000	
$\sum X$ = Sum of each $\sum X_n$					1660	
$(\sum X)^2$					2755600	
$\sum X^2$ = Sum of each $\sum X_n^2$					96880	
$\sum B^2$ = Sum of each $(\sum X_n)^2$					923600	

Number of values per condition (n) = 10

Total number of values (N) = 30 $df_{total} = 30 - 1 = 29$

Number of conditions (columns) = 3 $df_{between} = 3 - 1 = 2$

$$df_{within} = df_{total} - df_{between} = 29 - 2 = 27$$

$$SS_{within} = SS_{total} - SS_{between} = 5026.67 - 506.67 = 4520$$

and from this:

$$between\ conditions\ variance = SS_{between}/df_{between} = 506.67/2 = 253.33$$

$$within\ condition\ variance = SS_{within}/df_{within} = 4520/27 = 167.41$$

giving us an F value of $253.33/167.41 = 1.51$. This example is not that difficult to work out but the more conditions and/or more subjects we have then
the greater the chance of human error occurring in our calculations.
Thankfully, and as we have noted elsewhere, for example in **Pearson's**

Table 10.2 Excel calculation of ANOVA

Source of variation	SS	df	MS	F	p-value	F_{crit}
Between conditions*	506.6667	2	253.3333	1.513274	0.23828	3.354131
Within conditions*	4520	27	167.4074			
Total	5026.667	29				

*Excel uses the term Group rather than Conditions

Product Moment Correlation (r) and the *t-test*, computer technology can help with such calculations. The actual results of the three classes can be put into three columns of the spreadsheet Microsoft Excel and using the function ANOVA: Single Factor from the Tools–Data Analysis menu all the above details can be calculated in an instant. The summary table of results this produces is shown here (Table 10.2) as it exemplifies the standard format for the presentation of ANOVA results.

You can see how the Excel result matches our calculations. However, what it also shows us is whether the result is significant or not. Recall the teacher was using a *level of significance* of $p = 0.05$. The Excel result shows us that for this *level of significance* F_{crit} would need to be 3.35 or greater. Our value for F is 1.51. We cannot then reject the *null hypothesis* and there is no difference in the mean results for the varying teaching methods. The p value quoted is the *level of significance* at which the F result is significant. You will also note in the Excel result a term MS. This stands for mean square but is just the technical term used to describe variance, that is, $MS_{between}$ = *between conditions variance*. We have chosen not to introduce it as it only adds more detail but you will find the term used in some other texts.

What happens if we did not have Excel to test the significance of F? There are, as with other statistical tests (see the *t-test*) appropriate published *critical values tables* and consulting these would tell you if it were significant. It is worth noting how the results for F are written. In our case it would be $F(2, 27) = 1.51$ where the numbers associated with F correspond to the *degrees of freedom* in the calculation with that having the largest variance coming first. This order is important when looking up *critical values tables* for F.

You may remember we said we would consider what happens if we were taking measures on the same class. This would be a repeated measures one-way ANOVA. Although the calculations for this are similar to our independent measure one-way ANOVA there is not space here to undertake them nor to delve into the slightly different theory behind them. Both these aspects are readily available in other texts (Cohen and Holliday, 1996: 181–5; Hinton, 1996: 148–51). What we can do is show the results of the calculations for our example data by using Excel and the data-analysis tool ANOVA: Two Factor Without Replication. This gives Table 10.3.

Table 10.3 Excel ANOVA: Two Factor Without Replication calculation

Source of variation	SS	df	MS	F	p-value	F_{crit}
Individual*	4329.333	9	481.037	45.41259	1.5E-10	2.456282
Between conditions**	506.6667	2	253.3333	23.91608	8.54E-06	3.554561
Error***	190.6667	18	10.59259			
Total	5026.667	29				

*   This is the difference between subjects in rows and in Excel is labelled Rows
**   This is the difference between conditions in columns and in Excel is labelled Columns
***   Error variation = Within conditions variation – Individual variation

In this table the *between conditions variance* is as before. We would expect this since we have used the same results so the variation between each of the conditions will be the same. However, the denominator value now used to work out *F* is called the *error variance* which is calculated by subtracting the individual sum of squares from the within conditions sum of squares and dividing by the appropriate **degrees of freedom**. If you recall the within conditions sum of squares before was 4520 so you should be able to see where the value of 190.67 shown for the error variation comes from. In this case.

$$F_{between} = \frac{\text{between conditions variance}}{\text{error variance}} = \frac{253.33}{10.59} = 23.91$$

as the table shows. The important thing is to note at the **level of significance** set at $p = 0.05$ we now have a significant result. In short, removing all the individual variation gives us more chance of obtaining a significant result.

What we have seen is that ANOVA can tell us if there is a significant difference between the means of more than two samples. However, what it does not do is tell us where that difference lies. For example, is it between all the samples or only some of them? When a significant difference is found by ANOVA then further tests have to be completed such as the **Tukey test** to ascertain where the effect actually lies.

All our discussion so far has been about one-way ANOVA, where we are just looking at the effect of one *independent variable*. In many cases the effect of more than one *independent variable* is of interest. Such ANOVA calculations can be undertaken and are known by the generic term factorial ANOVA. So a two-way ANOVA refers to an analysis with two *independent variables*. Factorial ANOVA are important as they provide more information than one-way ANOVA and in particular enable the interaction between variables to be examined. Factorial ANOVA are beyond the scope of this text and the reader is directed to other readings such as Hopkins, Hopkins and Glass (1996) or websites such as http://www.statsoft.com for more details.

Table 10.4 Observed and Expected sales of samosas

	Square	Circle	Triangle
Observed purchases (O)	36	20	64
Expected purchases (E)	40	40	40

Central tendency

This is a measure of quantitative data, which summarises how the data is centred together. For descriptive statistics there are two measures of central tendency, namely the *mean* and the *median*. You will hear the term *mode* used as well but strictly speaking this is not a measure of central tendency as it only records the most frequent value, which could be far from the centre.

Chi square (χ^2)

This is a *non-parametric test* for *nominal* data and allows us to test if there is significant difference between the observed frequencies and expected frequencies for any data collected. For example a school canteen is interested in knowing whether, all other things being equal, changing the shape of its vegetable samosas influences their selection and it would like to know this for a *level of significance* of $p = 0.01$. That is, only 1 time out of 100 is the result likely to have occurred by chance. The *null hypothesis* is that the shape of the vegetable samosa makes no difference in its selection.

Vegetable samosas shaped as either a square, circle or triangle were made and displayed and sales recorded. The sales showed 120 samosas sold as shown in (Table 10.4). The expected purchases are just the total number sold divided by the number of alternatives. The value of Chi square is given by:

$$\chi^2 = \sum \frac{(Q - E)^2}{E}$$

which from our results gives

$$\chi^2 = \frac{4^2 + 20^2 + 24^2}{40} = 24.8$$

There are 2 *degrees of freedom* (Number of rows $-1 \times$ Number of columns -1) and by looking at a *critical values table* of chi square the critical value at $p = 0.01$ is 9.21. Our calculated value of 24.8 is greater than this. In other words the school canteen should reject the null hypothesis and conclude that the shape of a samosa is significant in selling it.

Confidence level

This term is linked with *normal distribution* and *standard deviation* and relates to the confidence we have that a particular result lies a certain distance (confidence interval) either side of the *mean* of the sample taken. The two confidence levels, which are most often used (although you could calculate any of them), are 95% and 99%. We have introduced confidence levels in terms of a percentage but they are typically quoted as a probability. A confidence level of 95% is the same as saying the result has a 0.95 probability, in other words a 95 in 100 chance of occurring inside the confidence interval. Equally, and this is more often than not what we are interested in, we could write a confidence level of 95% as a 0.05 probability, in other words a 5 in 100 chance of occurring outside the confidence interval.

We shall see later that for a *normal distribution* we can calculate its *standard deviation* (**SD**). The reason for introducing this here is that it is the *standard deviation*, which is used in various statistical tests and a *standard deviation* of ± 1.96 (either side of the mean) corresponds to a confidence level of 95%.

Correlation coefficient (*r*)

To understand what a correlation coefficient is, let's start from a graphical representation of the relationship of two variables which are from a *ratio scale* of measurement. Take the example graph shown (Figure 10.1) which plots age against the weight of a number of children.

This type of graph is known as a scatter plot, or scattergram, and provides a clear indication of whether there is any relationship between the variables being plotted against each other. In this case it shows that as the ages of the children increase so does their weight and so there is a positive relationship between the two. For other data there could equally have been a negative relationship or no discernible pattern. In each case we are really looking at whether there is a straight-line relationship between the two variables. A straight-line relationship is a strong one if the points lie close to the straight line, as they do here, and weak if they are widely scattered about the line (Moore, 1997: 307).

However, it is fairly unusual for researchers to report scatter plots and the usual convention is to calculate a number to represent the strength of the relationship, called a correlation coefficient. This number, usually written as *r*, tells us the strength and direction of the correlation and always falls between +1.00 and −1.00, though it is usual to omit the positive sign. A value of *r* of 0.87 would indicate quite a strong positive correlation whereas a value of −0.34 would indicate a weak negative correlation. The two extreme values for *r* seldom occur, especially in educational research. It is just possible that a value approximating 0.0 might happen if you were measuring hair colour

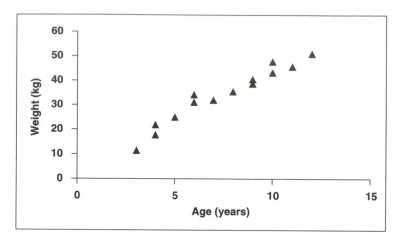

Figure 10.1 Relationship of weight against age for a group of children

against say, test scores, though even with an example as unlikely as this, a value around 0.0 would be highly suspicious because there is always the possibility of the impact of randomisation. Within this glossary are references to the following types of correlation calculations: ***Pearson's Product Moment, Kendall's tau*** and ***Spearman's Rank Order***.

Critical value tables

For all statistical tests there are tables which indicate the value that a test has to reach (or be greater than) for any particular *level of significance*. Part of the critical values table (Figure 10.2) is given here for the *t-distribution* used for *t-tests*.

Using such tables is quite easy. Let's assume for a particular *t*-test the *level of significance* was set at $p = 0.05$ for a ***two-tailed test*** and the ***degrees of freedom (d.f.)*** were 20. The critical value for *t* would be found by reading the table along the row corresponding to *d.f.* = 20 until you reached the column for $p = 0.05$ for a two-tailed test. This critical value is 2.086 and is highlighted. If, arising from the test you were carrying out, the value for *t* were calculated to be 2.027 then this would be below the critical value of 2.086 and so we would accept the ***null hypothesis*** associated with the test and conclude that the result *was not* significantly different. If on the other hand we calculated $t = 2.725$ we would reject the ***null hypothesis*** and conclude that the result *was* significantly different.

Critical tables values are available for all statistical tests and reading any of them follows a similar pattern to that indicated here.

d.f.	Level of significance for one-tailed test			
	0.05	0.025	0.01	0.005
	Level of significance for two-tailed test			
	0.1	0.05	0.02	0.01
1	6.314	12.706	31.821	63.657
5	2.015	2.571	3.365	4.032
10	1.771	2.160	2.650	3.012
15	1.753	2.131	2.602	2.947
18	1.734	2.101	2.552	2.878
20	1.725	2.086	2.528	2.845
40	1.684	2.021	2.423	2.704
60	1.671	2.000	2.390	2.660
120	1.658	1.980	2.358	2.617
∞	1.645	1.96	2.326	2.576

See **One-tailed and Two-tailed tests** for an explanation of these

See **One-tailed and Two-tailed tests**

See **t-test**

See **Z-scores**

Figure 10.2 Critical values for *t*-distribution and *t*-tests

Data reduction

Raw data is often not in a form, which gives any real 'feel' for how the research 'turned out'. For example, you may have 100 people's responses to a given question which might be in the form of 'yes' or 'no' or, if you have used a *Likert scale*, may be in the form of a number from 1 to 5. Presented as raw data though it is not usually particularly useful and what is needed is a means of summarising the data, for example, '84% said yes'. Such summarising is the basis of *descriptive statistics* and tables of *frequencies* or measures of *central tendency* are examples of these. Such summarising is known as data reduction 'since it results in the reduction of a large number of observations to a much smaller number of statistical indices' (Keppel and Saufley, 1980: 21).

Degrees of freedom (*d.f*)

This is in fact quite a difficult concept to understand (Walker, 1940) but simpler discussions of it are available (Hinton, 1996: 50–2). For our purposes we can define it as the number of values from a total number (*N*), which are free to vary. In other words the number that are not fixed by some restriction placed upon them.

Consider any six numbers. If there is no restriction on them, that is, they can be anything, then the degrees of freedom $d.f. = 6$. However, now let us place a restriction on these six numbers by saying the *mean* of their total has to be equal to 7. If the first five of these numbers were 4, 5, 8, 10 and 11 then in order for the *mean* of the total of all six to be equal to 7 the last number (n) will be fixed as follows:

$$\frac{4 + 5 + 8 + 10 + 11 + n}{6} = 7$$

giving the value $n = 4$. The last number is therefore fixed *due to the restriction placed upon the total of all six numbers* having to have a *mean* of 7. In other words the value of the last number is not free to vary. In this situation there are then only five numbers, which can vary, the sixth must be set from these. In this case the degrees of freedom $d.f. = 5$.

It might look like $d.f. = N - 1$, where N is the total number of data items; however, this is not always the case. For example, let's say for the above case we add another restriction – the first four numbers have to add up to 25. With this added restriction if you work out how many numbers are free to vary in the first four and add this to the restriction placed by the *mean* of all six being set to 7 you'll find the $d.f. = 4$. The more restrictions we place on the data the lower the degrees of freedom will be.

The degrees of freedom depend on the statistical test being considered and are crucial as it is used to determine the ***level of statistical significance*** of the test.

Dependent variable

This is the name given to the variable that a researcher is interested in studying. In studying examination results, after treating students with a particular teaching style it is the results, which are the dependent variable. The teaching style is the ***independent variable***.

Descriptive statistics

As the name implies these simply describe or summarise a number of observations and the following is an example of a descriptive statistic:

73% of people in the survey carried out indicated they were not opposed to genetic engineering where it was being applied to help find cures for certain diseases, e.g. muscular dystrophy.

Raw values of 24 students examination grades
A, A, A, B, B, B, B, B, C, C, C, C, C, C, C, C, C, C, D, D, D, D, E, E, F

which might be more conveniently presented as

Exam Grades	Frequency (f)
A	3
B	5
C	9
D	4
E	2
F	1

Figure 10.3   Examples of displaying frequencies

There is the issue about whether one uses percentages or actual numbers in such descriptions and which is used depends on the *sample size*.

Frequency (*f*)

This is a measure of the number of times a particular value occurs in any given number of values. It is one way of summarising data and frequency's can be recorded as shown in (Figure 10.3).

Independent variable

This is the variable that a researcher is in control of and manipulates in order to see how it affects a particular *dependent variable*. If one were interested to know if there was a relationship between the loss of weight and exercise then the researcher would manipulate the amount of exercise and measure the loss of weight. In this case the amount of exercise would be the independent variable and the measure of loss of weight the *dependent variable*.

Inferential statistics

Inferential statistics, in contrast to *descriptive statistics*, which simply summarise and organise large numbers of observations, are used to:

- make inferences from the sample data to the population from which it is drawn;

- examine relationships, through testing hypotheses, between different variables of the data being studied.

Inferential statistics therefore require further investigation of the data through appropriate statistical analysis and which analysis is used depends on the type of data being collected.

Interval scale

This refers to measurements which although separable by equal distances has limits in terms of what you can say about it. For example, examination scores provide interval data inasmuch as the difference between a score of 40 and 50 is the same as that between 70 and 80. What you cannot say though is that the person scoring 80 is twice as good as the person scoring 40.

Kendall's tau

This is a *non-parametric* measure of association of data measured on an *ordinal scale* to test if there is a one-to-one correspondence between variables, for example, the level of interest in a subject and final examination grades.

An explanation of Kendall's tau use and its calculation is beyond the scope of this text, but can be found elsewhere (Cohen and Holliday, 1996: 264–7). The calculation can be very complicated, especially with a large number of values and as such prone to human error. Thankfully there are statistical packages such as SPSS, which will undertake such tests on raw data and all we need to be sure of is that it is the correct test to use.

Kruskal-Wallis test

This is a *non-parametric test* used when one wants to find out if three or more independent groups belong to a single population. It is based on *median* results and the *null hypothesis* is that they are not from different populations. The data is assumed to be measured on the *ordinal scale* and is based on ranks. Table 10.5 shows the scores obtained (through the use of a *Likert scale*) from ten staff from three different departments within a school, of how important (5 = most important) they felt ensuring subject content was up to date was a characteristic for effective teaching. These scores were then ranked over all departments with equal scores being given the mean ranking, for example, the ranking for the five scores of 4 is $(3 + 4 + 5 + 6 + 7)/5 = 5$.

Table 10.5 Departmental scores for Kruskal-Wallis test

Department A		Department B		Department C	
Scores	Ranks	Scores	Ranks	Scores	Ranks
3	11.5	5	1.0	1	27.5
2	20.0	3	11.5	2	20.0
4	5.0	4	5.0	1	27.5
1	27.5	3	11.5	4	5.0
3	11.5	5	1.0	3	11.5
2	20.0	3	11.5	2	20.0
1	27.5	2	20.0	1	27.5
3	11.5	3	11.5	2	20.0
2	20.0	4	5.0	1	27.5
2	20.0	4	5.0	2	20.0

The Kruskal-Wallis test (H) is found from the following equation:

$$H = \frac{12K}{N(N+1)} - 3(N+1)$$

where N is the total number of cases and K is the sum of the squares of the total of the ranks of each of the groups divided by the number of cases in each group. In the case here:

- Squares of the total of the ranks in Department A = 30450.25
- Squares of the total of the ranks in Department B = 6889
- Squares of the total of the ranks in Department C = 42642.25

and as the number of cases in each group is 10

$$K = (30450.25 + 6889 + 42642.25) / 10 = 7998.15$$

Substituting for K in the equation above gives a value of

$$H = 10.20$$

Like other tests the significance of this result can be determined. For a *level of significance* of $p = 0.05$ and having 2 *degrees of freedom* a *critical values table* of *chi square* (χ^2) shows that a value of 5.99 is significant. Our value 10.20 is greater than this, which means we can reject the *null hypothesis* and state that these results are likely (at the 0.05 level of significance) to be from different populations. In other words the different departments do not share the same level of importance of ensuring subject content is up to date as a characteristic for effective teaching.

You will note that in our example there are a number of tied rankings. Consideration of these should be taken into account (Cohen and Holliday, 1996: 250), especially as the effect of ties is to increase the value of H and hence make the result more significant.

Level of significance (*p*)

This term is used in *inferential statistics* and refers to the predetermined probability (*p*) with which a researcher is willing to reject or not reject a *null hypothesis*. It is the value of p which is quoted in most research papers.

The question is, though, at what level should p be set? This is all tied up with *Type I (α) and Type II (β) errors* but where it is set must depend on the nature of the research problem. Most researchers tend to be cautious and set $p = 0.05$ indicating that only 5 times out of 100 is the result likely to have occurred by chance.

Likert scale

This is widely used in research and is the name given to a type of scale used in questionnaires, which while covering possible responses, also enables a degree of differentiation to be achieved between them. For example:

My secondary education prepared me well for my further education course				
Strongly Agree 1	Agree 2	No view 3	Disagree 4	Strongly Disagree 5

The data from such questions is *ordinal* and only provides a level of ranking. In other words no arithmetical analysis between the responses is possible and one respondent selecting 'Agree' may well have similar views to another selecting 'Strongly Agree'. Nevertheless with appropriate *nonparametric tests* the data from such scales can be used in various quantitative analyses, for example, the *Kruskal-Wallis test*.

Mean

This is the most familiar and most common measure of *central tendency* and is calculated by dividing the sum of the values by the total number of values. The mean (*M*) is therefore given as:

Values	Sum of the values ($\sum$)	Number of values (N)	Mean of values (M)
9, 10, 10, 12, 14, 15, 16, 18	104	8	104/8 = 13

Figure 10.4   Calculation of the mean as measure of central tendency

$$M = \frac{\sum X}{N}$$

where X is each value, N is the total number of values and $\sum$ indicates 'the sum of' as indicated in the example shown in Figure 10.4.

The mean is useful when the range of values is more or less symmetrically distributed about a central point and is essential where it forms part of other statistical measures, such as the *t-test*. Where there are extreme values the mean reflects these and is distorted accordingly. To convince yourself of this add the value 868 to the above example and recalculate the mean. You should get $M = 108$, which is not representative of the central point. In such cases the *median* is a better measure of *central tendency*.

Median

This is another useful measure of *central tendency* and is simply the middle value for a set of values. That is, the value at which for all the rest half are lower and half are higher. To work out the median first arrange all the values in order and then:

- if the total number of values obtained is odd just take the mid value;
- if the total number of values obtained is even you need to take the average of the middle pair of values.

as in the example shown in Figure 10.5.

Although not difficult to work out other considerations need to be taken in account in calculating the median where the *frequency* of the middle value is greater than one (Cohen and Holliday, 1996: 25).

From the way it is calculated the median, unlike the *mean*, does not reflect extreme values and so is used as a measure of *central tendency* where these occur.

Values	Values in order	Median
15, 7, 9, 18, 6, 14, 12	6, 7, 9, 12, 14, 15, 18	12

Values	Values in order	Median
15, 7, 9, 18, 6, 14, 12, 10	6, 7, 9, **10, 12,** 14, 15, 18	Average of 10 and 12 = 11

Figure 10.5 Calculation of the median as measure of central tendency

Mode

The mode records the highest *frequency* of any set of *nominal* data. The modal frequency value could occur anywhere within a distribution, which is why it is not considered as a true measure of *central tendency*. It does have its uses, for example in talking about the mixed race of a country. So it makes sense to talk about the modal race of Singapore as Chinese.

Nominal scale

Measurements which can only be placed in categories and nothing else, are regarded as nominal. For example, types of insects produce nominal scale data.

Non-parametric tests

If data collected is of an *ordinal* type and as such, although the order of any numbers is meaningful, any arithmetic analysis between them is not, then the type of test, which can be legitimately used on it, is known as non-parametric. As non-parametric tests make no assumptions about wider populations nor that any population being looked at has a *normal distribution* they are less powerful than *parametric tests* (e.g. *t-test*).

   Non-parametric tests are designed for specific populations, for example, a year group in a school or teachers of a particular subject. They are much quicker to apply and the calculations involved are often less problematic than for *parametric tests*. As such non-parametric tests are, as Cohen and colleagues note the 'stock-in-trade of classroom teachers' (2000: 317–18).

Normal distribution

If we were to take a large enough sample of measurable data, for example the weight of a large number of children at a particular age, and plotted

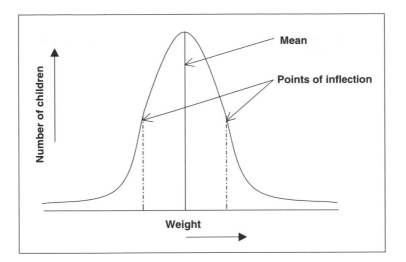

Figure 10.6   Normal distribution curve

these data it would produce a smooth bell-shaped curve, as shown here in Figure 10.6.

This curve is known as a normal curve and the distribution of values as a normal distribution. Although one talks of a normal distribution it is the mathematical properties of the normal curve which are of more importance to us. One of these is the fact that the curve has a point of inflection (that is, the point where the curve begins to fall off ever less steeply either side of the *mean*) and a perpendicular line drawn from this point to the base produces what is regarded as a standard unit of distance from the mean point known as the *standard deviation*. Knowing the *mean* and the *standard deviation* is all that is needed to describe any specific normal curve.

Null hypothesis (H₀)

This is the hypothesis, which is tested using *inferential statistics*, to determine the probability that it should be rejected or not rejected. Null hypotheses are stated such as to indicate that the expected outcomes will not show any statistically significant difference and that any differences that do occur will do so by chance. So, if we were interested in showing there was a significant difference between two sets of exam scores the null hypothesis, the one to be tested, would be:

There is no significant difference between the two sets of exam scores.

The point is that we should always be trying to disprove (rather than prove) a hypothesis, as this is consistent with the reality of probability. Employing

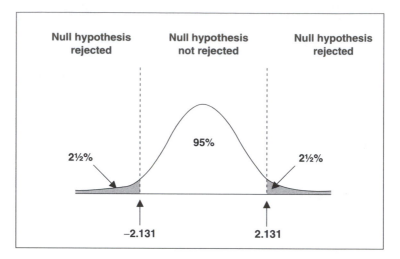

Figure 10.7   Diagram showing a two-tailed test

the appropriate statistical test to the data would tell us the probability of a difference occurring by chance. If this calculated probability were less than the predetermined probability set by the *level of significance*, then the result would be regarded as significantly different and the null hypothesis would be rejected. In other words a difference had been found between the two sets of exam scores, which was unlikely to have occurred by chance alone.

One-tailed and two-tailed tests

To find the significance for any statistical test one needs to set the *level of significance (p)* one is prepared to work to. For example, for $p = 0.05$ one is stating the result is only significant if it is likely to occur no more than 5 times out of 100 by chance. If we link this to *normal distribution* or *t-distribution* curves it means that the result would occur at the extremities of the curves, in fact in a total area under the curve corresponding to 5%.

Let us assume we undertake a *t-test* with 15 *degrees of freedom* and that we do not know whether the result will be below or above the *mean* value. The area corresponding to $p = 0.05$ diagrammatically would correspond to Figure 10.7.

The value 2.131 is obtainable from the *critical values table* for a *t-distribution*. The diagram shows there are two areas or 'tails' where a significant result could be obtained. This is typically the case as, unless we are confident we know if there is a difference which way the result will go we have to consider that the result obtained could be lower or higher than the *mean*. Such an analysis is called a two-tailed test.

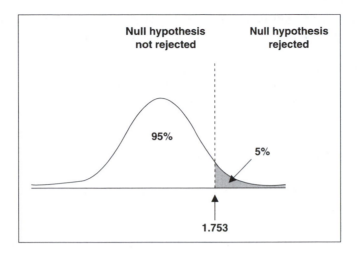

Figure 10.8   Diagram showing a one-tailed test

Now let us assume we know, or can be pretty certain, in which direction the result of the test will go. This is not usually the case but it could be that if several previous tests all gave results higher than the *mean* then it could be argued that if it were repeated with similar data the result would again be higher than the *mean*. Now we have no need to consider the lower half of the graph in Figure 10.7, and for $p = 0.05$ we would get Figure 10.8.

The value 1.753 is obtainable from the *critical values table* for a *t-distribution*. In this case the diagram shows there is only one area or 'tail' where a significant result could be obtained. Such an analysis is a one-tailed test.

Ordinal scale

This refers to measurements, which are ranked. With ranked data although the order of numbers is meaningful any arithmetic analysis between them is not. For example, with ranked school league tables you would not be able to say, on the basis of the ranking, the top school was twice as good as the second or the difference between the eight and ninth schools was the same as that between the tenth and eleventh.

Parametric tests

These are tests such as the *t-test* or, *Pearson's Product Moment Correlation*, which use *interval* data and are employed when one wishes to make inferences or predictions from sample data to the underlying population from which it came. They are generally much more powerful in detecting significant differences than *non-parametric tests*. There are, though, assumptions which need to be placed on parametric tests, which are that:

- a population has to have a *normal distribution*;
- samples come from distributions with equal *variance*;
- it involves *interval scale* or *ratio scale* data.

Pearson's Product Moment Correlation (*r*)

Correlation coefficients are quite easy to understand but calculating them can be prone to errors. Pearson's Product Moment Correlation (*r*) is a relatively straightforward calculation (Cohen and Holliday, 1996: 138) that allows us to find the strength of relationship between two *interval scale* variables:

$$r = \frac{n\sum XY - (\sum X)(\sum Y)}{\sqrt{\left[n\sum X^2 - (\sum X)^2\right]\left[n\sum Y^2 - (\sum Y)^2\right]}}$$

where n = the number of paired scores; X = values on one variable; Y = values on the other variable and Σ is the sum of these terms. Assume you had these values shown in Table 10.6, giving $\sum X = 560$, $\sum Y = 500$, $\sum XY = 29164$, $\sum X^2 = 33562$, $\sum Y^2 = 26432$ and $(\sum X)^2 = 313600$, $(\sum Y)^2 = 250000$. Putting these values into the above equation gives:

$$r = \frac{10(29164) - (560)(500)}{\sqrt{[10(560) - (313600)][10(500) - (250000)]}}$$

resulting in $r = 0.91$ to two decimal places indicating a strong positive correlation.

As with other tests the *level of significance (p)* would be set before the research and the significance of this result, namely, whether the null hypothesis should be rejected or not, found by consulting the appropriate *critical values table*. Let's say we set $p = 0.05$ then for 9 *degrees of freedom* as we have, the critical value for $r = 0.602$. Our value is greater than this so our result is significant for $p = 0.05$ indicating we should reject the *null hypothesis*. In other words there is a significant relationship between the two variables being looked at as only 5 times out of every 100 is this result likely to have occurred by chance.

It is worth noting again how the number of calculations required indicates how prone to error the result could be and here is where computers can

Table 10.6   Values for calculating Pearson's Product Moment Correlation

Student	Predicted A level result (X)	Actual A level result (Y)	(XY)	(X^2)	(Y^2)
A	30	34	1020	900	1156
B	38	36	1368	1444	1296
C	60	42	2520	3600	1764
D	65	60	3900	4225	3600
E	43	42	1806	1849	1764
F	50	48	2400	2500	2304
G	58	52	3016	3364	2704
H	72	66	4752	5184	4356
I	64	48	3072	4096	2304
J	80	72	5760	6400	5184

be of help. If the same results are put into two columns of the spreadsheet Microsoft Excel, it is simplicity itself (using the Pearson function) to get the software to calculate r, and give the result 0.9089152. This is a spurious level of accuracy and you would use $r = 0.91$ again, but the point of this example is to make you realise where computer technology can help in undertaking calculations which are prone to error. However, what is of more importance, as always, is that you know which is the correct test to use.

Power of a test $(1 - \beta)$

This is linked to *Type I (α) and Type II (β) errors* although more specifically with a *Type II error*. Whenever you are using *inferential statistics* you are working with probabilities and when you accept or reject a *null hypothesis* it is only on the basis of your research – other research may come up with a different outcome. Setting a *level of significance* only indicates the predetermined probability on which you have based your acceptance or rejection of your *null hypothesis* but you could still be wrong. A *Type II error* is where you *accept* the *null hypothesis* when it is *false*. The power of a test $(1 - \beta)$ tells you the probability of *rejecting* a *null hypothesis* when it is, in fact, *false*. This topic can get quite complicated and for more detailed information on it you are directed to Hinton (1996: 94–102).

Ratio scale

Like the *interval scale* this refers to measurements, which are separable by equal distances, but in this case you can draw a relationship between each of the data items. Weight, height, time and length are all examples of such data.

So a person 2m high is twice as high as someone who is 1m high. The key to the difference with an *interval scale* is that for ratio data each of the measurements has a *'meaningful zero'* (Moore, 1997: 178).

Some texts actually clump *interval scale* and *ratio scale* measurements together simply as data, which is separable by equal distances. While this is acceptable it is crucial one understands the difference of such data from *ordinal scale* and *nominal scale* measurements.

Sample size

For any sample this is just the number of observations taken and is a deceptively important factor in statistics.

The question, which is always asked, is 'How big should my sample be?' There is no easy answer to this and it will of course depend on the research you are doing. Normally the larger and more representative the sample is of the population you are interested in then the better. For purely *descriptive statistics* the sample size is not particularly crucial except in the way you present your data, for example:

> 75% of the people surveyed were in agreement that newly qualified hospital doctors should have their weekly working hours reduced.

Forgetting about who was sampled, which could of course significantly affect the results, the 75% appears to indicate a large number were sampled. It could be, though, this is the response from just three people out of a sample size of four. In such circumstances quoting percentages is misleading. Although there is no hard and fast rule it is usually accepted that percentages can be quoted when your sample size is ≥ 30. Less than this and you should quote actual numbers. For the above example, if it was the response from only three people it ought to read:

> Three out of the four people surveyed were in agreement that newly qualified hospital doctors should have their weekly working hours reduced.

Sample size, however, is important for *inferential statistics*. These use probabilities to make inferences and estimations with samples taken from much larger populations. Different statistical tests have been designed to cope with varying sample sizes and again it is important that the appropriate test is used with respect to the research you are undertaking. One particular effect of sample size in *inferential statistics* is on the *power of a test $(1 - \beta)$*.

Spearman's Rank Order

This is a *non-parametric test*, which allows us to find out if there is a significant relationship between two sets of *ordinal scale* data. It requires the rank ordering of data sets and then uses the calculation (where there are very few ties):

$$r_s = 1 - \frac{6\sum d^2}{n(n-1)(n+1)}$$

where d = the difference in rank between the items in a pair and n = the number of items.

The following example (Table 10.7) shows two departments' ranking of various characteristics for effective teaching, and are part of the findings from the research for a Phd (Chan, 1999).

The sum of the difference in ranks between paired items squared, Σd^2, is 237.25 and using this in our equation:

$$r_s = 1 - \frac{6\sum 237.5}{21(20)(22)}$$

giving a value for $r_s = 0.846$. A large number of ties requires a correction factor to be taken into consideration (Cohen and Holliday, 1996: 144–7), although in our case applying this correction factor results in a very minor difference $r_s = 0.845$.

The significance of this value as with other tests, such as the *t-test*, *Kruskal-Wallis test* and *Pearson's Product Moment Correlation (r)* can be obtained by consulting appropriate published *critical value tables*. In this case the result was found to be significant at a *level of significance* for a *two-tailed test* of $p = 0.01$. In other words the probability of this result occurring by chance is 1 in 100 and there is a strong agreement between the departments as to the characteristics perceived as important for effective teaching.

Standard deviation (SD)

Standard deviation is an important statistical measure of variability associated with the normal curve produced by a *normal distribution*. In other words how spread out the distribution of scores is from the *mean*.

Table 10.7 Values for the calculation of Spearman's Rank Order

Characteristic	Dept. A Ranking	Dept. B Ranking	*d*	*d²*
Clear and comprehensible lectures	1	1	0	0
Structured and organised lectures	2	3	−1	1
Shows thorough subject knowledge	3	2	1	1
Shows enthusiasm for their subject	4	4	0	0
Has a strong sense of responsibility	5	6	−1	1
Ensures current subject content	10	5	5	25
Welcomes students who need help	6.5	9	−2.5	6.25
Sets appropriate course objectives	6.5	11.5	−5	25
Gives useful handouts of notes	8	13.5	−5.5	30.25
Firm on class discipline	15.5	7.5	8	64
Relates theory to practice	12.5	7.5	5	25
Gives constructive feedback	12.5	10	2.5	6.25
Encourages self-learning	9	11.5	−2.5	6.25
Is friendly and approachable	11	13.5	−2.5	6.25
Gives appropriate homework	14	19	−5	25
Is fair in grading assessed work	15.5	15	0.5	0.25
Makes an effort to improve teaching	15.5	18	−2.5	6.25
Sensitive to students' feelings	20.5	20.5	0	0
Has a good sense of humour	18	16.5	1.5	2.25
Publishes articles and presents papers	19	16.5	2.5	6.25
Well groomed and appropriately attired	20.5	20.5	0	0

In particular it enables us to predict between what ranges various percentages of values observed should fall. So, just over 68% (the actual figure is 68.26%) of observed values fall within one SD of either side of the *mean* of a normal curve. This is just a mathematical property of a *normal distribution* curve, which we have already noted. Although the position of the standard deviation (SD) on a *normal distribution* curve is actually visible by the naked eye, it is for any given sample more accurately obtained from the following calculation:

$$SD = \sqrt{\frac{\sum fd^2}{N-1}}$$

where N is the number of values, d is difference obtained by subtracting the *mean* from each value and f is the frequency of occurrence of each value. The denominator $(N-1)$ is important to note and is linked in with *degrees of freedom*. All our statistical work revolves around SD calculations and it is therefore important that for any sample we make the best estimate we can for the SD. Smaller sample sizes increase the likelihood of errors creeping in and to

Table 10.8   Calculation of Standard Deviation

Values (X)	f (no. children)	fX	d (M–X)	d^2	fd^2
42	2	84	15.5	240.25	480.5
47	7	329	10.5	110.25	771.75
52	10	520	5.5	30.25	302.5
57	26	1482	0.5	0.25	6.5
62	15	930	–4.5	20.25	303.75
67	8	536	–9.5	90.25	722
72	2	144	–14.5	210.25	420.5
	$N = 70$	$\sum fX = 4025$			$\sum fd^2 = 3007.5$
	$M = 57.5$				

$$SD = \sqrt{\frac{\sum 3007.5}{70-1}} = 6.6$$

compensate for these the correction factor (N–1), which will increase the SD, is used.

As an example let us look at the weights of children and consider some actual values with weights in kg (Table 10.8). What this means then is that we would expect, for a normal distribution 68.26% of all children at the age chosen to have a weight between 50.9 kg and 64.1 kg, that is one SD either side of the *mean*.

t-distribution

Small sample sizes (< 30) do not reflect a *normal distribution* but in fact provide a distribution curve, which is flatter and is known as a *t*-distribution (Figure 10.9).

The crucial aspect to a *t*-distribution is that the point, either side of the mean, on the horizontal axis, which corresponds to 95% of the total area under the curve (95% of the sample), will be different from that for a *normal distribution*. For the latter we talk of a **Z-score** of ± 1.96 corresponding to 95% of the sample but this is no longer relevant for a *t*-distribution. Instead, the value quoted is the **t-score**. These vary depending on the sample size taken and are available in **critical values tables** for varying **levels of significance** but typically $p = 0.05$ and $p = 0.01$ are given. Once sample sizes are 30 or more **Z-score** and **t-score** critical values will be very similar.

t-score

As we have seen the shape of a *t-distribution* which reflect small sample sizes (< 30) varies according to the sample size. The consequence of this is

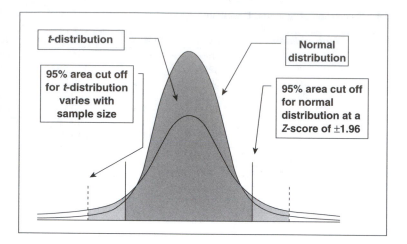

Figure 10.9   *t*-distribution curve

that the *t*-score from a *critical value tables* which indicates a statistically significant difference in any *t-test* will vary according to this sample size or the *degrees of freedom*. As you might expect as the sample size gets larger the value for a *t*-score will approach a *Z-score* for a normal distribution. We have already highlighted this point when we looked at *critical value tables* (p. 206) and more information on *t-scores* and how these values approach a *Z-score* can be found in Rose and Sullivan (1996).

t-test

This is just the generic name given to a range of statistical tests, which are available when sample sizes used are ≤30 and which are linked with the *t-distribution*. The calculation of various *t*-tests can get quite complicated but as we have noted elsewhere, computer technology can help and the most important thing is to know which test is the correct one to use.

   In the example of an experiment in educational research (see Chapter 5, p. 91) Lim (1997) set out to find if the differences in the *mean* between the results of his control and experimental group were significantly different. The particular *t*-test relevant to his work is given by the formula:

$$t = \frac{\dfrac{\sum X_1}{N_1} - \dfrac{\sum X_2}{N_1}}{\sqrt{\left(\dfrac{\sum X_1^2 - \left[\left(\sum X_1\right)^2/N1\right] + \sum X_2^2 - \left[\left(\sum X_2\right)^2/N_2\right]}{N_1 + N_2 - 2}\right)\left(\dfrac{N_1 + N_2}{N_1 N_2}\right)}}$$

Table 10.9   Calculation for a t-test

Scores for the control group (X_1)	Scores for the experimental group (X_2)	$(X_1)^2$	$(X_2)^2$		
0	4	0	16	$N1 =$	11
1	5	1	25	$N2 =$	9
3	7	9	49	$\sum X_1 =$	27
3	2	9	4	$\sum X_2 =$	51
0	3	0	9	$\sum X_1/N_1 =$	2.45
1	3	1	9	$\sum X_2/N_2 =$	5.67
1	7	1	49	$\sum (X_1)^2 =$	131
1	9	1	81	$\sum (X_2)^2 =$	363
3	11	9	121	$\sum (X_1)^2/N_1 =$	11.91
6	–	36	–	$\sum (X_2)^2/N_2 =$	40.33
8	–	64	–	$t =$	2.58

where X_1 is a score (value) of group 1, X_2 a score (value) of group 2 and N_1 and N_2 are the numbers in groups 1 and 2 respectively. His actual results were as shown in Table 10.9.

The value of t for the *level of significance (p)* set can be found by consulting appropriate published *critical values tables*. Say, before doing the research (as should be done), we set $p = 0.05$ then in the case for 18 *degrees of freedom* the critical value of t for a *two-tailed test* is 2.101. Our value of $t = 2.58$ is greater than that for t in the published *critical values tables* and so we would reject the *null hypothesis*. In other words the probability is that this result would only occur by chance in 5 out of 100 times. In actual fact Lim used a *one-tailed test* and set $p = 0.01$. For this the critical value of t is 2.552 so he was able to reject the *null hypothesis*.

As we have noted in other places, for example, the *Pearson Product Moment Correlation (r)*, the number of individual calculations means the whole exercise of calculating t is prone to error. Here again, using computers to help with the calculations is valuable. If the same results are put into two columns of the spreadsheet Microsoft Excel using the data-analysis tool t-Test: Two-Sample Assuming Equal Variances you can get the software to calculate t and part of the table of results produced are shown in Table 10.10. The results (taking into consideration the spurious level of accuracy) are identical to those already detailed.

Tukey test

The statistical test *Analysis of Variance (ANOVA)* allows you to test the difference between the *mean* of three or more samples. However, when it

Table 10.10   Excel calculation of a *t*-test

	Variable 1	Variable 2
Mean	5.666667	2.454545455
Variance	9.25	6.472727273
Observations	9	11
df	18	
t Stat	2.574245	
P(T<= t) one-tail	0.009552	
t Critical one-tail	2.552379	
P(T<= t) two-tail	0.019105	
t Critical two-tail	2.878442	

produces a significant difference, what it does not tell you is where that differ-ence lies. For example is it between all the samples or only some of them. The Tukey test allows you to compare each pair sample condition and from the result decide whether the difference is significant. For our repeated measures one-way ANOVA (p. 203) we did get a significant result so if we perform a Tukey test we should be able to determine where the effect of this difference is.

First, we need to do a pair-wise difference of the means for each condi-tion. As the means were $M_{Books} = 50$, $M_{WWW} = 56$ and $M_{Books + WWW} = 60$ the pair wise differences are:

$$M_{Books + WWW} - M_{WWW} = 4; M_{Books + WWW} - M_{Books} = 10; M_{WWW} - M_{Books} = 6$$

The Tukey test denoted by T is calculated from the formula:

$$T = (q)x \sqrt{\frac{errorvariance}{N}}$$

where q is found from consulting the appropriate Tukey test *critical values table*, the *error variance* was calculated in the ANOVA test (10.59) and N is the number of scores from which each mean was calculated (10).

We chose the *level of significance* as $p = 0.05$ and with this and the fact we had 3 conditions and 18 *degrees of freedom* looking up a Tukey test *crit-ical values table* gives us a value of q of 3.6. So the value of the Tukey test T is given by:

$$T = 3.61x \sqrt{\frac{10.59}{10}}$$

giving $T = 3.71$. If this T value is smaller than the difference between any two means, then the means are significantly different. This is the situation for all our cases so we can conclude that the test results are dependent on the style of teaching resource used.

Type I (α) and Type II (β) errors

Inferential statistics use probabilities and as such it is possible to make an error from the outcome of any such statistical test that is undertaken. Assume we have a *null hypothesis*, which says:

> There is no difference between the mean exam
> results of two groups of students.

and the *level of significance* at which a researcher is willing to reject or not reject this *null hypothesis* when it is in fact correct is set at $p = 0.05$. This allows for a 5% probability that the outcome could have occurred by chance. That is, 5 times out of 100 a researcher could reject the *null hypothesis* when in actual fact it is true. This is known as a Type I error:

> Rejecting a *null hypothesis* when it is true is a Type I error.

When a hypothesis is being tested the probability of a Type I error occurring is written as α. In order to minimise a Type I error researchers can set the value for α more rigorously. $\alpha = 0.01$ only allows for 1 time out of 100 of making a Type I error.

There is, of course, the possibility of making the converse error. That is we accept the *null hypothesis* when it is false. This is known as a Type II error:

> Accepting a *null hypothesis* when it is false is a Type II error.

In this case the probability of a Type II error occurring is written as β. It is important to note that a Type II error can only be made when the null hypothesis is accepted and is less likely to occur than when the less rigorous α (the probability of a Type I error occurring) is made. So $\alpha = 0.1$ is better for avoiding a Type II error.

The question, as with setting p the *level of significance*, is what does one set α at? There is no easy answer. There is a need to consider the *power of a test $(1 - \beta)$* but possibly the most important issue is to consider the repercussions of making a Type I or Type II error.

Assume funding will be allocated to your school in the form of new gym facilities if you can show you have a significantly greater percentage of children in your school who are overweight as compared to the national average. Also assume this funding is being competed for by three other schools. Setting α could be crucial. A Type II error is of no importance to you but you would want to minimise the occurrence of a Type I error (setting α as rigorously as possible, e.g. at 0.01 or even 0.001) so that you gave your school the best chance of securing the funding. Of course setting α at too high a level could also be self-defeating.

How would you set α if funding was guaranteed as long as you could show you have a significantly greater percentage of children overweight in your school compared with the national average? Now you don't want α set at too rigorous a level, being much happier to err on the side of a Type I error. There has to be a limit, though, as setting α too low is not likely to be acceptable to the funding body. In such cases and in research in general, setting α = 0.05 is regarded as a reasonable significance level.

Variance

This is just a measure of the variability, or how spread out, individual scores, are about their *mean*. It is calculated from the formula:

$$\frac{\sum(X - M)^2}{N - 1}$$

where X is each value, N is the total number of values and M is the *mean* of all the X values. Again the denominator $(N - 1)$ is associated with *degrees of freedom* and provides a correction factor for small samples. The two sets of data in Table 10.11 have an identical *mean* but the variance shows that the actual values are much more closely grouped in the second set than in the first.

Z-score

This indicates the number of *standard deviations* that any score falls on either side of the mean of the horizontal axis of a *normal distribution*. In our example of children's weights (p. 223) we calculated the *standard deviation* to be 6.6 kg and the *mean* was 57.5 kg. So, if we had children who weighed 64.1 kg this would be one *standard deviation* above the *mean*. They could be said to show a Z-score of + 1. It is easy to calculate the Z-score of any raw result (X) from the formula:

Table 10.11   Data showing differences in variance for identical totals

	First data set	Second data set
Actual (X) values	20 22 25 27 28 29 32 33 36 40 40 44 47 48 51 52 53 55 58 60	30 30 32 35 36 38 38 39 40 40 40 40 42 42 42 43 45 48 50 50
Total of all (X) values	800	800
Mean (M)	40	40
$\Sigma(X - M)^2$	3024	624
Variance	159.2	32.8

$$Z = \frac{X - M}{SD}$$

where M is the mean. So if a child weighed 49.25 kg, their Z-score would be equal to:

$$\frac{49.25 - 57.5}{6.6} = -1.25$$

that is 1.25 SD below the mean.

The Z-score is important because one of the properties of a normal curve is that a Z-score of ± 1.96 corresponds exactly to 95% of the total area under the curve, that is a 95% *confidence level*. So if we had a Z-score equal to or greater than ± 1.96 we could express this by saying the probability is that only 5 times out of a 100 is this result likely to occur by chance. This is in turn related to the **level of significance (p)** or probability and in this case would be expressed as $p = 0.05$.

The idea of Z-scores and normal distributions is important in the basic understanding of hypothesis testing in *inferential statistics*, such as *t-distributions* and *t-tests*.

Bibliography

Ausubel, D.P. (1963) *The Psychology of Meaningful Verbal Learning*, New York: Grune and Stratton.

Bailey, K. and Ochsner, R. (1983) 'A methodological review of the diary studies: windmill tilting or social science?', in K. Bailey, M.H. Long and S. Peck (eds) *Second Language Acquisition Studies*, Rowley, MA: Newbury House.

Bassey, M. (1984) 'Pedagogic research: on the relative merits of search for generalisation, and study of single events', in J. Bell, T. Bush, A. Fox, J. Goodey and S. Goulding (eds) *Conducting small-scale investigations in Educational Management*, London: Harper and Row.

Bassey, M. (1990) 'On the nature of research in education' – Part 1, *Research Intelligence*, BERA Newsletter, 36: 35–8.

Bassey, M. (1999) *Case Study Research in Educational Settings*, Buckingham: Open University Press.

Bell, J. (1999) *Doing Your Research Project* (3rd edn), Milton Keynes: Open University Press.

Bell, J. and Opie, C. (2002) *LEARNING FROM RESEARCH – Getting More From Your Data*, Milton Keynes: Open University Press.

Beynon, J. (1985) *Initial Encounters in the Secondary School*, Lewes: Falmer.

Black, T.R. (1999) *Doing Quantitative Research in the Social Sciences: An Integrated Approach to Research Design, Measurement and Statistics*, London: Sage.

Blumer, H. (1969) 'Sociological analysis and the variable', in H. Blumer, *Symbolic Interactionism: Perspective and Method*, Berkeley: University of California Press.

Borg, W.R. and Gall, M.D. (1996) *Educational Research: an Introduction* (6th edn), New York: Longman.

BPRS (2002) http://www.dfee.gov.uk/bprs/

BPS (2002) *Code of Conduct, Ethical Principles & Guidelines*, detailed on the web page http://www.bps.org.uk/documents/Code.pdf

Brewer, J.D. (2000) *Ethnography*, Buckingham: Open University Press.

Burrell, G. and Morgan, G. (1979) *Sociological Paradigms and Organisational Analysis*, London: Heinemann.

Buston, K. (1997) 'NUD•IST in action: its use and its usefulness in a study of chronic illness in young people', *Sociological Research Online*, 2(3), http://www.socreson line.org.uk/socresonline/2/3/6.html

Campbell, D.T. and Stanley, J. (1963) 'Experimental and quasi-experimental designs for research on teaching', in N. Gage (ed.) *Handbook of Research on Teaching*, Chicago: Rand McNally.

Carr, W. and Kemmis, S. (1986) *Becoming Critical*, Lewes: Falmer.

Carroll, T. (2001) *Educating the Critical Mind in Art: Practice-Based Research Into Teaching Critical Studies in A Level Art*, Unpublished Ed.D thesis, University of East Anglia.

Chan, T. (1999) 'Student evaluation of teaching effectiveness'. Unpublished Phd thesis, University of Nottingham.

Coffey, A. (1999) *The Ethnographic Self: Fieldwork and the Representation of Identity*, London: Sage.

Coffey, A., Holbrook, B. and Atkinson, P. (1996) 'Qualitative data analysis: technologies and representations', *Sociological Research Online*, 1(1), http://www.socresonline.org.uk/socresonline/1/4/lf.html

Cohen, L. and Holliday, M. (1996) *Practical Statistics for Students*, London: Paul Chapman.

Cohen, L. and Manion, L. (1994) *Research Methods in Education* (4th edn), London: Routledge.

Cohen, L., Manion, L. and Morrison, K. (2000) *Research Methods in Education* (5th edn), London: RoutledgeFalmer.

Crème, P. and Lea, M. (1997) *Writing at University: A Guide for Students*, Milton Keynes: Open University Press.

Cruickshank, D.R. (1987) *Reflective Teaching: The Preparation of Students Teaching*, Reston, VA: Association of Teacher Educators.

Denzin, N.K. (1997) 'Coffee with Anselm', *Qualitative Family Research*, 11(1): 16–18.

Denzin, N.K. (1998) 'The art and politics of interpretation', in N.K. Denzin and Y.S. Lincoln (eds) *Collecting and Interpreting Qualitative Materials*, Thousand Oaks, CA: Sage.

Denzin, N. and Lincoln, Y. (2000) 'Introduction: The discipline and practice of qualitative research', in N. Denzin and Y. Lincoln (eds) *The Handbook of Qualitative Research* (2nd edn), Thousand Oaks, CA: Sage.

Dey, I. (1993) *Qualitative Data Analysis: A User-Friendly Guide for Social Scientists*, London: Routledge.

DfES (2002) http://www.dfes.gov.uk/index.htm

ESRC (2001) http://www.esrc.ac.uk/esrccontent/postgradfunding/postgraduate_training_guidelines_2001.asp

Fan, G. (1997) 'An exploratory study of final year diploma nursing students' perceptions of their nursing education'. Unpublished MEd thesis, University of Sheffield.

Fielding, N.G. and Lee, R.M. (1998) *Computer Analysis and Qualitative Research*, Thousand Oaks, CA: Sage.

Fill, A.F. (1986) '"Divided Illocution" in Conversational and other situations – and some of its implications', *IRAL*, 24(1).

Fine, M., Weiss, L., Wesen, S. and Wong, L. (2000) 'For whom? Qualitative research, representations and social responsibilities', in N. Denzin and Y. Lincoln (eds) *The Handbook of Qualitative Research* (2nd edn), Thousand Oaks, CA: Sage.

Fisher, M. (1999) 'Using computers in qualitative analysis', in M. Henry (ed.) *I.T. in the Social Sciences: A Student's Guide to the Information and Communication Technologies*, Oxford: Blackwell.

Flanders, N. (1970) Analysing Teaching Behaviour, Reading, MA: Addison-Wesley.

Freire, P. (1972) *Pedagogy of the oppressed*, Harmondsworth: Penguin.

Further Education Development Agency, Institute of Education and The Nuffield Foundation (1997) *GNVQs 1993–1997, A National Survey Report*, London: FEDA.

Geerligs, T. (1995), 'Students' thoughts during problem-based small-group discussions', *Instructional Science*, 22(4): 269–78.

Glaser, B. and Strauss, A. (1967) *The Discovery of Grounded Theory*, Chicago: Aldine.

Griffiths, M. (1998) *Educational Research For Social Justice: Getting Off the Fence*, Buckingham: Open University Press.

Grundy, S. (1987) *Curriculum: Product or Praxis*, Lewes: Falmer.

Guba, E. (1990) 'The alternative paradigm dialog', in E. Guba (ed.) *The Paradigm Dialog*, Newbury Park, CA: Sage.

Hammersley, M. (1987) 'Some notes on the terms "validity" and "reliability"', *British Educational Research Journal*, 13(1): 73–81.

Hammersley, M. (1991) *Reading Ethnographic Research*, London: Longman.

Hargreaves, D. (1996) *Teaching as a Research Based Profession: Possibilities and Prospects*, London: TTA Annual Lecture.

Harland, J. and Kinder, K. (1999) *Crossing the Line: Extending Young People's Access to Cultural Venues*, London: Calouste Gulbenkian Foundation/NFER.

Hatton, N. and Smith, D. (1995) 'Reflection in teacher education: towards definition and implementation', *Teaching and Teacher Education*, II: 33–49.

Hinton, P.R. (1996) *Statistics Explained: A Guide for Social Science Students*, London: Routledge.

Hitchcock, G. and Hughes, D. (1989) *Research and the Teacher: A Qualitative Introduction to School-based Research*, London: Routledge.

Hopkins, K.D., Hopkins, B.R. and Glass, G.V. (1996) *Basic Statistics for the Behavioural Sciences*, Boston, MA: Allyn and Bacon.

Howard, K. and Sharpe, J.A. (1983) *The Management of a Student Research Project*, Aldershot: Gower.

Hume, D. (1992) *A Treatise of Human Nature*, Buffalo, IL: Prometheus Books.

Hyatt, D. (2000) *Assignment Feedback Seminar for Teaching and Learning Committee*, University of Sheffield: School of Education.

IATEFL, (2001) 'Feedback on teaching practice: what do trainees want?', *Teachers Trainers and Educators SIG Newsletter*, 2(3): 26–9.

Kelle, U. and Laurie, H. (1995) 'Computer use in qualitative research and issues of validity', in U. Kelle (ed.) *Computer-aided qualitative data analysis: Theory, methods and practice*, Thousand Oaks, CA: Sage.

Kemmis, S. (1997) 'Action research', in J.P. Keeves (ed.) *Educational Research, Methodology, and Measurement: an International Handbook* (2nd edn), Oxford: Elsevier Science.

Kemmis, S. and McTaggart, R. (eds) (1992) *The Action Research Planner* (3rd edn), Victoria: Deakin University Press.

Keppel, G. and Saufley, W.H. (1980) *Introduction to Design and Statistical Analysis: A Student's Handbook*, New York: W.H. Freeman.

Lakoff, R. (1990) '*The Grooves of Academe': Talking Power: The Politics of Language in Our Lives*, New York: Basic Books.

Lather, P. (1986) 'Research as Praxis', *Harvard Educational Review*, 56(3): 257–77.

LeCompte, M. and Preissle, J. (1993) *Ethnography and Qualitative Design in Educational Research* (2nd edn), Thousand Oaks, CA: Sage, and London: Academic Press.

Lee, R.M. and Fielding, N. (1996) 'Qualitative data analysis: representations of a technology: a comment on Coffey, Holbrook and Atkinson', *Sociological Research Online*, 1(4), http://www.socresonline.org.uk/socresonline/1/4/lf.html

Lees-Rolfe, P. (2001) 'Using the internet as a teaching medium for a section of the school chemistry syllabus: a case study'. Unpublished MEd thesis, University of Sheffield.

lesphinx-developpement (2002) http://www.lesphinx-developpement.fr/en/products/SphinxSurvey.htm, accessed January 2003. Offers a valuable overview of SphinxSurvey, a downloadable demonstration version.

Lim, C.P. (1997) 'The effect of computer-based learning (CBL) in support class on low-performance economics students'. Unpublished MEd thesis, University of Sheffield.

Lincoln, Y.S. and Guba, E.G. (1985) *Naturalistic Inquiry*, London: Sage.

Liu, D. (1998) 'Ethnocentrism in TESOL: teacher education and the neglected needs of international TESOL students', *ELT Journal*, 52(1): 3–10.

Manchester Metropolitan University Library (2002) *Bibliographic Citation* http://www.mmu.ac.uk/services/library/eresource/bibcit.html, Manchester.

McDonough, J. and McDonough, S. (1997) *Research Methods for English Language Teachers*, London: Arnold.

McKernan, J. (1991) *Curriculum Action Research*, London: Kogan Page.

McMillan, J. and Schumacher, S. (1984) *Research in Education*: *A Conceptual Introduction*, Boston, MA: Little Brown.

Measor, L. and Sikes, P. (1992) *Gender and Schools*, London: Cassell.

Microsoft (2002) http://www.microsoft.com/uk/office/excel/ and http://www.microsoft.com/uk/office/word/, accessed January 2003. Microsoft home pages to its spreadsheet programme Excel and word-processor Word.

Miles, M. and Huberman, A. (1994) *Qualitative Data Analysis*: *An Expanded Sourcebook* (2nd edn), Newbury Park, CA: Sage.

Milgram, S. (1963) 'Behavioural Study of Obedience', *Journal of Abnormal and Social Psychology,* 67: 371–8.

Moore, D.S. (1997) *Statistics: Concepts and Controversies* (4th edn), New York: W.H. Freeman.

Morrissey, S. and Marr, J. (1986) 'Cemetery Gates' from the album *The Queen is Dead,* (The Smiths), Rough Trade Records.

Nisbet, J. and Watt, J. (1984) 'Case Study', in J. Bell, T. Bush, A. Fox, J. Goodley and S. Goulding (eds) *Conducting Small-scale Investigations in Educational Management,* London: Harper Row.

OED (2001) http://dictionary.oed.com/

Oppenheim, A.N. (1992) *Questionnaire Design, Interviewing and Attitude Measurement,* London: Pinter.

Patton, M.Q. (2002), *Qualitative Research and Evaluation Methods*, London: Sage.

Pennycook, A. (1994) 'The politics of pronouns', *ELT Journal*, 48(2).

Pennycook, A. (1996) 'Borrowing other's words: text, ownership, memory and plagiarism', *TESOL Quarterly*, 30(2): 201–30.

Pomerantz, M. and Pomerantz, K.A. (2002) *Listening to Able Underachievers: Creating Opportunities for Change*, London: David Fulton Publisher.

Pring, R. (2000) *Philosophy of Educational Research*, London: Continuum.

Punch, M. (1994) 'Politics and ethics in qualitative research', in N. Denzin and Y. Lincoln (eds) *The Handbook of Qualitative Research* (2nd edn), Thousand Oaks, CA: Sage.

Qualifications and Curriculum Authority (2001) *The National Framework of Qualifications,* as shown on the QCA website, http://www.qca.org.uk, accessed 15 November 2001.

Qualitative Solutions and Research (1997) *QSR NUD•IST User Guide,* Victoria, Australia: Qualitative Solutions and Research Pty Ltd.

Richards, T.J. and Richards, L. (1995) 'Using hierarchical categories in qualitative data analysis', in U. Kelle, (ed.) *Computer-aided Qualitative Data Analysis*: *Theory, Methods and Practice,* Thousand Oaks, CA: Sage.

Richards, T.J. and Richards, L. (1998) 'Using computers in qualitative research', in N.K. Denzin and Y.S Lincoln (eds) *Collecting and interpreting qualitative materials,* Thousand Oaks, CA: Sage.

Rose, D. and Sullivan, O. (1996) *Introducing Data Analysis for Social Scientists* (2nd edn). Open University Press: Buckingham.

Samuel, S. (2002) 'How well are the visually impaired students integrated in a mainstream secondary school in Singapore: a case study'. Unpublished MEd thesis, University of Sheffield.

Sapsford, R. and Jupp, V. (1996) *Data Collection and Analysis*, London: Sage.

Schön, D.A. (1987) *Educating the Reflective Practitioner: Toward a New Design for Teaching and Learning in the Professions*, San Francisco, CA: Jossey-Bass.

Scolari (2002) http://www.scolari.co.uk/sphinx/sphinx.htm, accessed January 2003. Good introduction to the computer analysis programmes SphinxSurvey, ATLAS.ti and NUD•IST.

Seethepalli, V. (2002) 'The use of the internet websites as a teaching resource and teacher-pupil interactions in an integrated pre-school classroom: a case study'. Unpublished MEd thesis, University of Sheffield.

Shukor, S. (2001) 'Student's thinking: a comparison between conventional tutorials and problem-based environment'. Unpublished MEd thesis, University of Sheffield.

Sieber, J. (1993) 'The ethics and politics of sensitive research', in C. Renzetti, C. Lee and R. Lee (eds) *Researching Sensitive Topics*, London: Sage.

Sikes, P., Measor, L. and Woods, P. (1985) *Teacher Careers: Crises and Continuities*, Lewes: Falmer.

Sikes, P. (2000) '"Truth" and "Lies" Revisited', *British Educational Research Journal*, 26(2): 257–70.

Sikes, P. and Goodson, I. (2003) 'Living research: thoughts on educational research as moral practice', in P. Sikes, W. Carr and J. Nixon (eds) *Educational Research: Reconceptualising the Debate*, Buckingham: Open University Press.

Simpson, P. (1993) *Language, Ideology and Point of View*, London: Routledge.

Soh, L. (2001) 'A classroom case study on ways to create a motivating learning environment'. Unpublished MEd thesis, University of Sheffield.

Somekh, B. (1995) 'The contribution of action research to development in social endeavours: a position paper on action research methodology', *British Educational Research Journal*, 21(3): 339–55.

Sridhar, S.N. (1994) 'A reality check for SLA theories', *TESOL Quarterly*, 28(4): 800–5.

Stanley, L. and Temple, B. (1993) *Using Computers for Analysing Qualitative Datasets*, Manchester: University of Manchester.

Stanley, L. and Temple, B. (1995) 'Doing the business? Evaluating software packages to aid the analysis of qualitative data sets', *Studies in Qualitative Methodology*, 5: 169–93.

Stenhouse, L. (1975) *An Introduction to Curriculum Research and Development*, London: Heinemann.

Strauss, A. and Corbin, J. (eds) (1997) *Grounded Theory in Practice*, London: Sage.

Strauss, A. and Corbin, J. (1998) *Basics of Qualitative Research: Techniques and Procedures for Producing Grounded Theory* (2nd edn), London: Sage.

Sturman, A. (1999) 'Case study methods', in J.P. Keeves and G. Lakomski (eds) *Issues in Educational Research*, Oxford: Pergamon.

Swales, J. (1990) *Genre Analysis: English in Research and Academic Setting*, Cambridge: Cambridge University Press.

TES (1999) 'High Art: "bald men with cellos"', *Times Educational Supplement* (17/12/1999).

TES (1999) 'We're not all old or bald!', *Times Educational Supplement* (28/1/2000).

Tooley, J. with Darby, D. (1998) *Educational Research – A Critique: A Survey of Published Educational Research*, London: OFSTED.

Travers, M. (2001) *Qualitative Research Through Case Studies*, London: Sage.

Troyna, B. (1994) 'Blind faith? Empowerment and educational research', *International Studies in the Sociology of Education*, 4(1): 3–24.

Usher, R. (1996) 'Textuality and reflexivity in educational research', in D. Scott and R. Usher (eds) *Understanding Educational Research*, London: Routledge.

University of Sheffield Library, (2002) *Harvard Referencing Guide*, http://www.shef.ac.uk/library/libdocs/hsl-dvc1.html, Sheffield.

Walliman, N. (2001) *Your Research Project: A Step-by-step Guide for the First-time Researcher*, London: Sage.

Walker, H.M. (1940) 'Degrees of freedom', *Journal of Educational Psychology*, 31: 253–69.

Weitzman, E.A. and Miles, M.B. (1995) *Computer Programs for Qualitative Data Analysis,* Thousand Oaks, CA: Sage.

Wellington, J.J. (1996) *Methods and Issues in Educational Research*, Sheffield University: USDE Papers in Education.

Wellington, J.J. (2000) *Educational Research: Contemporary Issues and Practical Approaches*, London: Continuum.

Whitehead, J. (1985) 'An analysis of an individual's educational development: the basis for personally orientated action research', in M. Shipman (ed.) *Educational Research: Principles, Policies and Practices*, Lewes: Falmer.

Wiseman, S. (1966) *Correlation Methods*, Manchester: Manchester University Press.

Woods, P. (1999) *Successful Writing for Qualitative Researchers*, London: Routledge.

Wragg, E.C. (1999) *An Introduction to Classroom Observation* (2nd edn), London: Routledge.

Wright, D.B. (1997) *Understanding Statistics: An Introduction for the Social Sciences*, London: Sage.

Zeichner, K.M. and Liston, D.P. (1987) 'Teaching student teachers to reflect', *Harvard Educational Review*, 57(1): 23–48.

Zuber-Skerritt, O. (ed.) (1996) *New Directions in Action Research*, London: Falmer.

Index